Ordnance Survey/Jarrold
Landranger Guidebook
to

Shakespeare
Country

and North Cotswolds

Compiled by Peter Titchmarsh, M.A., F.R.G.S.

Companion to Landranger Map 151

Jarrold Colour Publications

How to use this Guide.

Space has not allowed us to include every place on Landranger Map 151, in the 'Places of Special Interest' section (pages 18-77). But the items have been selected to provide you with a varied and interesting companion in your travels around the Shakespeare Country and the Northern Cotswolds. Places of exceptional interest have been highlighted by being printed in blue.

Each entry is identified with a four figure map reference, identifying the map square in which the feature lies. The first 2 figures are those which appear in blue in the top and bottom margins of the map. The second 2 figures are those which appear in the left and right hand margins of the map.

The Key Map on page 4 identifies the suggested starting points of our eleven Tours and eight Walks, and in the Tours and Walks Sections, all places which also have a separate entry in the 'Places of Special Interest' Section are in bold type. Each Tour and Walk is accompanied by a map, and there are cross references between Tours and Walks on both the maps and in the text.

Acknowledgements

We would like to thank Dr Levi Fox, the Director of the Shakespeare Birthplace Trust, for his article on *The Shakespeare Connection*, and for his invaluable advice on the references to William Shakespeare and the Shakespeare Birthplace Trust properties in the *Places of Interest* section. We are also most grateful to David and Maria Titchmarsh for their work on the *Walks* section, which involved their walking over the routes concerned and providing the detailed directions for walkers.

First published 1985 by Ordnance Survey and Jarrold Colour Publications

Ordnance Survey
Romsey Road
Maybush
Southampton SO9 4DH

Jarrold Colour
Publications
Barrack Street
Norwich NR3 1TR

Printed in Great Britain by Jarrold and Sons Ltd., Norwich. 185

Contents

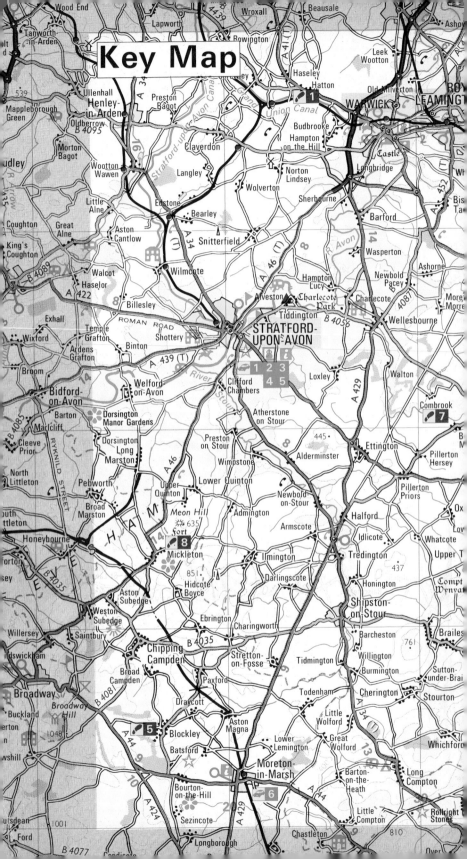

Key Map

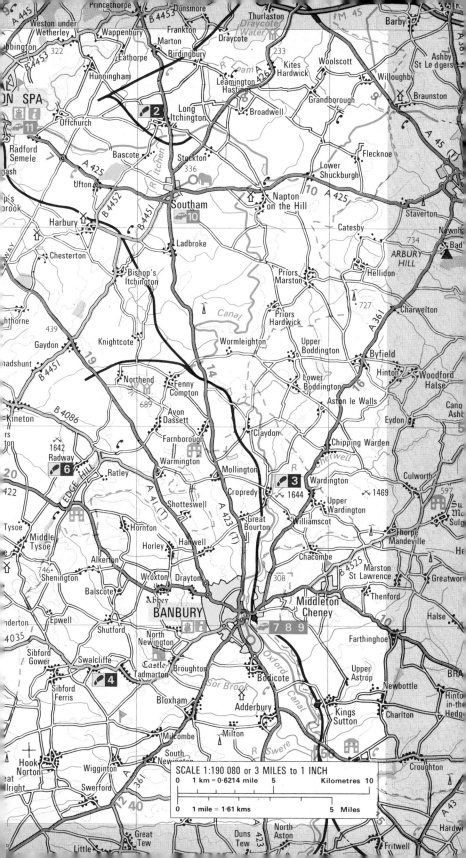

SCALE 1:190 080 or 3 MILES to 1 INCH

0   1 km = 0·6214 mile   5   Kilometres 10

0   1 mile = 1·61 kms   5   Miles

Introduction

Lying in the very heart of England, this is a largely rural area, situated on the divide between the southern bounds of the great Midland Plain and the northern confines of the limestone belt that stretches right across England, from Devon to Lincolnshire. This limestone belt is known as the Cotswolds in part of our area, but it stretches beyond the Cotswolds, north-eastwards across the less well defined ironstone country of North Oxfordshire, and into the borders of Northamptonshire. The Cotswolds may be better known than its neighbour, but there are many hidden gems to be found in this quieter ironstone country.

The outstanding feature of the 'plain' country to the north of these hills, is the valley of the lovely River Avon, together with that of its tributary the River Leam, which stretches westwards across largely flat countryside, where lias clay has over the years, provided material for several massive cement works. To the north-west of the Avon valley, north of Shakespeare's Stratford-upon-Avon, lies the countryside of deep, narrow lanes, and low rounded hills that were once clothed by the Bard's beloved 'Forest of Arden'. Here a number of oak trees may still be found beside the lanes, together with small scattered woodlands, amongst which there are a bewilderingly large number of minute hamlets; but the great forest itself is now only a distant folk memory. Beyond the Avon, the agricultural lands of south Warwickshire have been noted for their abundant richness for centuries, and this area has always been known as the Feldon, with it's own 'cathedral' in the form of the fine parish church at Brailes.

Although largely rural in flavour, the area does have its busy towns .... Stratford-upon-Avon itself, a market town and pre-eminent tourist centre; the county town of Warwick, with its great castle poised above the Avon, and its considerable industry; and Royal Leamington Spa, still elegant in parts, but also industrialised to an extent. To the south-east, lies the busy and ever growing town of Banbury.

Banbury in fact lies beyond the Severn-Thames watershed, upon the banks of the little River Cherwell, which flows south from here to join the Thames at Oxford. Apart from the Cherwell and its tributaries, the only other river of note that flows south towards the Thames is the Evenlode, which rises in the exquisite gardens of Sezincote, near Moreton-in-Marsh. All other rivers; the Leam, the Stour, and the Alne, flow into the Avon, which itself flows west and south to join the mighty Severn at Tewkesbury.

Here then is a richly diverse landscape, within which are small market towns like Henley-in-Arden, Shipston-on-Stour, Moreton-in-Marsh, and of course Chipping Campden, together with the four larger towns mentioned above. Beyond these lie a multitude of attractive villages, each with a character of its own. Some have the obvious appeal of a tourist favourite, but many more deserve to be better known. Beyond these villages again, are other special places of interest ... beautiful gardens, fine country houses and ancient sites ... and these will prompt further exploration into the quiet countryside in which they lie.

With these factors in mind we have devised a series of tours to guide you to the best features that this area has to offer, but if you purchase Landranger Map 151, you will be able to vary these tours to suit your own requirements. They have been designed primarily for motorists, but they are also suitable for cyclists, especially those classified as such. Walkers would of course find these tours too long and too 'road-orientated', but to whet your appetite, we have also provided a series of eight walks in widely varied countryside, and each of these link on to at least one of the tours. We cannot stress too strongly that your car is an ideal means to 'arrive' at an area, but to gain real enjoyment and satisfaction, it is infinitely preferable to explore the area on foot when you have arrived. So, if you do decide the use the Tour Section, please do so with discretion, and take your walking gear with you.

We do hope that you enjoy yourselves.

History Revealed...
A Short Survey of the Area's Past.

Moving inland along the upland ridges of Britain, Neolithic (or Stone Age) farming communities from the Continent had begun to settle here by the mid fourth millenium B.C. By 2500 B.C. these Stone Age farmers were firmly established in the hilly limestone country on the southern half of our map, although visible remains of their civilization, such as long barrows, are scanty here. About 2000 B.C. the so-called 'Beaker Folk' moved westward from the Continent, heralding the Bronze Age, a culture that gradually replaced that of their Neolithic predecessors. This culture was characterised by worship at stone circles or henges, the most famous of which are at Stonehenge and Avebury. On the far south of our area there is a modest henge monument, known as the Rollright Stones, and close by are the exposed remains of a typical Bronze Age round barrow, known as the Whispering Knights (page 53).

A third wave of settlers, the Iron Age peoples, moved westward from the Continent between about 550 B.C. and 50 A.D. They organised themselves into larger and more cohesive groups, and not only were they able to construct and maintain large, well-sited forts, such as those at Wappenbury (page 69), Meon Hill (page 52), Nadbury (page 94), Madmarston (page 47) and Rainsborough (page 27), but they also started a process, to be continued later by the Romans and Anglo-Saxons, of extending their farming into the lower and more difficult valley country. A great hoard of Iron Age currency bars was discovered at Meon Hill, and there is no doubt that these Iron Age peoples were in general far more sophisticated than the Roman propagandists would have us believe.

The Romans landed in 43 A.D., and they advanced with considerable speed as far as the line that was to become the Foss Way, the great road that almost exactly bisects our area. The country to its south and east was soon consolidated, and by 47 A.D. the legions were then able to move on to the task of pacifying the wilder parts of Britain, far away to the north and west. Roman settlement in our area must have been considerable, and several Romano-British sites have been excavated, as at Swalcliffe (page 66), Wappenbury (page 69), and Kings Sutton (page 43). Roads were built, westwards from Kings Sutton, to Worcester, and north towards the distant Derbyshire hills (the Ryknild Street); and a marching camp was built astride the Foss Way at Chesterton. With improved techniques, agriculture was further extended in the valleys, although most known villa sites are restricted to the south of the area, to the hillier areas of Gloucestershire and Oxfordshire, and none are open to inspection.

Anglo-Saxon remains in the area are very scanty, but the churches at Wootton Wawen (page 76), Barton-on-the-Heath (page 21), and Tredington (page 68), all contain at least a small proportion of work regarded by experts as Anglo-Danish in origin; evidence of Danish influence straying further south and west than is normally to be expected. Norman work is to be found in many churches, but some of the finest examples are to be found at Halford, where there is a fine tympanum over the north doorway (page 37), at Hook Norton with its fascinating font (page 41), and at Barford St Michael which has a splendidly carved north doorway (page 21). The round headed Norman arch gradually gave way to the pointed, but still simple 'Early English' equivalent, and this style predominated throughout most of the 13th century. A good specimen of this rugged style is to be found at Pillerton Hersey (page 51). However the first flowering of English Gothic, known as the 'Decorated' period, dates approximately from 1290 to 1350, and our 'Decorated' favourites in the area are the tomb chest at Cherington (page 27), the little church at Ratley (page 53), and the fine spired church at Todenham (page 67). There is also a fascinating series of mid-14th century sculptures on at least four north Oxfordshire churches ... Hanwell (page 38), Adderbury (page 18), Alkerton (page 18), and Bloxham (page 23) ... all probably carried out by the same team

The Great Hall, Warwick Castle.

of craftsmen.

The late-14th and the whole of the 15th century was an age of great prosperity, derived largely from wool, and this affected the southern, hillier half of the area more dramatically than the valley country to the north. It was fortunate indeed that this prosperity coincided so closely with the final flowering of English Gothic, the style now known as 'Perpendicular'. The great 'wool church' at Chipping Campden (page 29) is one of the finest Perpendicular churches in the country, but there are many others in the area that must not be missed; St Mary's at Warwick, with its superb Beauchamp Chantry Chapel (page 72), and both the Parish Church and the Guild Chapel at Stratford-upon-Avon. To the south of Banbury are three churches with outstandingly beautiful spires; Adderbury, Bloxham and superlative Kings Sutton. Thanks to this coincidence of prosperity and piety the Perpendicular period was also a great time for the detailed improvement and enrichment of so many

other churches. This was the time when roofs were raised and clerestory windows added, bringing more light into interiors now being enriched with opulent brasses, noble tombs and handsome aisle chapels.

Monastic remains in the area are not of great interest. There were priories at Wroxton (41-41) and Chacombe (49-43), a Cistercian nunnery at Pinley (21-65), a Gilbertine Priory with a hospital for lepers, at Clattercote (45-49), and a Friary at Warwick; but these buildings have either disappeared, or their fragmentary remains have been incorporated in later buildings.

All these monastic institutions were swept away by Henry VIII in the years immediately after 1539, but in the centuries that followed, our parish churches continued to reflect a strong religious tradition. Their content was often enriched in the 17th and 18th centuries with many splendid monuments. See especially Little Rollright (29-30), Honington (26-42), Chesterton (35-58), and Charlecote (26-56). In the 19th century, many churches were re-built or restored by Victorian architects, who were often brilliantly inspired by the past in cold academic terms, but who seldom had any regard for the patina of age and character that they so often swept away. It was not until the closing years of the 19th century that it became clear to William Morris, his friends and some of his contemporaries, that steps should be taken to reverse this trend, and where restoration has been carried out after this time an atmosphere of the past can often still be savoured. See Burton Dassett (39-51).

To return to the secular front .... The Normans built several castles in the area, the finest being the great castle of Warwick. The earthworks of other medieval castles may still be traced at Brailes (30-40), Swerford (37-31), Deddington (47-31), Kineton (33-50), and Fulbrook (25-60), and the remains of other castles have been incorporated into later buildings at Hanwell (43-43), and at Broughton (41-38), the latter being a beautiful, still moated Tudor mansion. Other 16th century houses include Charlecote (26-56) and Compton Wynyates (33-41), but two other fine manor houses, at Chipping Campden and Wormleighton, were burnt down in the Civil War. This bitter conflict had a strong impact on our area, with the first encounter of the war being at Bascote Heath (39-62), and major battles taking place at Edge Hill (33-51) and Cropredy Bridge (46-46).

The 17th and 18th century produced many fine houses in the area, including Upton House (36-45), Farnborough Hall (43-49), Honington Hall (26-42), and, just into the 19th century, exotic Sezincote (17-30), all of which are open to the public. Great parks were created, follies were built, and the landscape in general was changing fast, with the acceleration of the enclosures. This was a movement that had been started by the great sheep graziers of the 16th century, and which was largely completed by the beginning of the 19th, as a result of those sweeping changes in agricultural methods, now known collectively as the Agricultural Revolution.

The Industrial Revolution on the other hand, did not have a great impact on our area, which has always remained a largely rural one, but the 18th and early 19th century did see the building of canals across its hills and valleys. By the end of the 19th century however, the railways had gained supremacy, with a network of lines carrying passengers and freight, and the canals were already in decline. Now many of the railways have been closed, and the roads, many of which started as turnpikes in the 18th century, have been improved out of all recognition. At the time of writing no motorways pass through the area, but the M40 Extension is planned to run up the Cherwell valley, to the east of

The Whispering Knights. Part of the Rollright Stones.

Banbury, and then north-west through the hills, and down to a point near Warwick.

The main roads through the area are busy with constant traffic, but once away from these no doubt essential arteries, visitors will find that it is still possible to move quietly through its small towns and villages, and to appreciate the rich diversity of its past.

The Shakespeare Connection.

by **Dr. Levi Fox**, O.B.E., M.A., F.S.A.
The Director of the Shakespeare Birthplace Trust

All over the world people instinctively link the names of Stratford-upon-Avon and Shakespeare. Though possessing a fascinating history as an English market town in its own right Stratford has become famous as an international tourist and cultural centre because of its association with William Shakespeare, the greatest dramatic writer of all time. Shakespeare was born in the house in Henley Street preserved as his birthplace in 1564 and both his parents came from farming stock. His mother Mary Arden, was the daughter of Robert Arden, a substantial yeoman farmer of Wilmcote, where the family farmstead may still be seen (see Wilmcote, page 74); his father, John Shakespeare, was a glover and wool dealer, also described as a yeoman, who took an active part in local public affairs and held the office of bailiff or mayor of the Borough in 1568.

Though little is known of William's childhood, there is every reason to believe that he received a sound classical education at the town's grammar school and it is likely that as a boy he witnessed some of the plays produced by companies of travelling actors who visited the town and played in the guildhall.

At the age of eighteen William married Anne Hathaway, daughter of Richard Hathaway of Shottery (see Anne Hathaway's Cottage, page 58) and for reasons not known he left Stratford. Within a short time he can be traced in London, first as an actor and then as a reviser of plays, and there is evidence to show that by 1592 his work was already attracting the admiration and envy of some of his contemporaries.

A great deal is known about Shakespeare's activities in London. He became a leading member of the official company of players which provided entertainment for the Court and he was one of the consortium of theatre people who built and managed the Globe playhouse on Bankside. As a writer of plays his output was exceptional both in amount and quality, and with the wealth his success brought him he invested in property in London and Stratford. In 1597 he purchased New Place (see page 63) and it was here, in the familiar setting of his native town that he lived in retirement from about 1610 until he died at the age of 52 in 1616. He was buried in the parish church of Stratford, where he was baptised, and where his grave and monument may be seen.

Seven years after Shakespeare's death a complete edition of his histories, comedies and tragedies — the First Folio of 1623 — was published by his friends and shortly afterwards the first literary pilgrims made the journey to Stratford to see his grave. The growing recognition of Shakespeare's genius and his association with Stratford can be traced from this time onwards and during the first half of the 18th century the increased national interest in the poet's life and work reflected itself in the larger numbers of people coming to Stratford to visit the places associated with the bard. In 1756 the owner of New Place cut down the mulberry tree planted by Shakespeare because visitors wishing to see it had become so numerous as to be a nuisance.

It was, however, the Garrick Jubilee of 1769 which firmly established Stratford's position as the shrine of literary pilgrimage. The celebrated actor, David Garrick, then at the height of his popularity, came down to Stratford to take part in a three-day festival in honour of Shakespeare. A magnificent temporary amphitheatre on the banks of the Avon provided the setting for a programme of ceremonies and social activities which attracted national patronage and publicity on a scale hitherto unknown. The Jubilee has been described as one of the splendid occasions of English history.

From this time onwards Shakespeare's Birthplace became the object of special attraction. Travellers, like the Hon. John Byng in 1785, recorded their impressions of it and when Washington Irving visited the house in 1815 he was shown a collection of spurious personal relics which the guide assured him had belonged to the poet.

It was to prevent exploitation of this kind that when Shakespeare's house was offered for sale in 1847 sufficient money was raised by public subscription to purchase the property for preservation as a national memorial. There then came into existence the Shakespeare Birthplace Trust, an unusual kind of educational institution of charitable status, which during the intervening years has contributed greatly to the preservation of the physical Shakespearian heritage. In addition to the Birthplace the Trust has acquired and administers New Place, Anne Hathaway's Cottage, Mary Arden's House and Hall's Croft. Each year these properties are visited by well over a million people, three quarters of whom come from abroad, representing nearly every country in the world. The income from visitors' admission fees provides for the upkeep of the properties and at the same time enables the Trust to maintain library, archive and museum collections, and to provide study and research facilities at its headquarters, the Shakespeare Centre.

Apart from the influence of the Birthplace Trust the greatly increased popularity of Stratford as an international tourist and cultural centre owes much to the development of the festival idea and the establishment of a permanent theatre specialising in the presentation of Shakespeare's plays. During the 18th and early 19th centuries various temporary buildings were used by visiting theatrical companies and the tradition of celebrations set by the Garrick Jubilee was continued with particular emphasis on the poet's birthday. The tercentenary celebrations of 1864 inspired the formation of the Shakespeare Memorial Association and in 1879 Stratford's first memorial theatre was built by Charles Edward Flower. From that time to the present not a single year has passed without the production of a season of Shakespeare's plays. At first this lasted for a few weeks only; now it runs for the greater part of each year.

When the theatre was destroyed by fire in 1926 Shakespeare lovers all over the world, particularly Americans, built and endowed the present Royal Shakespeare Theatre, opened in 1932. Since then the story of the theatre has been one of almost uninterrupted progress. The productions of the Royal Shakespeare Company at Stratford now attract an international audience of upwards of half a million people each year; in addition the company has a London theatre at the Barbican and also undertakes tours in this country and abroad.

The international regard in which Shakespeare and his birthplace are held is supremely illustrated by the traditional celebrations which take place at Stratford each year to commemorate the poet's birthday. From small beginnings originally intended to give local people an opportunity to honour the memory of their famous townsman, these celebrations are now attended by diplomatic representatives of overseas countries together with personalities of art, literature and the theatre, and have become a unique international event. The unfurling of the flags of the nations, the floral procession and the laying of flowers on the poet's tomb, together with the traditional toasts at the luncheon are symbols of a universal recognition of the enduring genius of the great Englishman, William Shakespeare.

'William Shakespeare, 1564-1616'. Attributed to Gerard Soest (1637-81). In the collection of the Shakespeare Birthplace Trust.

Leisure Activities . . . A Brief Summary.

The area covered by this guide provides a bewildering variety of sport and leisure activities and we have listed some of those which we feel will be of particular interest to visitors.

Motoring. You will probably have arrived in your own car, but if you wish to hire a self-drive car or chauffeur-driven car, there is a wide choice available. Try Guide Friday, Waterside, Stratford-upon-Avon, *Tel: (0789) 294466*; Welcome Garages (chauffeur-driven cars), *Tel: (0789) 204393*; Arden Garages (self-drive), *Tel (0789) 67446*. If they are unable to help, use the local Yellow Pages, or Thompson Directory.

Bus. Local bus services can be fun if you are prepared to fit in with their schedules, which are normally governed by local transport needs. A timetable giving details of times and routes may be obtained from the Midland Red (South) Travel Centres at Stratford-upon-Avon *(Tel: 204181)*, Leamington Spa *(Tel: 22593)*, and Banbury *(Tel: 62368)*. Stratford-upon-Avon and the Shakespeare

Country is also well served by Guide Friday (see above), who offer a variety of guided tours.

Train. Details of train services in the area may be obtained from the railway stations at Stratford, Leamington and Banbury. The best telephone number for enquiries is *Leamington Spa (0926) 22302*. However it must be said that trains will not reach many of the places mentioned in the guide, and they are probably more suitable for 'long-haul' routes either in or out of the area.

Caravanning and Camping. There are a number of suitable sites in the area. Enthusiasts will no doubt wish to refer to club booklets or other specialist publications, but here is a list of some well established sites, with map references and telephone numbers:

Caravans and Tents.

Dodwell Trailer Park, *Stratford-upon-Avon (2 miles west on A439, Evesham road) (16-53) Tel: (0789) 204957*

The Elms Camp, *Stratford-upon-Avon. (On B4086) Tiddington road (21-55) Tel: (0789) 292312*

Holt Farm, *Southam. (On road from Southam to Priors Marston) (43-60) Tel: (0926-81) 2225*

Long Compton Mill, *Long Compton (On Barton-on-the-Heath road) (27-33) Tel: (0608-84) 663*

At the Shakespeare Countryside Museum, Mary Arden's House, Wilmcote.

Lock at the union of the Stratford-upon-Avon Canal and the River Avon, at the Bancroft Gardens, Stratford-upon-Avon.

Long Marston Airfield *(To west of A46) (17-48)* Tel: *(0789) 299868*
Park Hill Farm, *Halford (Turn south-east off Foss Way in Halford, farm is at first T-junction) (26-44)* Tel: *(0608-61) 452*

Caravans only.
Berryfield Farm, *Newbold-on-Stour (Turn north at X-rds between Armscote and Ilmington) (22-45)* Tel: *(0608-82) 248*
Wilkem Lawns, *Upper Quinton (To east of A46) (17-46)* Tel: *(0789) 720446*

Cycling. This is a splendid way of looking around the area, and once off the main routes (which is the object of most of our listed tours) the little 'unclassified' roads (yellow on the Landranger map) are relatively peaceful. If you do not have your own machine, these can be hired from:
Pashleys Store, *Guild St., Stratford-upon-Avon,* Tel: *(0789) 297044*
Knotts, *15, Western Rd., Stratford-upon-Avon,* Tel: *(0789) 205149*
Jeffrey's Toyshop, *Moreton-in-Marsh,* Tel: *(0608) 50756*

Walking. This is the ideal way of exploring the area, and may be combined with any of the above means of transport. You will find eight walks described on pages 000-000, and we hope that these will provide a pleasant introduction to the pleasures of walking with map and guide in this wonderfully unspoilt countryside. Stout shoes and waterproof clothing are desirable, and during the wetter part of the year, walking boots, or even wellies can widen the scope of your journeys, taking in more of those sodden fields and footpaths than might otherwise be possible. Small rucksacks are worthwhile, and while a a compass is useful even in this gentle, well charted landscape, it is not essential. Do not always expect to find well-defined paths across this pastoral countryside. Rights of way are clearly shown on both the Landranger map and on the Pathfinder extracts, but these may not show up too clearly on the ground... and as always, some of the footpath signs put up by the local authorities do not always stay put too long. We leave you to guess why! While there may not usually be a right-of-way on canal towpaths, British Waterways welcome walkers. They do not hold themselves responsible for maintaining these paths for walkers, but in our view the possible problems involved are outweighed by the rewards usually to be obtained.

Horse Riding. Details of riding facilities may be obtained from:
The Warwick School of Riding, *Guys Cliff, Coventry Rd., Warwick,* Tel: *(0926) 494313*
The Windmill Hill Riding Academy, *Warwick Rd., Stratford-upon-Avon,* Tel: *(0789) 731202*

Fun on the Water. This area has much to offer those who, in some way or other, love to 'mess about in boats'. Narrow boats and cruisers may be hired to explore the canals, and the Avon westwards from Stratford-upon-Avon. Local firms include:

Western Cruisers, *Stratford-upon-Avon,*
Tel: (0789) 69636

Stratford-upon-Avon Marine,
Tel: (0789) 69636)

Bidford Boats, *Bidford-on-Avon,*
Tel: (0789) 77305)

Gordon's Pleasure Cruisers, *nr Napton,*
Tel: Southam 3644

Fenny Marine, *Fenny Compton*
Tel: Fenny Compton 461

Two national organisations that offer a booking service are:
Boats of Oxford
Tel: (0865) 727288
U.K. Waterway Holidays, of Rickmansworth
Tel: (09237) 78231)

Hotel Boats which take passengers for a day or a week, are also available via the two organisations above.

Punts, rowing boats and canoes may be hired by the day or the hour, at Stratford, Warwick and Leamington. If you have your own canoe, the Avon is well worth exploring, and the canal system offers a pleasant alternative, with its still waters and reed-bordered towpaths. The Stratford-upon-Avon Canal, and the Oxford Canal southwards from Napton (46-62) offer some of the most pleasant canal cruising to be found anywhere, and there is also the Grand Union Canal to be explored. Sailing on inland waters is largely a club activity, but if you wish to become involved, there are clubs at Draycote Water (46-69), Napton Reservoir (46-62) and at Boddington Reservoir (49-53).

Golf. There are two courses at Stratford-upon-Avon, the Stratford-upon-Avon G.C., *Tel: (0789) 205677 (21-55),* and the Welcome G.C., *Tel: (0789) 295252 (21-56),* two at Leamington Spa , the Leamington & County G.C., *Tel: (0926) 20298 (32-62),* and the Newbold Comyn Municipal G.C., *Tel: (0926) 21157 (33-66),* a Municipal G.C. at Warwick, *Tel: (0926) 494316 (27-64),* one at Middleton Cheyney, near Banbury, the Cherwell Edge G.C., *Tel: (0295) 711591 (49-42),* and a fine private course at Tadmarton, near Banbury, *Tel: (0608) 737278 (39-35).*

Places to Visit.... A summary list showing page number followed by map reference.

Prehistoric and Roman Sites, open to public.
The Rollright Stones (53, 29-30)

Battlefields.
Danesmoor (34, 51-46)
Bascote Heath (22, 39-62)
Edge Hill (34, 35-49)
Cropredy Bridge (32, 47-46).

Castles.
Broughton Castle (25, 41-38)
Deddington Castle Earthworks (32, 47-31)
Warwick Castle (71, 28-64).

Historic Houses.
Anne Hathaway's Cottage, Shottery (58, 18-54)

Broughton Castle.

Lord Leycester's Hospital, and the West Gate, Warwick.

Aynhoe Park (19, 51-33),
Charlecote Park (NT) (26, 26-56)
Farnborough Hall (NT) (35, 43-49)
Hall's Croft, Stratford-upon-Avon (63, 20-54)
Harvard House, Stratford-upon-Avon (62, 20-54)
Honington Hall (40, 26-42)
Lord Leycester's Hospital,Warwick (72, 28-64)
Mary Arden's House, Wilmcote (74, 16-58)
New Place, Stratford-upon-Avon (63, 20-54)
Sezincote (56, 17-31)
Shakespeare's Birthplace (61, 20-55)
Upton House (NT) (68, 36-45)
Wroxton Abbey (77, 41-41)

Gardens and Parks.
Bancroft Gardens, Stratford-upon-Avon (64, 20-54)
Batsford Park Arboretum (22, 18-33)
Hidcote Manor Garden (NT) (39, 17-42)
Jephson Gardens, Leamington Spa (56, 32-65)
Kiftsgate Court Gardens (42, 17-43)
Recreation Grounds, Stratford-upon-Avon (65, 20-54)
St Nicholas Park, Warwick (72, 28-64)

'History brought alive' ... at Stratford-upon-Avon's 'World of Shakespeare'.

Wildlife Parks and Zoos.
Dorsington Manor Gardens (33, 42-61)
Southam Zoo (60, 42-61)

Country Parks.
Burton Dassett (25, 39-51)
Draycote Water (33, 46-69)

Museums and Art Galleries.
Arms and Armour Museum, Stratford-upon-Avon (62, 20-54)
Banbury Museum (21, 45-40)
Bygones Museum, Aston Magna (19, 19-35)
Elizabethan Model Village, St. Nicholas Park, Warwick (72, 28-64)
Leamington Spa Art Gallery (56, 31-65)
Museum of Country Bygones, Marton (47, 40-68)
New Place, Stratford-upon-Avon (63, 20-54)
Royal Shakespeare Theatre Art Gallery, Stratford-upon-Avon (64, 20-54)
St John's House, Warwick (72, 25-65)
Shakespeare Countryside Museum, Mary Arden's House, Wilmcote (74, 16-58)
Stratford-upon-Avon Motor Museum, Stratford-upon-Avon (62, 20-55)
Warwick Doll Museum, Warwick (72, 28-64)
Warwickshire Museum, Warwick (72, 28-64)
Woolstaplers Hall Museum, Chipping Campden (29, 15-39)
The World of Shakespeare, Stratford-upon-Avon (65, 20-54)

Craft Activities.
Campden Pottery, Chipping Campden (31, 15-39)
Campden Weavers, Chipping Campden (31, 15-39)
Hatton Craft Centre, Hatton, nr Warwick (39, 23-66)
Stratford Brass Rubbing Centre, Stratford-upon-Avon (64, 20-54)

Special Events and Old Customs.
Dover's Games, Dover's Hill (33, 13-39) On the Friday following the Spring Bank Holiday, followed by the Scuttlebrook Wake, on the Saturday.
Maypole Dancing, Welford-on-Avon (72, 14-51). May 1st.
Royal International Agricultural Show, at Stoneleigh, north of Leamington Spa, first week in July.
Shakespeare's Birthday Celebrations, each year on the Saturday nearest April 23rd.
Shakespeare's Plays at the Royal Shakespeare Theatre, Stratford-upon-Avon. Season from end of March to end of following January.
Stratford-upon-Avon Festival, latter half of July.
For a list of other fascinating events, dates of which change annually, see Heart of England Tourist Board's leaflet 'Events in the Heart of England', obtainable from Tourist Information Centres, listed above.

Shakespeare's Birthday celebrations. These are held here each year on the Saturday nearest 23rd April.

Further Information.

Tourist Information Centres.

Banbury. *8, The Horsefair. Tel: (0295) 59855)*
Chipping Campden. *Woolstaplers Hall Museum, High St.(Summer only) Tel: (0386) 840289*
Moreton-in-Marsh. *The Council Offices, High St. Tel: (0608) 50881*
Royal Leamington Spa. *Jephson Lodge, The Parade. Tel: (0926) 311470 27072*
Stratford-upon-Avon. *Judith Shakespeare's House, 1, High St., Tel: (0789) 293127*
Warwick. *Court House, Jury St. Tel: (0926) 492212*

Other Useful Addresses, and/or Telephone Numbers.

Heart of England Tourist Board, *P.O.Box 15, Worcester WR1 2JT*
Thames and Chilterns Tourist Board, *8, Market Place, Abingdon, Oxon OX14 3UD*

Guide Friday Ltd., *13, Waterside, Stratford-upon-Avon. Tel: (0789) 294466 This is a useful local tour and travel service.*
Royal Shakespeare Theatre, *Stratford-upon-Avon, CV37 6BB. Tel: (0789) 295623. Credit Card Bookings Tel: (0789) 297129*
National Exhibition Centre, *Birmingham. Tel: 021-780-4141*
National Agricultural Centre, *The Royal Show Ground Tel: (0203) 555100*
National Trust Regional Office, *Tewkesbury Tel: (0684) 297747. OS map agent if required.*
Warwickshire Nature Conservation *Trust Tel: (0926) 496848*
R.A.C. 24 Hour Breakdown Service *Tel: 021-430-3232*
A.A. 24 Hour Breakdown Service *Tel: 021-550-4858*

Ordnance Survey Agent:

J. Gould, 9 High Street, Warwick. *Tel: (0926) 492904.*

Places of Special Interest

Places of outstanding interest are printed in blue.

Adderbury (47-35) Handsome ironstone village, much of which is astride the busy Banbury to Oxford road, with a quiet tree-lined street leading down to the Sor Brook. The church has a fine spire and tower, and around the tower and beneath the aisle parapets there is a splendid series of nearly a hundred medieval carved figures, ranging from a man ringing handbells, to a boy with dogs on a lead and a dragon with two tails. These carvings are thought to be the work of a mid-14th century mason, or group of masons, who also worked at Alkerton, Bloxham and Hanwell. Medieval doorways open into an equally fascinating interior, with a fine early-15th century chancel screen, and several interesting monuments.

Adderbury House, at the end of a small avenue of trees opposite the green, was the home of John Wilmot, Earl of Rochester, the dissolute 17th century poet. Walk westwards from here to Bloxham, partly along the disused line of the old Banbury and Cheltenham Direct Railway; or northwards over the fields to Bodicote, passing an old windmill at Bloxham Grove (45-36).

Alderminster (23-48) Small village astride the ever busy Stratford to Oxford road, with an interesting church of Norman origin, looking out over the River Stour to the little turreted church of Whitchurch, standing by itself in water meadows, amid a circle of trees. Alderminster church has a stout 13th century central tower and several Norman features, but beware, some of these are in fact the work of a late 19th century restorer.

Alkerton (37-42) Looks across the deep valley of the little Sor Brook, to the larger village of Shenington. There are several attractive Hornton stone houses, all on steep slopes, with views westwards over the valley. Within the church, with its 13th century tower, there is a real flavour of medieval times, with steps ascending from the nave to the chancel beneath the tower crossing. Do not overlook the fascinating carvings around the outside cornice to the south aisle, with men and dogs, and a bear among the many figures. These are thought to be the work of a mid-14th century mason, or group of masons, who also worked at Adderbury, Bloxham and Hanwell. The rectory was built by Thomas Lydyat, a 17th century scholar and Fellow of New College, Oxford, who was tutor to Charles I's brother Henry.

Walk south from here, down the valley of the Sor Brook, to Shutford, or northwards to the Temple Pool, and on to Upton House, making partial use of the road.

Alscot Park (20-50) Elegant early Gothic revival house in a well wooded park on the banks of the lovely little River Stour. This was built in the mid-18th century by James West, the Joint Secretary to the Treasury. It appears that it was largely the work of father and son, Thomas and Edward Woodward, architects, builders and quarry owners of nearby Chipping Campden; although two London craftsmen were also involved. We also suspect that Sanderson Miller (see Radway, page 52) must have had some influence upon its design. The house, which is occupied by the West family, is not open to the public, but there are pleasant views of it from the Stratford to Oxford road, and also from the minor road to Preston on Stour. (Stop awhile on the bridge over the Stour.)

Alveston (23-56) Tranquil 'residential' village situated amongst trees within a deep bend of the River Avon, two miles to the north-east of Stratford-upon-Avon. The ferry from which the cheerful little

Cottages at Alveston.

inn takes its name is sadly no longer in existence, but it is possible to walk northwards along a track, to an old weir, and south-eastwards beside the river to join the road to Charlecote just beyond the village. The Victorian church is not of great interest, but the surviving 18th century chapel of the old church contains several interesting features, including a fine late-16th century effigy of Nicholas Lane, 1595. There is a Youth Hostel on the B 4086, on the edge of the village, a valuable facility for young visitors to Stratford-upon-Avon.

Armscote (24-44) Attractive mellow stone village situated no more then three miles from the northern bastion of the Cotswolds, Windmill Hill, above Ilmington. There is a fine Jacobean manor house, very Cotswold in flavour, and several no less pleasing houses of the same period. There is no church, but there is an early-18th century Friends Meeting House, with a simple, unspoilt interior, and a hospitable inn, the Wagon Wheel. Do not miss the delightful converted 'railway-carriage' on the road towards Halford.

Aston Cantlow (13-59) Small village of black and white timbering and mellow brick, with the little River Alne just to its west. There are ancient earthworks in the water meadows, possibly the remains of an early medieval castle. One of the village's best known features is the richly timbered King's Head Inn, which has been in the same family for many generations, and which is noted for its mouth-watering 'duck-suppers'. The church, with its Perpendicular tower and late-13th century chancel, is believed to have been the scene of the marriage in 1557 of John Shakespeare of Snitterfield and Mary Arden of Wilmcote, the parents of William Shakespeare. But apart from this, the church is well worth visiting, to look at the 15th century font, the medieval bench ends and the early 17th century pulpit. There is a pleasant walk northwards along the Alne valley to Wootton Wawen, from whence one can walk along the towpath of the Stratford-upon-Avon Canal, either north towards Lowsonford and Lapworth (off Map 151), or south to Stratford-upon-Avon itself.

Aston Magna (19-35) Attractive stone village on hill slopes, looking out over the flat country that runs towards the valley of the Stour. It has a few pleasant houses and barns, and a little green, on which stands the base and lower part of a medieval cross. Overlooking the green is a church built in 1846 and not of particular interest to visitors. The circular earthworks to the south of the church are the remains of a medieval 'Homestead Moat', possibly connected with the Jordans, tenants of the Bishop of Worcester, recorded there in 1182. There is an interesting collection of old dairy equipment,

Aston Magna.

farm implements, and craftsmen's tools at the **Bygones Museum at Bank Farm** *(tel. 0608 50487 for details)*. Walk south-eastwards from here, across fields and over the Foss Way, to the pleasant little hamlet of Lower Lemington (see page 46).

Aston Subedge (13-41) This quiet village is situated beneath the wooded Cotswold edge, with a small stream beside the road that leads up over the hill towards Chipping Campden. Houses, farms and a little church are situated amongst orchards, reminding us that we are on the very edge of the Vale of Evesham... one of the great fruit and vegetable areas of England. The little church was built in 1797 and surprisingly there are signs of Greek influence about its bell turret and cornice. There is a delightful old clock, a small gallery and a canopied pulpit, all contemporary with the church itself. Opposite the church is the charming 17th century manor house, once the home of Endymion Porter (1587-1649), who was an ambassador of Charles I, and well known at the courts of both James 1st and Charles 1st. It was here that he entertained Charles's brother, Prince Rupert, when he came to the Cotswold Games organised by Porter's friend, Captain Robert Dover (see Dover's Hill, page 33).

Summertime at Avon Dassett.

Avon Dassett (41-50) Built on the southern slopes of the little Dassett Hills, this pleasing stone village is dominated by the tall spire of its Victorian church. This building is likely to have been made redundant by the time you come this way, but if by a lucky chance this has not happened, climb the steep stone steps to look inside at the 13th century tomb of Deacon Hugo, with his likeness in high relief upon the dark marble lid. Trees overhang the road up beyond the church, which leads eventually to the Burton Dassett Country Park (see Page 25), but we prefer to walk down the village, past flower-filled cottage gardens, with views out over the valley to the wooded slopes of Edge Hill. There is a pleasant walk across the fields to Burton Dassett church, and beyond to the Country Park.

Aynho (51-33) A beautifully trim village perched on high ground above the Cherwell valley, with wide strips of grass between the A41 road and the houses and cottages that border it. Many of their walls are covered with apricot trees, evidence of a long standing tradition by which the Lord of the Manor was paid a toll in this unusual fruit. Handsome Aynhoe Park mansion, standing on the edge of a park landscaped by Capability Brown, was the home of the Cartwright family for over three hundred years, but it is now in the hands of the Mutual Households Association, who have a series of flats here. The Cartwrights built a Jacobean house, but this was burned down by Royalist troops retreating from the battle of Naseby, and Aynhoe Park today reveals itself as a late 17th century mansion, much altered in the early 18th, and the early 19th centuries, the last alteration being by Sir John Soane in 1802. Parts of the elegant interior are open to the public at certain times *(For details, Tel: (0869) 810636)*. The nearby church retains its 15th century tower, but it is otherwise the work of a local architect in the 1720's, and is well worth visiting for its unspoilt 18th century interior, complete with box pews and gallery. Robert Wylde was appointed Rector here in 1646, but only after having to submit to a competition with a rival candidate as to who could preach the best sermon. On being told that he had won, Wylde retorted, *'We divided it, I have got the Ay and he the No'*. So all was not universal gloom at the outset of the Cromwellian period at Aynho! On a sadder note, Pesthouse Wood (52-33) is believed to have been used to shelter those with the plague, food being left at the edge of the wood by cautious villagers for their less fortunate friends living in its

The Oxford Canal at Aynho, near Banbury.

centre, to collect later. Do not miss a visit to the delightful Cartwright Arms.

Banbury (45-40) A busy market town for many centuries, Banbury is now also an important industrial centre, and has grown very considerably in size since the 1950's. Despite much re-development it still has a few old alleys and quiet corners which bring some relief to the super efficient shopping areas. Four of Banbury's famous old inns have also survived ... the White Lion, in the High Street, in the yard of which is a wisteria, which is said to be the largest in the country; the Flying Horse and the Reindeer in Parsons Street, and the Unicorn, with its attractive courtyard, in the Market Place. The large 17th century Whateley Hall Hotel in the Horsefair, used to be called the Three Tuns, and the many well-known people who have stayed here include Jonathan Swift, who is believed to have taken the name Gulliver from a tombstone in the nearby churchyard.

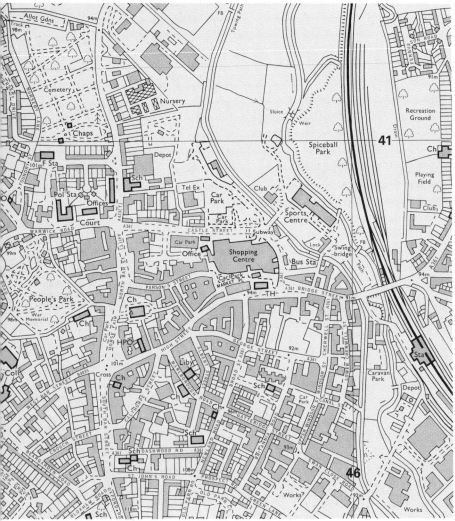

Banbury.

SCALE 1:10 000 or 6 INCHES to 1 MILE

There is a fine sports centre, Spiceball Park, and the old canal wharf nearby is busy with holiday boats throughout the summer months. Banbury Cross, situated at a cross roads, on the broad Horsefair, is a mid-19th century replacement of a medieval cross destroyed by the Puritans in the early 17th century. A well known nursery rhyme refers to the cross...

Ride a cock-horse to Banbury Cross
To see a fine lady on a white horse;
With rings on her fingers and bells on her toes
She shall have music wherever she goes.

This only appeared in print in the 18th century, but it is probably much older, and may possibly have referred to a visit here by Queen Elizabeth I. The cross stands in a wide street, which is overlooked by several pleasant old houses, amongst which is the Banbury Museum and Information Centre. (See the interesting exhibition, *A Changing Landscape — Banbury and the Cherwell Valley.) (Tel: (0295) 59855 for opening times.)*

Not only did the citizens of Banbury destroy their old cross, but they also, in 1792, blew up their medieval church with gunpowder, on the grounds that it was unsafe.This was replaced by an elegant church designed by S.P.Cockerell, the architect of Sezincote (see page 56), and his son C.R.Cockerell, who completed the tower and handsome portico by 1822. Unfortunately the interior was over restored later in the 19th century and is not of great interest to visitors. Banbury Cakes, which are eliptical in shape, and made of light pastry lined with currants, have been made in Banbury for at least three hundred years, but only became well known due to the efforts of local entrepreneur, Betty White, in the

Banbury Cross.

later years of the 18th century. They are of course still on sale here, and are delicious, especially when eaten fresh from a Banbury oven.

Barcheston (26-39) Minute hamlet just across the Stour from Shipston, with a manor house, rectory and church. The present manor house is largely 17th century, but it was here in about 1560 that William Sheldon set up his tapestry weaving enterprise, having first sent his man, Richard Hicks, to Flanders to learn the craft. The best known

productions from the Barcheston looms were the Sheldon tapestry maps, fascinating examples not only of tapestry, but also of the early cartographer's art. Several of these have survived, and good examples are to be seen at the York Museum and in Oxford's Bodleian Library. However a fine map of Warwickshire itself, is to be found at the Warwickshire County Museum at Warwick (see page 000), and Stratford's New Place Museum has two delightful tapestry panels, with allegorical scenes (see page 000). Barcheston church has a 14th century tower, and an interesting medieval interior, the content of which includes the tomb of William Willington and his wife carved in alabaster, and a brass to Richard Humphray ... both from the 16th century. There are pleasant walks beside the Stour, north to Shipston, and south to Willington and Burmington.

Barford (27—60) Disturbed by traffic on the busy A429, and considerably enlarged by modern housing, Barford still retains a certain charm. It has an old bridge over the Avon, a street lined with timber-framed and mellow brick houses, leading to a church with a Perpendicular tower, but which is otherwise Victorian. It was in fact rebuilt in 1884 at the expense of Miss Louisa Anne Ryland, of nearby Sherbourne Park (see page 57). Light floods in through clear glazed windows, and there are several pleasant monuments. See also the box pews and the east window, which is a good example of the Victorian stained-glass maker's art. Barford was the home of Joseph Arch, the man who fought so hard for the rights of the agricultural worker, at a time when they were so heavily exploited. His cottage still stands near the church, and there is a monument to him in the churchyard, put there by the National Union of Agricultural Workers (see also Wellesbourne, page 000).

Barford St.Michael (43-32) The church here has a squat Norman tower, and a Norman north doorway which is one of Oxfordshire's outstanding art treasures. This has fantastic carvings of beak heads and chevrons, and intertwining decoration on its capitals and tympanum. Do not miss the bench ends with their poppy heads, the chancel screen, nor the minute brass of William Fox and his wife, all placed in this delightful church in the 15th century. The long, low, thatched George Inn is also worth visiting.

Barton-on-the-Heath (25-32) Quiet village on a small rise, with a tree shaded green, on which stands a little well house, with an urn beneath a stone dome supported by three columns. This green is overlooked by handsome 17th century Barton House, and beyond this lies a modest little Norman church, with small saddle-back tower. Two sculptural details, one on the outside of one of the north chancel windows, and one on the inside of the same window, provide clues to the possible presence of an earlier Anglo-Danish building. These were common in the north and east of England, but it is unusual to find one so far to the south-west. Other features of interest include an amusing fragment of Norman sculpture, a little pig running up the chancel arch; a small brass to Edmund Bury (1559) in the chancel floor, the 15th century font, and the pieces of beautiful medieval stained glass in

The Village Green, Barton-on-the-Heath.

the chancel's north windows. Lawyer Robert Dover, the founder of the *'Cotswold Olympicks'* (see Dover's Hill, page 33), and his wife Sibilla, came here in 1650, to live with their son John, who had served as a Captain of Horse under Prince Rupert in the Civil War. Robert died in 1652 and was buried here, but his son continued to live at Barton until his death in 1696. Walk south from here, either on field path or road, to Little Compton, or south and east, up on to the high country where the Rollright Stones lie (see page 53).

Bascote Heath (39-62) It was here on 23rd August 1642, exactly two months before the Battle of Edgehill (see page 34), that the first skirmish of the Civil War took place. Parliamentary troops under Lord Brooke of Warwick Castle set upon a Royalist force, killing about fifty of them, and capturing some artillery. It was two days after this that Charles I raised his standard at Nottingham ... an act that most regard as the real starting point of the war. All is now peaceful at Bascote, an unexceptional, but pleasantly wooded area, with canal-side walks along the Grand Union not far away.

Batsford (18-33) A compact little estate village at the gates of Batsford Park, a large 19th century neo-Tudor mansion (1888-92), which can best be

SCALE 1:25 000 or 2½ INCHES to 1 MILE

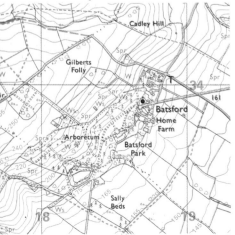

viewed from its arboretum (see below). The church is slightly older than the house (1861-62), and is an ambitious neo-Norman building, with tall spire and apsidal chancel. It is worth visiting for the sake of the handsome wall monument to Thomas Edward Freeman (1808) by the sculptor Joseph Nollekins. Do not overlook the other monuments, to members of the 'Mitford family, the Lords Redesdale, the forbears of the fabled Mitford sisters, whose early years at Swinbrook, a village on the Windrush beyond Burford, are so delightfully chronicled in Jessica Mitford's book *'Hons and Rebels'*.

Batsford Park Arboretum (18-33) Here are fifty acres of splendid woodlands, with scenic walks giving fine views eastwards out over the broad valley towards the Oxfordshire Cotswolds. There are over a thousand different species of trees, bamboos and shrubs, together with bronze statues from the Orient. Plants may be purchased from a nursery by the car park, which is approached from the A44 to the west of Moreton-in-Marsh. *Tel: (0386) 700409 for opening times.*

Bearley (18-60) The village itself is not of great interest to visitors, but the little church was rebuilt as late as 1962, and the result is most satisfying. See the Norman north doorway, and the little mellow brick tower, with its timbered gables. Bearley Aqueduct (16-60) lies well to the west, but is worth visiting. It was built in 1813, to carry the Stratford-upon-Avon Canal over a small valley, and is a massive structure with no fewer than thirteen large brick piers carrying a cast-iron channel complete with tow path. Delightful tow-path walks from here, north to Wootton Wawen and south to Wilmcote.

Bidford-on-Avon (Map 150) (09-51) This large village lies to the west of the main area covered by our guide, but it may be located on the Key Map on page 4, on the A439, to the west of Stratford-upon-Avon. We have included it here as it was possibly one of William Shakespeare's drinking haunts, and figures in a little verse which is attributed to the poet, which runs thus:

> *Piping Pebworth, dancing Marston,*
> *Haunted Hillborough, hungry Grafton,*
> *With dodging Exhall, papist Wixford,*
> *Beggarly Broom and drunken Bidford.*

There is a wonderful story that tells of, Shakespeare having a meeting at the Falcon Inn with a merry band of local topers calling themselves the 'Bidford Society of Sippers', who apparently drunk the poet and his friends under the table, and who then placed these vanquished drinkers under a crab-apple tree to cool off. This would of course account for the description in the verse, 'drunken Bidford', but unfortunately it is not possible to substantiate this. Bidford is pleasantly situated on the banks of the River Avon, and its High Street, after half a century's battering by heavy traffic, is now quiet once again, thanks to a much needed relief road. Its fine 15th century bridge marks the point where the Roman Ryknild Street (see page 56) forded the Avon. It was partly destroyed in the Civil War, but some of its medieval cutwaters have survived, and provide much welcome shelter for pedestrians trying to cross the bridge. The 'riverside' beyond the bridge provides car parking, picnicing and other recreational facilities for large numbers, especially at week-ends. The church, the tower of which makes an attractive picture upstream from the bridge, is almost entirely mid-19th century, but its contents includes a handsome 17th century monument to Lady Dorothy Skipwith, with a bust of the lady in question in a circular, garland-encircled niche. The Falcon, where Shakespeare and his friends may have drunk (see above), is an inn no longer, but it survives as a fine mullioned and gabled building of Cotswold stone and grey lias. It is possible to walk eastwards, partly beside the river, to Hillborough (see page 40), or south-westwards, through Marlcliff, and beside the river to Cleeve Prior and Offenham.

Binton (14-54) Attractively sited village, with a long street dropping down to a deep-set roadway, overlooked by flower-filled cottage gardens, an ornamental drinking well, and a rather severe Victorian church. This was built in 1875 in blue lias and Cotswold stone, a combination that does not appear to have suited Binton too well. However there are delightful views out over the Avon valley from the churchyard, and inside can be found a stained glass window, dedicated to Scott of the Antarctic, who had married the rector's daughter in

Cottage at Binton.

1908, and who was to die so tragically a few years later. There is a good walk north from here, via Red Hill and Withycombe Wood (14-57), to Aston Cantlow.

Bishop's Tachbrook (31-61) Small village not far to the south of Leamington Spa, with several half-timbered cottages, and a church with Norman origins and a substantial Perpendicular tower. Inside will be found several monuments to members of the Wagstaffe family, and a memorial to Robert and Walter Savage Landor composed in Latin by the latter. Walter Savage Landor, author and poet, was born at Bishop's Tachbrook in 1775, the family having lived here since the 16th century. His stormy life is of considerable interest, but his works are

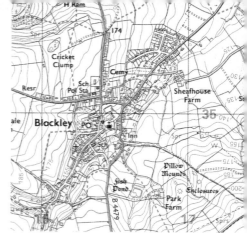

SCALE 1:25 000 or 2½ INCHES to 1 MILE

now seldom read. He died in Florence in 1864, having been involved in an unhappy scandal (the last of many) a few years earlier.

Blockley (16-34) A delightful village, owned by the Bishops of Worcester in medieval times, and built on the steep slopes of a hollow beneath the high wolds, near the head of a small but prolific stream. It was this stream that provided the power required for no fewer than six silk mills, when Blockley was at the height of its prosperity in the early years of the 19th century. These mills provided much of the silk required by the ribbon manufacturers of Coventry, and at one time they employed well over five hundred people. See the old mill beyond the pool below the church, now a private house.

Unspoilt by tourism, Blockley's steep little streets and terraces are full of character, with 17th and 18th century houses accompanied by dignified 19th century buildings. Despite Blockley's prosperity, the limitations of geography prevented the railway coming any closer than Paxford, but the village was not to be put off entirely, for there remains to this day, an inn of character, still proudly entitled 'The Great Western Arms'. The church has a large airy interior, with plenty of plain glass and a flat ceiling. There is a Norman chancel, which was probably once vaulted, and a tower built as late as 1725, by Thomas Woodward, who appears to have copied certain features from the fine tower of his own parish church at Chipping Campden. Inside the church, do not overlook the series of handsome monuments to various owners of Northwick Park, at least two of which are by the celebrated 18th century sculptor, J.M.Rysbrack, nor the two monumental brasses, both of priests, one in the chancel floor, and one (unusually) in the centre of the sedilia.

Explore the delights of Blockley on foot, and if possible walk to the south-western end, and up a track into Dovedale Woods **(Following Walk 5)**. This makes a very pleasant walk, although you will have to use a short stretch of the busy A44 to return via Warren Farm (15-34), if you wish to avoid a return journey on the same track through Dovedale. There are also attractive walks south-eastwards to Batsford and Bourton-on-the-Hill.

Bloxham (43-35) A large ironstone village strung out along the undulating A361 with enough strength of character to overcome the disadvantages of too much traffic. It has well built houses, cottages and inns, no two of which are at the same level. At the Banbury end of the village stands Bloxham School, most of which was designed by one of our favourite Victorian architects, G. E. Street. Street also had a hand in the restoration of the fine parish church at the other end of the village, a building of considerable scale, with a magnificent 14th century spire and an austere but dignified interior, which was not spoiled by Street's very restrained restoration work. Here will be found a fascinating series of 14th century carved figures, probably the work of the same mason, or group of masons, who worked at Adderbury, and also possibly at Alkerton and Hanwell. See also the very grand 18th century tomb of Sir John Thorneycroft, and the east window of 1869, which was the work of William Morris and his friends, Edward Burne-Jones and Philip Webb. Walk north-west from here across the fields to Broughton (see page 25), or eastwards, partly along a disused railway line (the old Banbury and Cheltenham Direct Railway) to Adderbury.

Boddington, Lower & Upper (48-52 & 48-53) Two small villages on the western slopes of a low hill, with views out over flat countryside on the borders of Northamptonshire, Oxfordshire and Warwickshire, through which runs the delightful Oxford Canal. There are no special features in the lower village, but Upper Boddington, to its north, has an inn of character and a 14th century church with a late Perpendicular tower. Inside the church will be found a six foot long, iron-bound chest hewn out of a single piece of oak. A mile to the east of these villages, on the other side of the hill, there is a reservoir feeding the summit level of the Oxford Canal at a point to the north of Claydon, by way of a long channel running around the contours below Lower Boddington. Boddington Reservoir is quietly situated, and there are colourful sailing dinghies to be seen from the road in summertime, and bird watching opportunities in winter.

Bourton-on-the-Hill (17-32) If only this village could be by-passed, all would be perfection. But even so, traffic rumbling up Bourton's steep and none too wide street does not entirely spoil this charming village. At the top of the hill stands an 18th century stone built inn, the Horse and Groom; then down the road goes, past pretty little terraces of 17th and 18th century cottages, past the warm stone church , to the bottom of the village, which is here enriched by elegant Bourton House, in the grounds of which stands a fine 16th century barn (dated 1570). The church had a clerestory added in the 15th century and this, together with its handsome three stage tower gives it a totally Perpendicular look. However once within the pleasant cream washed interior, the massive arcade columns reveal its Norman origins....the pointed arches were probably a 12th or 13th century alteration. There are old stone floors and a minute 18th century gallery near the north door. The beautiful bell-metal Winchester Bushel and Peck, dated 1816, are a rare survival of these English standard measures, and were used by local magistrates in the settlement of disputes (usually those relating to the payment of the hated tithes). Do not overlook the 15th century octagonal font, nor the colourful 18th century wall tablets.

Brailes Church... 'the Cathedral of the Feldon'.

Brailes (30-39) Upper and Lower Brailes make up a village of considerable size, strung out along the winding B4035, Shipston—Banbury road. In medieval times it was an important market town, with the protection of a castle, the earthworks of which are clearly visible from the road, and which may be visited on foot. In medieval times it was almost certainly the third largest town in Warwickshire, after Warwick and Coventry, and slight signs of many roads and buildings are visible from the air, in fields adjoining the present main road. There are many pleasant old houses in the village and also two attractive inns, the 16th century George in Lower Brailes and the Gate in Upper Brailes. However Brailes is best noted for the splendid Perpendicular tower of its large church, known locally as the 'Cathedral of the Feldon', the Feldon being the rich pastoral area of southern Warwickshire in which the village lies. The lofty interior was unfortunately scraped in 1879, and has a rather cold feeling, but the sheer size reminds the visitor of the long vanished importance of Brailes. The village lies in some delightful countryside beneath the shelter of Brailes Hill, itself topped by a small clump of trees, a landmark which is visible from many parts of the north-eastern Cotswolds. There are many fine walks across the fields, northwards to Winderton and Compton Wynyates and south-westwards alongside a brook to Sutton-under-Brailes and Stourton.

Broad Campden (15-37) Quieter and much smaller than Chipping Campden, Broad Campden is tucked away in a small valley, with woods never far away ... a delicious little village well removed from the dangers of mass tourism. It has a series of delightful old houses, a small Victorian chapel and an 18th century Friends Meeting House, with much of its original furnishings intact. Charles Ashbee (see Chipping Campden, page 29) converted a derelict Norman chapel into a house for himself soon after his arrival in the area in 1905. Broad Campden has a warm little inn, the Baker's Arms, and an outstandingly good guest house, the Malt House.

Broom (Map 150) (08-53) This village lies to the west of the main area covered by this guide, but can be located on the Key Map, on page 4, almost due west of Stratford-upon-Avon, and about a mile north of Bidford-on-Avon. We have included it here, because in the oft quoted verse attributed to William Shakespeare (see Bidford-on-Avon, page 22), it is referred to as *'Beggarly Broom'*. Why 'beggarly' ? We can only assume that it was for reasons of alliteration alone, and that the inhabitants of this small village on the River Arrow did not, and do not, deserve the unfortunate label that appears to have been hung on them for all time.

Broughton (42-38) The small village on the B4035 is itself unexceptional, but the castle and church are of great interest. A fortified manor house was built here in the early 14th century, and in 1377 it came into the ownership of William of Wykeham, Bishop of Winchester and founder of New College, Oxford and Winchester School. In 1405 Thomas Wykeham turned the manor house into a true castle, and also built the gate-house. His granddaughter married Sir William Fiennes, Lord Saye and Sele in 1451, and Broughton has remained in the hands of the Fiennes family until the present day. The castle was modified in the 16th century, being turned into a house, by removing most of the battlements, altering the roof lines and heightening the great hall. It has remained largely unchanged since that time. It is surrounded by a wide moat, and is one of the most romantically situated castles we have encountered. The interior is full of interest and a visitor here will learn much of England's history from the part that various members of the Fiennes family have played, especially in the period leading up to, and during the Civil War. Celia Fiennes whose diary gives such a fascinating insight into travel in England in the late 17th century, was a member of the family, and although she was the daughter of a second son, she was a frequent visitor here. Writing in 1687 she refers to Broughton thus '. . . *its an old house moted round and a parke and gardens, but were much left to decay and ruine, when my brother came to it . . .*'. *(Tel: (0295) 62624 for opening times.)*

The adjoining church has a fine chancel screen and a splendid series of monuments, largely of members of the Fiennes family, but also of earlier owners of Broughton Castle. Despite restoration work carried out by Sir Gilbert Scott and his son G. G. Scott in the 19th century, this church is still full of atmosphere and well worth visiting.

Burton Dassett (39-51) There was once a substantial little town here, with its own market every Friday, and consequently known as *Chipping Dassett* ('Chipping', being the Old English word for 'market'). This stretched northwards over the now bare hills to Northend, but it declined due both to the Black Death, and later to enclosures by sheep graziers, notably Sir Edward Belknap, who in the early 16th century disposed of no fewer than twelve tenant farmers, to make way for his large and highly profitable flocks of sheep. Now only a church and a few houses survive, but the church here should on no account be missed. It is a Hornton stone building with Norman origins, and has many delightful carvings upon its 13th century north arcade capitals. The interior was restored late enough in the 19th century (1890), for it to have escaped the excesses that were so commonplace amongst the Victorian restorers of only a year or two previously. (William Morris started to turn the tide of opinion when he founded the Society for the Protection of Ancient Buildings in 1877.) There are medieval tiles, old plaster covered walls, traces of medieval wall paintings, and a wonderful atmosphere of the past. The church stands in a churchyard with many charming 18th century tombstones, and there is a

pleasant walk south-eastwards from here over the fields to Avon Dassett. On the green outside the church stands a little Victorian Holy Well. For Burton Dassett Country Park, see below.

Burton Dassett Country Park (39-52) A hundred acre area of small bumpy hills, with open grassy country to be enjoyed by all who long for the type of countryside more usually to be found in the Peak District or the Yorkshire Dales, but found here on a very much smaller scale. There is an old 'beacon tower', probably the base of a medieval tower mill, which until a few years ago kept company with the ruins of an old wooden post mill. Ironstone was quarried here during the last half of the 19th century, it being moved to the railway line beyond Northend by aerial ropeway, but all signs of this activity have long disappeared. On Magpie Hill, to the south of the beacon tower, there is an A.A.Viewpoint, enabling visitors to identify features on the distant skyline. However most come here to walk, to enjoy the views, to fly kites, or on quieter days, to simply sit on the turf and to listen for the skylark's song.

Burton Dassett Country Park.

Byfield (51-53) The quiet and hilly countryside around Byfield is dominated by a great concrete 'lighthouse', one of a chain of 'Post Office Towers' that provide microwave links between the major centres of Britain. Byfield itself used to be of considerable importance, but in the 19th century it became overshadowed by the new railway town of Woodford Halse, which lies a few miles to its east, and which has now itself very much declined. It is a village of much character, with stone houses and small tree-shadowed greens. The tall five stage church tower is topped by a modest spire, and the interior of the church contains a good series of 15th century bench-ends, a west doorway with ball-flower ornament, and the headstops of its chancel arch depicting a demon and a mouse respectively. Walk westwards from here to Boddington Reservoir (see page 24).

Campden Railway Tunnel (16-40) The best road between Chipping Campden and Hidcote Manor Garden passes a wooded embankment created by spoil taken from a tunnel excavated for the Oxford, Worcester and Wolverhampton Railway, built between 1845 and 1853. This tunnel was the site of the so-called 'Battle Of Mickleton', when the great railway builder and engineer, Isambard Kingdom Brunel, led a gang of no fewer than 2000 navvies armed with picks, shovels and even pistols, in an eventually successful attempt to take over from the navvies of the original contractor, who had refused to leave the site. Read the full story of the battle, and of Brunel's fascinating career, in L. T. C. Rolt's outstanding biography. (See Book List.)

Catesby (Upper and Lower) (51-59) Two minute villages in hilly country near the headwaters of the River Leam. Lower Catesby has a small, moated Victorian church, in which will be found some very pleasing Jacobean furnishings, including a handsome pulpit with tester, a reader's desk, stalls and a communion rail. To the south-east of the church there are some massive red brick stables, which were part of the Catesby House estate. Catesby House, in Upper Catesby is a substantial Victorian building, on the site of a Benedictine priory, founded in about 1175. At the Dissolution of the Monasteries in 1539, the Commissioners pleaded for this establishment to be saved, claiming that it was *'in verry perfett order, the priores a sure wyse discrete and very religious woman'*, but this plea

Quiet countryside near the Catesbys.

was rejected out of hand by the ever intractable Thomas Cromwell, and malicious persons appear to have implied that the commissioner concerned, Sir Edmund Knightley, may have been on terms of some intimacy with the *'wyse priores'*. The last major railway line to be built in Britain, the Great Central, ran under the Catesbys in a massive tunnel, and it is said that those dining at Catesby House could then hear the trains rumbling beneath them. .The railway has long vanished, for it never paid its way; and now all that remains are the old air shafts and spoil heaps, visible from the road south towards Hellidon. Walk north from the Catesbys to Flecknoe, and then link on to the Grand Union Canal, less than half a mile beyond. Do **not** try to explore the old tunnel.

Chacombe (49-43) Compact village standing just to the east of the Cherwell valley, and less than three miles from busy Banbury. It has an attractively signed inn overlooking a minute green, the George and Dragon, which has a reputation for excellent meals. Its old stone houses are dominated by a largely 14th century church which was over-restored by the Victorians. There is a Norman font with cablework carving, box pews and a small 16th

Chacombe Priory.

century brass in the north side of the chancel floor to London merchant, Michael Fox. Chacombe Priory, a 17th and 18th century house, stands on the site of a priory of Augustinian canons, founded by a certain Hugh Chacombe, who was Justiciary to Henry II in Normandy. Good walk north from here, across fields to Upper Wardington, and beyond to Edgcote.

Charlecote (26-56) A small, but very charming village with a few mellow brick houses and cottages looking out across its only road, to Charlecote Park. The church, which is also on the edge of the park was completed in 1851, having been paid for by Mrs Mary Elizabeth Lucy of Charlecote Park , who in her words, *'had long wished to pull down the wretched old church in the park and build a new one'*. It is in the Decorated style and typically Victorian, but is well worth visiting on account of the three fine 17th century monuments, to three Sir Thomas Lucy's, and their respective wives, which were moved here from the earlier church. The monument to the Sir Thomas dated 1640, in black and white marble, is the work of Nicholas Stone, the finest English 17th century sculptor, and should on no account be missed.

Charlecote Park was landscaped by Capability Brown, who made full use of the Elizabethan mansion's setting on the banks of the Avon, close to the point where it is joined by the little River Dene (itself crossed by an elegant bridge carrying the road towards Loxley). The mellow brick 16th century Gatehouse provides a delicious break

SCALE 1:25 000 or 2½ INCHES to 1 MILE

Charlecote ... trim gardens, massive cedars and a mansion full of memories.

between the wide deer park and the trim gardens and house beyond. The porch of the house is also part of the original Elizabethan structure, as are the Stables and Brewhouse. Considerable alterations were made to the house in the 19th century and its interior is now largely Victorian in flavour. To fully appreciate this, you should read the fascinating and often rather tragic memoirs of Mary Elizabeth Lucy, published as *Mistress of Charlecote* and introduced by Lady Alice Fairfax Lucy. Mary came to Charlecote as a young bride in 1823, and lived there until her death in 1889. Her personality and her influence are evident at every turn, and the interior of the house very much reflects her life and that of her family during the 19th century. Visitors to Charlecote can see a fascinating video film, based on extracts from *Mistress of Charlecote*, on show in a room above the Tack Room off the stable yard, and it is strongly advised that this is viewed at the start of any visit.

Charlecote had been in the hands of the Lucy family since the early 13th century, and it was given by them to the National Trust in 1946. Queen Elizabeth I stayed here for two nights while on the way to Kenilworth in 1572 and there is a much related, but sadly unsubstantiated tale, of the young William Shakespeare being caught poaching deer by Sir Thomas Lucy in 1583. Justice Shallow in *Henry IV, Part Two* and *The Merry Wives of Windsor* is thought to be a take-off of Sir Thomas, with the playwright's mockery of the knight's pride in his coat of arms incorporating a *'dozen white luces'*. But quite apart from these associations a visit to Charlecote is well worthwhile, with a walk down through the park, with its herd of fallow deer, a view of the video film (see above), a visit to the house, the stables with its collection of Lucy family carriages, the brewhouse, a walk round the gardens on the banks of the Avon, a visit to the National Trust shop, and a light meal in the excellent Orangery restaurant. *Tel: (0789) 840277 for opening times.*

Charlton (52-36) This small stone village is now the busy part of Newbottle parish, although the church of Newbottle (see page 50) lies about a mile to the north. However in the cemetery at Charlton will be found the altar tomb of the celebrated conservative statesman and lawyer, F.E.Smith, Earl of Birkenhead, who died in 1930. This memorial was designed by the equally celebrated Sir Edwin Lutyens, perhaps best known for his other more public memorial, the Cenotaph in Whitehall. Rainsborough Camp, a mile to the south of Charlton, and reached by a bridle path, was an Iron Age hill fort, which was later used by the Romans. It looks westwards out over the Cherwell valley, which it must have controlled most effectively.

Cherington (29-36) This modest stone village is situated in the upper Stour valley between Brailes Hill and Stourton Hill. It has a a handsome 17th century manor house, further enriched by a charming 18th century Gothick porch. The largely 13th

SCALE 1:25 000 or 2½ INCHES to 1 MILE

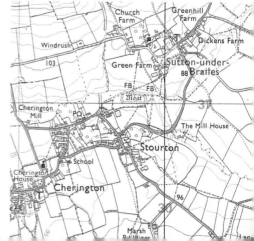

century church is full of interest. It has a well proportioned tower, fine Perpendicular windows, some with interesting medieval glass, a Jacobean altar table and rail, and a delightful series of carved corbel figures beneath the roof beams. However Cherington's greatest treasure is the lovely 14th century canopied tomb chest, topped with an effigy of a 'civilian', whose name is unfortunately not known . . . a fine specimen of the Decorated period. There is a pleasant, partly open road leading south from here across Weston Park, towards Long Compton. This park once contained a fine early 19th century mansion, but it was pulled down in 1934. Its site is marked on the map (28-34), but no trace remains above ground. Read the fascinating story of Weston in *A Prospect of Weston in Warwickshire*, by Michael Warriner, published by the Roundwood Press, but now out of print. Walk on this road, or use the bridle-path running roughly parallel with it, up to Margett's Hill, and on, partly through Long Compton Woods, to Long Compton.

Chesterton (35-58) Apart from a few houses at Chesterton Green, this is almost a deserted village. There was once a great 17th century mansion here, built for the Peyto family, probably by John Stone, son of the great sculptor Nicholas Stone. Old prints reveal that it had a facade with eleven bays, and it appears to have been inspired by Inigo Jones's Banqueting Hall at Whitehall Palace, a building on

Chesterton Windmill.

which Nicholas Stone had previously worked as mason. The mansion was pulled down in 1802, and all that now remains is an isolated archway in the churchyard. The elegant watermill (34-59) was probably also designed by Stone, for the mansion

SCALE 1:25 000 or 2½ INCHES to 1 MILE

Chipping Campden ... with its splendidly towered church.

must have overlooked its millpond cum ornamental lake. For many years the design of the very handsome windmill (34-59) was ascribed to Inigo Jones, as it was built in 1632, some twenty years earlier than the mansion. However it is now thought to have been the work of the squire himself, Sir Edward Peyto. It is without doubt a fine piece of work for an amateur, even in a county, which a century later, was to produce Sanderson Miller, squire of Radway and architect extraordinary (see page 52). Walk across the field from the T – junction to visit the windmill, which has been restored in recent years, and which now stands complete with a handsome set of white painted sails. There are fine views from this dome-topped building upon its Tuscan columns, and below it to the north west are the earthworks of a Roman marching camp, astride the Foss Way.

The church, which looks across an open field to a small lake with waterfowl usually in residence, is a long, low building, entered through a Decorated south doorway. The interior is full of character, with a black and white chequered floor, old plastered walls and three fine monuments to members of the Peyto family, one of which is by the outstanding 17th century sculptor, Nicholas Stone, and one by his son John, the builder of the long vanished mansion. A study of the map will show various walking possibilities in the vicinity of Chesterton, especially towards the south and east, but please respect landowner's rights and keep all dogs on leads.

Chipping Campden (15-39) Chipping was an Old English word meaning 'Market', and Campden had a weekly market, and no fewer than three annual fairs as early as the mid 13th century. It was without doubt the most important trading centre for wool in the north Cotswolds in the 14th and 15th centuries, and its name must have been familiar to wool merchants on the quays of Bruges and Antwerp, and most other cloth-trading ports of western Europe. William Grevel, described as *'the flower of the wool merchants of all England'* on his memorial brass in the parish church, built 'Grevel's House' in about 1380. With its splendid Perpendicular style two-storeyed, gabled window, this was to become one of the first of a bewilderingly beautiful series of buildings in the honey-coloured local stone, that were erected in the following centuries, by succeeding townsmen grown prosperous on wool. Grevel's House is in private hands, but the Woolstapler's Hall, built at about the same time by wool merchant, Robert Calf, now houses an interesting small museum, which also incorporates a helpful Tourist Information Centre *(Tel: (0386) 840289)*.

The lovely Market Hall was built in 1627 by Sir Baptist Hicks *'for the sale of cheese, butter and poultry'*. He had made his money in the cloth trade, not in Chipping Campden, but in the southern Cotswolds and in London; for by this time Campden's wool trading prosperity had almost ceased, due to the fact that since Edward III's reign, Flemish weavers had been encouraged to come to England, and wool was handled directly by the clothiers in the Stroud valley and elsewhere, rather than by exporting merchants. Sir Baptist built himself a fine mansion not far from the church, but sadly this was later burnt down by Royalists during the Civil War to prevent it falling into the hands of Cromwell's forces, and the only survivals are the lodges and gatehouse, two ruined pavilions and an almonry. However just below the church is Sir Baptist's most

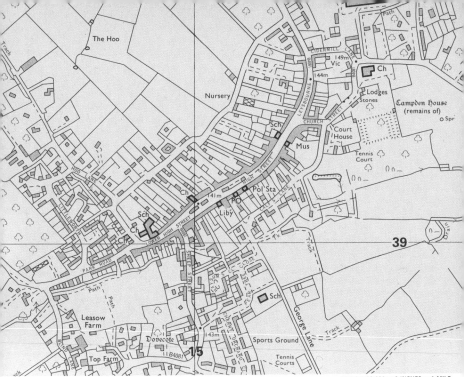

Chipping Campden.

SCALE 1:10 000 or 6 INCHES to 1 MILE

enduring legacy, a row of delightful almshouses built by him in 1612. Sir Baptist became Baron Hicks and Viscount Campden in 1628 (an appointment no doubt arising from the substantial loans that he had made to his sovereign) but sadly he died only a year later. He and his wife are buried beneath a splendid marble monument in Campden church. This is one of the great Cotswold wool churches, a fine Perpendicular style building with a handsome 15th century pinnacled tower. Its interior is perhaps a little cold in feeling, but it contains some interesting monumental brasses, a series of monuments in the Noel Chapel, and an outstanding collection of medieval English embroidery, including copes and altar hangings.

Chipping Campden's prosperity declined greatly in the 18th and 19th centuries, although local quarry owner and builder, Thomas Woodward, left an enduring mark on the High Street, with the building of the elegantly classical Bedfont House in about 1745. However Campden appears to have slept largely undisturbed by intrusions until the early years of the 20th century. Then, in 1902, a disciple of William Morris and Ruskin, Charles Ashbee, moved his 'Guild and School of Handicraft' from London's East End to Chipping Campden. This migration of fifty craftsmen and their families was a brave endeavour and full of ideals, but the Guild did not survive the rigours of economic depression, the World War, and above all, the mutual suspicion arising between the Cockney craftsmen and the countrymen of Campden. However Ashbee's ideals have in part survived, thanks largely to the artist and architect F. L. Griggs, who established the Campden Trust in 1929, and who did so much to preserve the Chipping Campden that we see today; thanks also to George Hart, the craftsman in metal, his son and grandson, who have kept the tradition of the Guild alive; and also more recently, to Robert Welch, the talented industrial designer whose work may be seen at his studio shop in the High Street.

Chipping Campden's present day character still owes much to F. L. Griggs and his friends, and remains largely unspoilt. There are now more tourist shops, restaurants and hotels than there were in Griggs's day, but there are still a few genuine 'country-town' shops and small inns left, and it remains a pleasure to walk the length of the High Street and up past the almshouses, to the splendidly towered church, and on to the open land beyond, which belongs to the National Trust. Do not overlook the garden opened in memory of Ernest Wilson, who was born at Chipping Campden

High Street, Chipping Campden.

in 1876, and who became one of the great plant collectors, on a series of expeditions to the Far East in the first thirty years of this century. This is situated in the lower half of the old Vicarage garden, and fronts on to the Main Street. See also Campden Pottery *(Tel: (0386) 840315)*, and Campden Weavers *(Tel: (0386) 840864)*.

Chipping Campden is the northern terminus of the long distance footpath, known as the Cotswold Way, which runs from here following the approximate line of the western scarp, down to Bath, a distance of about 90 miles. Why not walk the first few miles at least, up over the fields to Dover's Hill (see page 33). Start by walking west, down the High Street, and turning right into Back Ends and Hoo Lane, and then follow sign to left marked 'Cotswold Way'.

Chipping Warden (49-48) This pretty ironstone and thatch village is situated in the upper Cherwell valley, and, like Chipping Campden, was once a busy market town, 'Chipping' being the Old English word for 'market'. There are at least two inns here, one of which, the Rose and Crown, serves the delectable Hook Norton Ale (or 'Hooky' to the locals). There are the remains of an old market cross on the green, behind which is the large Decorated and Perpendicular church. Inside will be found an elegant 18th century pulpit, with canopy and iron hand-rail, and brasses to William Smarte, a 15th century rector, and to Richard Makepiece and his wife and their fifteen children . To the south-west of the village, just to the west of the A361, there are earthworks, known as Arbury Banks, which are probably the remains of an Iron Age camp. There are attractive views across the Cherwell valley to Edgcote Park (see page 34), and an opportunity to walk across fields, south and west, latterly beside the Cherwell, to a point where its course is joined by the Oxford Canal, just beyond Prescote Manor (47-46).

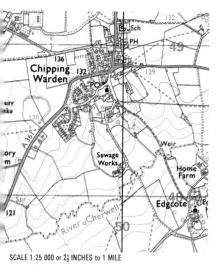

SCALE 1:25 000 or 2½ INCHES to 1 MILE

Claverdon (19-64) A village much enlarged by modern development, situated in a countryside of small lanes and scattered woodlands, with a series of smaller settlements within a mile or two of its

centre. The church has a Perpendicular tower and a chancel arch of the Decorated period, but is otherwise the result of 19th century rebuilding. There is a memorial tablet to Sir Francis Galton (1822-1911), a cousin of Charles Darwin and a scientist who made significant advances in such widely assorted disciplines as meteorology, heredity and the science of finger-printing. See also the tomb of Thomas Spencer, a second son of one of the Althorp Spencers, who were all descended from the Spencers of Snitterfield. He lived in a large house on the north-east of the village, the only remains of which are now known as the Stone Building, a 'tower-house' which may at one time have been semi-fortified, in a style more often found in the wilder parts of the North Country. Neither the Stratford-upon-Avon Canal, nor the Grand Union are far away, and their tow paths make some of the best walking in the area.

Claydon (45-50) Oxfordshire's northernmost village sits on a quiet hilltop less than two miles south of 'Three Shires', where the boundaries of Warwickshire, Northamptonshire and Oxfordshire meet. To the east there is gently undulating countryside through which the lovely Oxford Canal winds on its way south towards the Cherwell valley. The towpath walk from here to Cropredy is particularly attractive, passing several locks, where in summertime, boats may usually be seen, being 'worked through' by enthusiastic amateur crews who will often welcome a little help from passing walkers. Claydon church has a little saddlebacked tower, and within will be found Norman arcading with supporting pillars no more than five feet high. Incorporated in a farm at Clattercote (45-49), there are the slight remains of a priory founded in the 12th century, but this is **not** open to the public.

Clifford Chambers (19-52) Delightful village not far from the Stour's confluence with the Avon, with a single wide street, bordered by tree shaded grass verges, ending at the gates of a manor house. This was late 17th century, but was largely re-built by the renowned Sir Edwin Lutyens soon after the end of the 1914-18 War. Stone, mellow brick, half timbering . . . all play their part in Clifford village, and all are enhanced by colourful gardens, many with a cottage flavour. The church has Norman origins, but it has a thin Perpendicular tower and a chancel that was over-restored by the Victorians. However do not overlook the pulpit and communion rail, which are both Jacobean, nor the two 15th century brasses to Sir Henry Rainsford and his wife and children. It is known that the 16th century rectory was the home of a John Shakespeare, at the time when William Shakespeare was growing up. There is an attractive walk, mainly over the fields, to Stratford-upon-Avon, and one leading south, and parallel with the Stour, to Atherstone on Stour, and on to Preston on Stour.

Combrook (30-51) Beautifully sited in a deep wooded valley, the little village of Combrook stands below a grass covered dam. This we assume to be the work of Capability Brown, who created two lakes in the valley as part of the landscaping of the Compton Verney estate, in which the village lies. Here are a few old farms and thatched cottages, but many of the buildings were put up by the estate in the mid 19th century... a charming little Gothic church much ornamented with angels, a school, and several estate houses. But all is mellow in this quiet valley and the Victorian work does not offend the eye. It is possible to take a circular walk (see Walk 7) from here, up by the dam and roughly parallel with the western shore of the lake, and return beyond the other side, partly through woods. This allows for a fine view of Compton Verney from the bridge on the road between the two lakes (see below). It is also possible to walk south and east, over the fields and across the little River Dene, to Butlers Marston.

Compton Verney (31-52) Dignified early-18th century mansion in a wooded valley, with two lakes. There was an old manor house here in the 15th century, but the present house was built in about 1714, and alterations were carried out in 1760 by Robert Adam. About ten years later Capability Brown was called in to transform the gardens into a landscaped park, complete with two lakes; and a chapel was built, the decaying interior of which contains several interesting monuments to the Verney family. Unfortunately Compton Verney is not open to the public, but it is well worth stopping to obtain glimpses of the house and bridge across the lake, from amongst the trees on the road between Wellesbourne and Kineton, but do not park near the bridge. It is possible to walk south from here parallel with the west side of the lower lake, to the delightful little village of Combrook, and then back, partly through woodland, beyond the other side of the lake. **(See Walk 7).**

Compton Wynyates (33-41) A beautiful Tudor mansion of mellow brick in a lovely setting amongst wooded hillsides. The unusual occurrence of brick in this predominantly stone countryside is probably accounted for by King Henry's gift to William Compton, of the ruined castle of Fulbroke (site at ref 25-60, near Sherbourne, which is itself near Warwick), and Sir William's subsequent use of the salvaged materials at Compton. Royal visitors to Compton Wynyates included not only Henry VIII, but also Elizabeth I, James I and Charles I. Most of the moat was filled in at the end of the Civil War, and the famous clipped yews are alas no more. The house is no longer open to the public, but there are enchanting glimpses of it down from the road to its immediate west. On the skyline behind the house there is a stone tower-windmill complete with sails,

and this can be reached by a path that starts from a tree lined track off the road well to the north east of the house. It is possible to walk down the other side of the hill into Upper Tysoe. Compton Pike (32-41), to the south-west, looks like the top of a spire peering over the edge of the hillside until it is encountered close by, when it is revealed as a sharp pyramid-like structure. Was it built to confuse and amuse, or was it the base of a beacon ? Opinions are divided.

The Cotswold Way (See Chipping Campden, page 31)

The Red Lion Inn, Cropredy.

Cropredy (46-46) Here the Cherwell and the Oxford Canal start a parallel run, which lasts almost the whole way to their union with the Thames at Oxford. The canal has more impact than the river, and it brings much flavour to an already attractive village. The churchyard has many beautifully lettered 17th and 18th century tombstones, and is overlooked by the hospitable Red Lion Inn. The largely Perpendicular church contains fragments of a wall painting of the Last Judgement above the chancel arch, a fine 15th century lectern in the form of a brass eagle on a globe, early oak screens in the side chapels and a beautiful old roof, well lit by clerestory windows.

Cropredy Bridge was the site of one of the fiercest minor battles of the Civil War, when on 29th June, 1644, the Royalists under King Charles himself became engaged with a Parliamentarian force lead by Sir William Waller. Initially it appeared that Waller would triumph, but eventually the Royalists prevailed, and a quantity of artillery and many prisoners were taken. This victory removed the Parliamentary threat to the Royalist stronghold at Oxford for the remainder of the year, and was thus of considerable significance. Read more about this in the *Ordnance Survey Guide to the Battlefields of Britain*. The best walks from here are inevitably north and south along the canal towpath, but it is also possible to walk across fields to Wardington and Chipping Warden **(see Walk 3).**

Deddington (46-31) A trim ironstone village, much of which is astride the busy A423, Banbury to Oxford road, and which still awaits relief from the proposed M40 motorway extension. The grassy ramparts are all that remain of a large medieval

SCALE 1:25 000 or 2½ INCHES to 1 MILE

motte-and-bailey castle. It was here, on June 10th 1312, that Edward II's favourite, Piers Gaveston, already a prisoner of the Earl of Pembroke, was seized by the Earl of Warwick, who Gaveston had rather unwisely nicknamed 'the black cur of Arden'. The prisoner was then taken on mule-back to Warwick Castle and on July 1st was beheaded on Blacklow Hill , just to the north of the town (see Gaveston's Cross (28-67), page 37). The fine Decorated and Perpendicular style church lies between the castle mound and the main road. It has a well proportioned interior, with clerestory windows and a window over the chancel arch, all 15th century work. The contents of the interior is not of outstanding interest, but do not miss the Jacobean pulpit, nor the small 14th century brass. Sir Thomas Pope, founder of Trinity College, Oxford, friend of Sir Thomas More, and one time guardian of the young queen-to-be, Elizabeth, was born at Deddington in 1508. He is buried in Trinity College chapel.

Other pleasant old buildings in Deddington include the little Town Hall (for this was a market town until the 18th century), the Jacobean Kings Arms, and the 18th century Three Tuns.

Dorsington Manor Gardens (12-50) These are situated to the north-east of Dorsington village, and are just off our map. Here is the home of the Domestic Fowl Trust, which has a collection of domestic birds from many parts of the world. There is also a collection of 'Domestic Household Appliances' a model railway, picnic area, restaurant and gift shop. *Tel: (0789) 772442.*

Dover's Hill (13-39) This is a delightful crescent-shaped field-walk poised on the very edge of the Cotswold scarp, and was acquired by the National Trust in 1928, thanks to the efforts of Chipping Campden's F. L. Griggs, and to the generosity of that great historian, G. M. Trevelyan. There is a small car park here, and one can walk along the hillside, down to the edge of dense woodland below, or even back down to Chipping Campden, on the footpath shown on the map, which is part of the Cotswold Way. On a clear day views out over the Avon valley and the Midland plain extend to Bredon, the Malverns, and the distant outlines of the Black Mountains and the Long Mynd. Identification of these distant hills is made easier and more interesting by a well engraved viewing topograph not far beyond the car park.

Dover's Hill was the site of the famous 'Cotswold Olympicks', founded in 1612 by local lawyer Robert Dover, with the approval of James I, having been approached through Dover's friend at Court, Endymion Porter, who lived at nearby Aston Subedge (see page 19). These games, held on the Thursday and Friday after Whit Sunday, included the usual horse racing, hare coursing, dancing and wrestling, but there were also two essentially local contests of a more violent nature; single-stick fighting, in which the contestants fought with one arm tied behind their backs, sometimes for hours at a time, with the sole intention of 'breaking the other's head'; and the other; shin-kicking, the purpose of which was to reduce one's opponent to such agonies that he was forced to withdraw defeated. The more enthusiastic shin-kickers used to 'harden-up' by beating their own shins with planks, or even in extreme cases, with hammers, in the weeks prior to the games.

Although temporarily suppressed during the Cromwellian period, the Games were otherwise held regularly each year until the mid-19th century. By this time they had become the scene of considerable violence and drunkenness, a state greatly worsened by the presence of Irish navvies, who were then building the nearby tunnel (see page 25), and they were discontinued in 1853, following an Act of Parliament enclosing the land. In 1951, the Games were again revived, and since then they have been held each year on the Friday following the Spring Bank Holiday, followed by the 'Scuttlebrook Wake', on the Saturday, a colourful fair which culminates in a torch-light procession from Dover's Hill, back down into Chipping Campden.

Draycote Water Country Park (46-69) This is situated at Hensborough Hill on the south-eastern shore of the large Draycote Water reservoir, and lies on the A 426 Southam to Rugby road. There is a car park, picnic area and adventure playground for children. There is also a Fishing Lodge, and facilities for both boat and bank fishing. Sailing here is a club activity, but the movement of sailing dinghies over the sparkling water always provides a pleasant spectacle. In winter-time there are bird-watching possibilities here, but only with a permit. *(Apply to Avon Treatment Works, Mill Road, Rugby).*

Dinghies at Draycote Water.

Ebrington (18-40) A beautiful village overlooking a valley through which the little Knee Brook flows on its way to join the Stour above Shipston. 'Yubberton', as many of the locals still call it, has many attractively thatched, stone cottages lining its little sunken roads leading to the centre, which is overlooked by a war memorial and the handsomely signed Ebrington Arms.

The church stands on a small ridge close to the largely 17th century manor house, and above the rest of the village. It has a good solid tower and a Norman south doorway with a geometric design upon its tympanum, rather similar in style to the one at Great Rollright (see page 37). Inside the church there are a few medieval bench-ends, and a large, heavily restored pulpit, dated 1679. In fact the whole interior has been over-restored, but there are several fine monuments to members of the Keyte and Fortescue families. See especially the monument to Sir John Fortescue, who was Lord Chief Justice of England during some of the most troubled years of the Wars of the Roses. Despite a reversal of his fortunes after the defeat of the Lancastrians at Tewkesbury in 1471, he was allowed a gentle retirement at Ebrington until his death some years later, at the age of ninety. This was most unusual in an age when defeated enemies were usually despatched without hesitation, in a variety of highly barbarous methods.

The two 17th century Keyte monuments are equally interesting and we particularly like the notice reading, *'William Keyte Esq., A.D. 1632, left by will the milk of ten good and sufficient kine to the poor of Ebrington from May 10th — November 1st for ever'*. It is sad to read a note below that indicates that *'This charge was redeemed 1952'*; no doubt a practical step, but how dull ! William Keyte's son, Sir John Keyte, must also have been a man of substance, as it is known that he raised a troop of horse *'at his own expense'* in support of his sovereign, during the Civil War.

The best walk from Ebrington leads north-eastwards, past Foxcote House, to Ilmington, and returning via Nebsworth and Ebrington Hill. Links may also be made to the road northwards over Lark Stoke, or across to Hidcote. All these walks are over windy, often open wold country, with fine views out over the Midland plain, the Northamptonshire uplands and the line of hills on the borders of

Oxfordshire. They are some of the best to be found in the area covered by this guide.

Edgcote (50-47) Here is a handsome 18th century manor house, an old rectory, a few cottages, and a church with 13th century origins, all on the edge of parkland bordering the infant Cherwell, and looking across to the village of Chipping Warden. The present manor was built in 1747-52 by Sir Richard Chauncey, probably to the plans of William Smith of Warwick, to replace a house, which had sheltered Charles I and his two sons on the night before the Battle of Edgehill, and which had been in the Chauncey family for centuries. In the church there are monuments to two Elizabethan Chaunceys, and an elegant marble bust of Sir Richard, the builder of the present manor, by the celebrated Flemish-born sculptor, J. M. Rysbrack, who was also responsible for three wall tablets in memory of other Chaunceys. See also the 18th century pulpit and box pews, the manorial pew, and the rather sad little inscription to a spinster, who died in 1730, *'Under this marble stone lies whatsoever was mortal of Bridgit Chauncy, of whom man was not worthy'*.

On July 26th 1469, during the Wars of the Roses, a battle was fought at Danes Moor, to the south-

Edgcote House and Church.

east of Edgcote, when Robin of Redesdale, a northern rebel, probably backed by the Earl of Warwick, defeated Edward IV's troops under the command of the Earl of Pembroke. Pembroke and his brother, Sir William Herbert, were taken prisoner, and soon put to death by the rebels. For further details, read the *Ordnance Survey Guide to the Battlefields of Britain*. Traditionally Danes Moor is said also to be the site of a much earlier battle, between Danes and Saxons, but there appears to be little evidence to substantiate this. Walk across the Cherwell valley to Chipping Warden, or south across the fields to Upper Wardington and Chacombe.

Edgehill (37-47) Small village just behind the scarp face from which it takes its name. There are two buildings of interest, a thatched cottage, and a 'castle'. Both are the work of Sanderson Miller, 18th century squire of neighbouring Radway (see page 52), and are in the *'Picturesque Gothick'* style, for which Miller was noted. (See also Radway, page 52.) The 'castle', which is now a lively local inn, was built on the point where Charles I's standard was raised on Sunday morning, 23rd October in the year 1642, at the start of the first major battle of the Civil

Monuments in Ebrington Church.

The Castle Inn, Edgehill.

War. The story of the battle is well summarised in the *Ordnance Survey Guide to the Battlefields of Britain*. But briefly, the Parliamentarian forces under the Earl of Essex, had come from the north and west, and the Royalists from the south and east, and on that fateful Sunday morning, they were facing each other across the broad country that lies between Kineton (33-51) and Edgehill, with the Parliamentarians based on Kineton and the Royalists on Edgehill. Initially it appeared that the cavalry, under the command of the King's younger brother, Prince Rupert, had triumphed, but lack of discipline led to much impetus being lost while Rupert's horsemen plundered the baggage train of the Parliamentarian commanders in Kineton. So Edgehill's results were not as decisive as they might have been, and although there were heavy casualties on both sides, the two armies withdrew at the end of the day, both remaining as effective fighting forces.

The actual site of the battle is now largely in the hands of the Ministry of Defence, but there is a small modern monument beside the road to Kineton (35-50), and good views over the country where the battle must have raged may be had from the bottom of the woods that clothe part of Edgehill's slopes. These woods were planted by Sanderson Miller, along the upper edge of his park at Radway. There are two paths down through these woods to Radway, and together they make a delightful circular walk. **(See Walk 6.)** It is also possible to walk along the top of the woods to Sun Rising Hill and beyond, dropping down eventually into Tysoe (34-44). Celia Fiennes (see page 25), coming to see Edgehill in about 1690, *'where was the famous Battle fought in Cromwells tyme'*, further remarked in her diary that, *'the Ridge of hills runs a great length and so high that the land beneath it appears vastly distant.... tho' formidable to look down on it and turnes ones head round, the wind allwayes blows with great violence there'*. It is happily still very much the same.

Epwell (35-40) A small Hornton stone village tucked away in a hollow not far behind the scarp face of the Oxfordshire Cotswolds, the top of which

is followed here by the boundary between Oxfordshire and Warwickshire. There is a small ford just below a row of cottages, one of which used to be the Three Horseshoes Inn. The church has a small central tower, a thin Jacobean pulpit, a Perpendicular roof, and a pretty little 14th century piscina. Although not clearly defined at this point, the course of a Roman road running eastward from Worcester, through Alcester and Stratford-upon-Avon towards the Kings Sutton area, must have passed almost directly through Epwell. Its course is much clearer about two miles to the south-east, in the vicinity of Swalcliffe and Madmarston Hill (38-38). The Chandler's Arms serves Hook Norton Ales, and it is possible to walk south-westwards from here, past Blenheim Farm, and then linking on to a track following the course of the Roman road (see above), to arrive at Swalcliffe.

Exhall (Map 150) (10-55) This lies beyond the west of the main area covered by this guide, but it may be located on the Key Map on page 4, due west of Stratford-upon-Avon, and about two miles north of Bidford-on-Avon. We have included it here as it is referred to in an oft quoted doggerel verse, attributed to William Shakespeare (see Bidford-on-Avon, page 22), as *'dodging Exhall'*. We are not sure what the inhabitants of Exhall were dodging, but it is thought that the verse may have been referring to the remote, scattered nature of its houses, cottages and farms... a delightful feature of Exhall that has survived to this day. It is quietly situated in a broad valley below wooded Oversley Hill, with timber-framed cottages and substantial farm houses, and a largely Norman church, much restored in about 1862. There are views southwards to the wooded ridge on which Ardens Grafton stands.

Farnborough (43-49) A charming Hornton stone hillside village, with cottages and pathways poised above its winding street. Do not let the impressive Victorian spire deter you from visiting the church, which is apart from this feature, a largely medieval building. It has an interesting Norman south doorway, and an attractive and poignant memorial to a Mrs Wagstaffe, who died in 1667, which tells us that, *'Ten children of their mother are bereft'*.

Ambrose Holbech commenced the building of Farnborough Hall in 1684, and it was from his descendants that it passed to the National Trust in 1960. It is a handsome largely 18th century house set in modest parklands, with lakes and a delicious terrace walk along the hillside above and beyond. Here will be found a little classical temple, an oval pavilion and, at the far end, a tall obelisk. Knowing how close Farnborough is to Radway, the home of

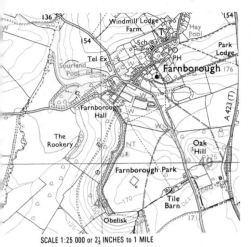

Windmill Lodge
Farm
Hay
Pool

Sch
PO
PH
Tel Ex
Sourland
Pool

Farnborough

Park
Lodge
176

A 423 (T)

Farnborough
Hall

The
Rookery

Oak
Hill
175

Farnborough Park

Tile
Barn

Obelisk 171

SCALE 1:25 000 or 2½ INCHES to 1 MILE

Sanderson Miller (see page 52), it is hard to ignore the possibility that he was in some way involved with the layout of this terrace. Views from here, out over the valley towards Warmington and Edge Hill are a delight, and it is a sad business visualising the changes that would take place, if the M40 motorway extension comes this way. The interior of Farnborough Hall is equally beguiling, especially the dining room, with its marble chimney-piece, and its panels framing copies of paintings by Canaletto and Pannini, panels which once framed the originals. *Tel: (0684 297747) (The National Trust, Tewkesbury Regional Office) for opening times.*

Fenny Compton (41-52) Small village of Hornton stone and mellow brick, sitting quietly beneath the Burton Dassett hills with several pleasing old houses. These include, by the church, the handsome early-18th century Red House, once the rectory, and in nearby Bridge Street, the stone Woad House, which has a 14th century window in the Decorated style. The church of St. Peter and St. Clare, standing above most of the village, has a stout little tower topped by a short spire. The Victorians built the south arcade, as a copy of the Decorated north arcade, and the overall effect is rather heart-warming, with views of the chancel through a minute chancel arch, and light coming in from the small clerestory windows above. To the east of the village, just beyond a factory making concrete products, there is a busy marina on the lovely Oxford Canal (see page 50). To its south is a long, deep cutting which was once a tunnel, but the best canal walks are north-east, past the George and Dragon, towards Wormleighton. Other walks from Fenny Compton lead south-west, up over Gredenton Hill, from which there are fine views; and on to the Burton Dassett Country Park (see page 25), or south- eastwards over Hall's Hill and Windmill Hill to Farnborough.

Foss Way This runs diagonally across our map, from Moreton-in-Marsh (20-30), north-eastwards to Eathorpe (39-69) which lies to the east of Leamington Spa. The permanent Roman occupation of Britain commenced in 43 A.D., almost a hundred years after Julius Caesar's brief invasions in 55 and 54 B.C., and within only four years the new

Governor, Ostorius had concluded its first stage by establishing his civil boundary along the line that was soon to become the Foss Way. This then became a temporary frontier between the subjugated Iron Age tribes of the south and east, and their wilder, still to be conquered counterparts in the hillier and less easily controlled north and west.

The Foss Way ran from Lincoln to Exeter, a total distance of 182 miles, and in the years that followed its construction, its purpose must have been largely military, with forts and marching camps established upon it at regular intervals, and with roads leading off it to the north and west carrying the legions towards the more troubled regions that lay beyond. It is one of the most direct of all Roman roads, and between Lincoln and Axminster in Devon, it is never further than six miles away from a theoretical straight line joining these two points. Thomas Codrington, writing in 1903, stated that in Leicestershire and Warwickshire the Foss Way was *'now an unimportant road mostly grass covered, or little more than a lane or field road'*, and the writer recalls this still being the case until the late 1940's. Today however it is a much used, but strangely still unclassified road from Halford northwards. The only site of any interest connected with the Foss in the area covered by this guide, is the shallow rectangular earthwork below Chesterton Windmill (34-59), all that remains of a Roman marching camp. The best accounts of the Foss Way, and the other Roman road in the area, that between Stratford-upon-Avon and the King's Sutton area (see Epwell, page 35), is to be found in I. D. Margary's classic work, *Roman Roads in Britain*.

The Four Shire Stone (23-32) A handsome 18th century monument topped by a sundial and ball, marking the meeting point of four counties, Oxfordshire, Gloucestershire, Warwickshire and Worcestershire. This still applies to the first three, but the

The Four Shire Stone.

isolated 'island' of Worcestershire, no doubt originally due to the once wide domains of the Bishops of Worcester, has been swallowed up in Gloucestershire many years ago.

Foxcote (19-41) This fine early-18th century mansion, possibly built by Edward Woodward of Chipping Campden, is only open to visitors by prior written appointment with Mr C. B. Holman, but there is a public right-of-way for walkers down its long curving drive, and beyond it on a rougher track, to the village of Ebrington. Starting from the road between Ilmington and Charingworth, this is an attractive walk, and a return journey may be made via Ebrington Hill and Nebsworth (19-42).

Gaveston's Cross (28-67) This solid stone cross on four large piers, was erected on Blacklow Hill to the north of Warwick in 1832, to mark the spot where the unfortunate Piers Gaveston was beheaded in 1312 (see Deddington, page 32). Part of the rather bleak inscription upon it reads, *'The base minion of a hateful king, in life and death a memorable instance of misrule'*. One wonders why the builders of this dark monument ever bothered to record such a gloomy and remote event. There is no path to it, but the monument is normally just visible from the busy A46, in a small wood.

Grand Union Canal (19-69 — 52-65) This amalgamation of several older waterways, runs from Birmingham to the Thames at Brentford, a total distance of 137 miles. It crosses our map from the vicinity of Rowington (19-69) to the hamlet of Wolfhampcote (52-65), with a junction at Napton, linking on to the Oxford Canal (see page 50). The most dramatic flight of locks, is at Hatton (24-66), and there is a short tunnel at Shrewley (21-67), less than two miles to the west. The best known canalside inns are the Blue Lias at Long Itchington (42-64), the Boat on the A 426 near Stockton (43-65), and the Waterman, near the top of the Hatton flight of locks, west of Warwick (24-66). British Waterways welcome walkers on the canal towpaths, even where no statutory right-of-way exists, but it does not hold itself responsible to walkers for the state of these paths. In some cases they may be partially obstructed, or rather overgrown, but they are so attractive that, in our opinion, walking along them is a risk well worth taking. **(See Walks 1 and 2.)**

Great Rollright (32-31) Windy upland village just over the county boundary into Oxfordshire, with fine views south over a broad valley towards rolling hill country around Chipping Norton. There are no real features of interest here, apart from the Norman church. This has some grotesque gargoyles on its well proportioned Perpendicular tower and a Norman doorway whose tympanum has a fish inserted amongst various geometric carvings. The porch in which it shelters is two storeyed and its cornice is richly carved with an assortment of animals, flowers and the heads of men and women. Inside there is much evidence of over-zealous Victorian restoration, but do not overlook the brass to John Battersby, rector here until his death in 1522; nor the pleasant roof with the names of the churchwardens in the year 1814 on one of its beams. Walk north from here, down the scarp slope, across a valley, and beside a great wood, to the village of Whichford in Warwickshire.

Great Wolford (24-34) This modest village looks out towards neighbouring Little Wolford, across a valley through which the Nethercote Brook flows

north to join the Stour, and so on to the Avon and Severn; but less than two miles away, streams flow south to join the Evenlode, which flows into the Thames. So, although the village stands less than four hundred feet above sea level, this is watershed country, and it was perhaps for this reason that a small Iron Age hill fort was built here, the earthworks of which may be seen to the immediate south-east of the village. Wolford's medieval church was destroyed by fire in the early 19th century, and was replaced by a broad building, with a short chancel containing some monuments to the Ingram family. Its best feature is the tall spire, which is an outstanding landmark in this gentle south Warwickshire landscape.

Guy's Cliffe (28-66) The ruined 18th century mansion and 15th century chantry chapel, both beside the River Avon, unfortunately appear not to be open to the public. There is however a pleasant walk starting from the 'Saxon Mill' (a largely 19th century building which has been a restaurant for many years), leading over the Avon, and across fields to Old Milverton, on the northern edge of Leamington Spa. Guy's Cliffe, is the place where the legendary Guy, a Saxon Earl of Warwick, lived out his declining years as a hermit. In the 15th century Richard Beauchamp, Earl of Warwick, built a chantry chapel here, and this still incorporates an eight foot high statue of Guy, carved out of the rock, against which the chapel stands.

The ruined mansion (visible from the little footbridge carrying the path from the Saxon Mill) stands on a rock above the Avon. Sarah Siddons was employed here as a lady's maid for a few months in 1772-3, the owner, Lady Mary Greatheed being much taken by her. After Sarah's marriage to William Siddons and subsequent rise to fame as an actress, she was a frequent guest of the Greatheeds at Guy's Cliffe, and Mr Greatheed wrote a play in her honour, *The Regent*, in which she appeared at Drury Lane.

Halford (26-45) Pretty stone village astride the busy Foss Way, which crosses the River Stour just to its south. The lovely medieval bridge was by-passed some years ago, but it still stands beside the modern bridge, providing the visitor with an opportunity to lean over its old stone parapets and gaze at the reed bordered, willow shaded river beyond. Up to the east of the new bridge is a fascinating early-19th century octagonal house known as 'The Folly', and in the village, away from the Foss, a stone and partly timbered manor house. The church of St. Mary, to the south of the manor, was heavily restored in the 19th century, but contains several items of considerable interest. The Norman tympanum over the north doorway is carved with the head of an angel, with wings and flowing drapery, and is probably the best example of Norman work in the area covered by our guide, reminding us of the superb levels to which the craftsmen of the 11th and 12th centuries could sometimes rise. See also the Norman chancel arch, the attractive 16th century font cover, topped by the carvings of five bishops' heads, the two long fire-hooks for pulling down burning thatch, and the 15th century choir stall with its carved misericord. There is an inn on the Foss Way with an archway indicating that it must once have given shelter to coach travellers, and which today is still warmly welcoming. There is an interesting walk northwards from Halford, starting beside the Stour, then keeping to the right of Ettington Park, and after crossing a road, through woods at Rough Hill. Here one can sometimes see deer which run wild in most of the woodlands of south Warwickshire. The path ends at a point where the A 422, crosses the course of an old railway line (24-50).

Hampton Lucy (25-57) Although much enlarged by modern development, this village, shown on 17th century maps as *Bishop's Hampton*, retains a certain elusive charm, with several thatched, half-timbered cottages, a bright little inn, and a handsome early-18th century rectory in mellow brick. Here lived the Reverend John Lucy, a member of the Lucy family of Charlecote Park, which is clearly visible across the fast flowing River Avon. The Reverend John paid for the complete re-building of Hampton Lucy church by Thomas Rickman and Henry Hutchinson in about 1825. Their best known work is the 'Bridge of Sighs' at Cambridge, but Hampton Lucy is without doubt their finest church, an outstanding example of early-19th century Gothic. This church with its splendidly pinnacled west tower, and richly Decorated style interior, was further enhanced by George Gilbert Scott, who added the apsidal chancel about thirty years later. Rickman is not as widely known as the Gilbert Scotts, but it was he was responsible for the original classification of English medieval architectural styles into 'Early English', 'Decorated', and 'Perpendicular'. This was perhaps an over-simplification, but as readers of this guide will note, it is a classification still much used today.

The Avon is crossed here by a cast-iron bridge, built, like the church, at the expense of the Reverend John Lucy, and just beyond it there is a lovely mellow brick watermill, which has recently been restored to working condition. Flour is now being ground here again, and the mill is open to the public at certain times *(see the local press for details)*. Walk north from the village side of the bridge, parallel, but above the river, or beyond the mill, and over the fields to Wasperton; although this latter walk is somewhat involved with gravel workings in its middle stages.

Hanwell (43-43) Pretty ironstone village on hilly slopes, looking eastwards over a broad valley, just to the north of Banbury, with a small inn called 'The Moon and Sixpence'. Here is a house incorporating a mellow brick and stone tower, the only remains of a large castle built by William Cope, Cofferer to Henry VII, in the closing years of the 15th century,

SCALE 1:25 000 or 2½ INCHES to 1 MILE

and pulled down in about 1780. The most noteworthy member of the Cope family was Sir Anthony Cope, who in the reign of Queen Elizabeth, spent some time in the Tower for presenting a Puritan revision of the Book of Common Prayer to the Speaker of the Commons. He was eventually pardoned, sat as member for Banbury in several parliaments, and entertained James I twice at Hanwell. Sir Anthony and his first wife lie together in a large canopied tomb in the chancel of the nearby church, which has an exceptionally wide east window, and a most entertaining series of medieval stone carvings on its arcade capitals, and on a cornice on the wall of the chancel. These carvings are thought to be the work of a mid-14th century mason, or group of masons, who also worked at Adderbury, Alkerton and Bloxham. Do not miss the unusual chimney disguised as a pinnacle.

Harbury (37-59) This is situated in countryside much ravaged by cement workings, but most are now at least covered over by thin turf. A fossilised icthyosaurus was found in these workings, and this prehistoric beast is now to be found in the Natural History Museum, South Kensington. It is only too easy to get lost in the bewildering pattern of Harbury's streets, as it is a village of considerable size, without any apparent logic in its plan. There are shops and inns, the remains of a fine six-storey windmill, the sails of which have long since gone, and a mullioned 17th century school, which is now a private house. This was founded in 1611 by Jane Wagstaffe, a memorial to whom may be seen in the large 13th century church. This has a stone tower, capped by Georgian brickwork, which is a most unusual feature. The best walks from Harbury are to the south-west, to Chesterton, with its windmill and its lakes (see page 28).

Haseley (23-67) Minute hamlet with a neo-Tudor manor house, built in 1875, and a delightful little church with a remarkably unspoilt interior. Here will be found 18th century box pews and pulpit beneath a pleasing ceiled wagon roof, and a tomb chest monument to Clement Throckmorton and his wife (1573), with their portraits in brass. These two brasses are palimpsests, ones that have been used a second time on the reverse side, and like many more to be found in England, they came from Flanders, one of them having 14th century Flemish work on its reverse. It appears that there was a thriving trade in these palimpsests, but it has never been proved if those indulging in it were honest men or villains. Do not miss the 15th century stained glass in the west window, below the tower.

Hatton (23-67) A scattered parish, the largest features of which are the long flight of locks, taking the Grand Union Canal down into the Avon valley, and the massive mid-19th century Central Hospital. The beautiful 18th century rectory, was further enlarged by Dr. Samuel Parr, a Harrow schoolmaster, who came here as rector after failing to secure the headmastership. There is a plain monument to him in the church, dated 1825, and several 18th century monuments, but apart from the Perpendicular west tower, with its interesting west window containing German 16th century glass from a Tree of Jesse, the rest of the church was re-built in about

1880. (See **Walk 1**, for a pleasant canal-side walk.)

There is an interesting Craft Centre at George's Farm, which houses a variety of craft workshops including ones devoted to ceramics, metalwork and graphic design. If coming from Warwick, fork left off A41, on to B4439, take first left at cross roads, over canal and railway bridge, and farm is on left (It is marked 'Hatton Farm' on our map, at ref 23-66). *Tel. Claverdon (092684) 2096 for details.*

Hellidon (51-58) Small stone village in delightful, wooded, hilly country just over the Warwickshire border into Northamptonshire. In a pool to the east of the village, the River Leam starts its short journey to Leamington Spa, where it joins the Avon after a mere twenty five miles meandering through flat meadow country. The 14th century church retains its stout stone tower, but its interior was ruthlessly restored by that prolific and over-thorough architect, William Butterfield, best known perhaps for his work at Keble College, Oxford. Walk north-west to Napton on the Hill, or south to Byfield. In winter time, when the fields are too wet under foot, try the pleasant circular road walk taking in Hellidon and the Catesbys.

A walk in the sunshine, Hellidon.

Henley-in-Arden (15-65) This busy little market town is strung out for almost a mile, along the ever busy A34, but hopefully one day it will be relieved, either by a by-pass or a motorway. Despite the traffic it is well worth exploring on foot, for it has a wealth of old buildings in a variety of materials, from half timbering, to stone and mellow brick. It grew up beneath the protection of Beaudesert , a 12th century castle of the De Montforts', the grass covered 'motte and bailey' earthworks of which, are still visible to the east of the town, just across the little River Alne. Below the castle earthworks is the largely Norman church of Beaudesert, while only a hundred yards to its west, in Henley-in-Arden High Street, there is Henley's own church of St John Baptist. This is late-15th century, and its grey stone tower stands out as an effective foil to the half-timbered buildings around it, notably the Guildhall, which is its approximate contemporary. There are bright shops, and a number of inns, some of which bear witness to the importance of Henley-in-Arden as a coaching stop in days gone by. Another small clue is attached to house No. 185. . . a milestone

Half-timbered cottages in Henley-in-Arden High Street.

stating, *'From London CII miles, from Stratford VIII, from Birmingham XIV 1748'.* The best walk from Henley is south-east, over the fields, past Blackford Mill Farm, beside the Alne, across a minor road, over the Stratford-upon-Avon Canal, through part of Austy Wood; then turning north past Cutler's Farm, passing Kington Grange, and back across the fields, over the canal to Preston Green, to return via Beaudesert to Henley.

Hidcote Boyce (17-41) Here is a pleasant hamlet below the western slopes of high Ilmington Downs. It has a single, gently sloping street bordered by flower-filled cottage gardens. Some distance to its north, the road is overlooked by Hidcote House, a delicious 17th century manor house, with attractive gable ends and mullioned windows, and pretty fan-tailed doves flying to and from their nesting boxes overlooking the gateway.

Hidcote Manor Garden, Hidcote Bartrim (17-42) This was given to the National Trust in 1948 by the great horticulturalist, Major Lawrence Johnson, who had by then devoted forty years of his life to its creation. When he came to Hidcote in 1905 there was a 17th century manor house, and only a cedar tree, a clump of large beeches and a few walls. The garden that we see today was created from eleven acres of open Cotswold hill country. In fact he made not one garden, but a series of small gardens, separated by now mellowed walls, and hedges of hornbeam, yew, green and copper beech, box and holly. Amongst these magnificent hedges are such delights as the Fuchsia Garden, the White Garden, the Bathing Pool Garden, and in contrast to these formal creations, a wild garden beside a stream. These are enriched by grass walks and lawns, mellow brick gazebos and wrought-iron gates through which one can glimpse distant views of Bredon Hill and the Malverns, across the blue haze

39

of the valleys through which the Avon and Severn flow. See also the Theatre Lawn, which is usually the scene for an open air Shakespeare play at some time each summer, the Long Walk in the Kitchen Garden, which contains a fine collection of old French roses, the alley of lime trees, and the fine avenue of beech trees. The National Trust describe Hidcote as *'one of the most delightful gardens in England'*, and it would indeed be hard to dispute this claim. The Trust have one of their excellent gift shops here, and refreshments available include coffees, light lunches and cream teas. *Tel: (038677) 333 for opening times.*

There is a track up the hill from here, which leads over the top of Ilmington Downs; for details, see **Walk 8.** But do not use the car park, which is for the use of those visiting the gardens.

Hillborough (Map 150) (12-52) This lies to the west of the main area covered by this guide, but it is situated to the south of the A 439, Stratford-upon-Avon to Bidford-on-Avon road, just over a mile to the east of the latter village. We have included it here as it is featured in the oft quoted verse attributed to William Shakespeare (see Bidford-on-Avon, page 19) as *'Haunted Hillborough'*. There was a substantial village here in medieval times, just to the north of the river Avon, but like so many others it was depopulated, largely in the 15th and 16th centuries, by the twin scourges of plague and enclosure. So, by Shakespeare's time it must have been a sad, deserted place, and a likely haunt for ghosts. This tradition appears to have lived on for several centuries after, and there are tales of ghosts until comparatively recent times. The fine 16th century manor house has been well restored, and to its south east there is a fine circular dovecote providing nesting places for about nine hundred birds. Walk westwards from here, partly beside the river, to Bidford-on-Avon.

Hinchwick (14-30) An early-19th century manor house, on the line of the Roman road, the Ryknild Street (see page 56), at the southern end of a tranquil, wooded valley, with a series of small lakes amongst the trees. (Please do not trespass.) There is a bridle-way north from here through woods, and over the wold country of Bourton Downs, and beyond this by crossing the busy A424, Blockley can be reached, along a track, past Warren Farm.

Honington (26-42) A most attractive village grouped around a wide, tree-shaded green with a beautiful assortment of houses and cottages in timber, mellow brick and stone, blending together to produce a highly satisfying scene. Honington is approached from the A34, Stratford to Shipston road, by a small road leading over a pretty five arched bridge with balls upon its parapet. It is probably contemporary with the late-17th century Honington Hall, an exceptionally handsome mellow brick mansion visible well over to the left, in parkland beside the River Stour. This was built in 1685 by a London merchant, Sir Henry Parker, and is enriched by a series of oval recesses between the upper and lower windows, in which busts of the twelve Caesars sit most comfortably. The house was lovingly restored in the mid 1970s, and incorporates a wealth of richly contrived 18th century plasterwork, especially in its entrance hall and octagonal Saloon. *Tel: (0608) 61434 for opening times.*

Honington.

SCALE 1:25 000 or 2½ INCHES to 1 MILE

Apart from its 13th century tower, the adjoining church is contemporary with the house, and its elegantly decorated interior reminds one of a Wren city church. It was also restored in the '70s and is enriched with several opulent monuments to members of the Parker and Townsend families. See especially the self-important, but sumptuous monument to Sir Henry Parker and his son Hugh, a piece of work that typifies the spirit of the age in which they lived. In contrast, there are two monuments by the 19th century sculptor, Sir Richard Westmacott, less exciting, but also less worldly, the one to Lady Elizabeth Townsend, depicting a mourning male figure by an urn; a typically poignant Westmacott treatment.

There is a pleasant little road north from Honington, to Halford, with views out over the River Stour from its northern end.

Hook Norton (35-33) A large village situated in remote hilly country that once yielded great quantities of ironstone. The old Brymbo Ironworks have long since vanished, but other evidence of Hook Norton's past importance as an ironstone centre may still be seen.... a series of dramatic piers , the only remains of a massive railway viaduct that once spanned the broad valley to its east, carrying the long vanished 'Banbury and Cheltenham Direct Railway'. There is also a red brick Victorian brewery here; an unusual intrusion into the Cotswold scene, which still brews the most delectable Hook Norton ale. This beer, like the village in which it is brewed, is known far and wide as 'Hooky', to all those who know a thing or two about 'real ale'.

This village, with its orange-brown stone and thatched roofs, is well worth exploring. 'The Green' and 'East End' are both very pleasant, but we particularly favour the terrace in the centre of the

SCALE 1:25 000 or 2½ INCHES to 1 MILE

village looking southwards, with the Bell Inn at one end and the church at the other. The latter is a large building of Norman origin with a finely pinnacled Perpendicular tower and a spacious, pleasantly bare interior, the contents of which include a fascinating Norman font, complete with sculptured figures of Adam and Eve, Saggitarius the Archer, and other signs of the Zodiac. Walk south-east from here, across the broad valley over which the viaduct once ran, and up over the hill to the delightful little village of Swerford in the next valley.

Hooky... 'a most delectable ale'.

Horley (41-43) Situated on the slopes of a small valley just below open ironstone country so typical of north Oxfordshire, Horley is a delightful, small village with its church poised at the top of a street lined with old stone houses and cottages. The church, with its Norman tower and chancel, was exceptionally well restored as recently as 1949, when a rood loft and screen were added. In the north aisle will be found Horley's greatest treasure, an unusually well preserved 15th century wall painting of St. Christopher fording a stream. With details including two anglers both of whom have made a catch, this still seems to breathe the very spirit of late medieval England, and is well worth seeing. Walk up the valley from here, to Hornton, and then on over the hills to Ratley and Edgehill.

Hornton (39-45) Here, to the north of the church were the quarries that gave their name to Hornton stone... the slightly orange, toffee-coloured ironstone that has given the villages and towns of this area their unique flavour. These quarries have been closed for many years, but 'Hornton' stone is now quarried at Edgehill, two miles to the north-west, across the border into Warwickshire. Hornton is a quiet, pleasing village in a hollow at the head of a small stream flowing south-eastwards in the general direction of the Cherwell. It has a small green, many stone houses and cottages, some of them thatched, two 17th century farmhouses and a manor house of the same period.

The church dates back to the 12th century, although the tower and many other features are Perpendicular. Like the church at neighbouring Horley, it also has a medieval wall painting...the one here being a late-14th century 'Doom' depicting the *Last Judgement*. The purpose of Doom Paintings was to instil into the parishoners, who were without exception illiterate, a fear of hellfire and damnation if they transgressed in any way from the required 'God-fearing' standards required of them. The 'Doom' at Hornton is comparatively mild in its content, but many others that survive are quite horrific, and it is no wonder that the church was so successful in maintaining its hold over the peasant mind for so long. Walk north from here, to Ratley and Edgehill, or south-east, down the valley to Horley.

Idlicote (28-44) Deliciously situated on a small hill, with a tree-shaded pool and with views eastwards, out over flat countryside to the dark outline of Edge Hill, Idlicote is little more than a hamlet, but it does however have a small church. This has Norman origins, but its Norman doorway is filled with a Georgian door, and this provides a foretaste of the interior, which is full of 18th century flavour, with a little west gallery, a three-decker pulpit and an ogee-shaped font cover, the latter probably being 17th century in origin. There is also a pleasant 17th century chapel, with Tuscan columns dividing it from the chancel. Idlicote House, off the drive to which the church lies, is a dignified early 19th century building, while close to it, is a fine 18th century octagonal dovecote, which provided shelter for no fewer than 1002 nesting birds. The best walk from Idlicote is southwards, over Idlicote Hill, past St Dennis Farms, and across to Brailes. By turning right before reaching St Dennis, it is possible to make a circular walk, including the lovely village of Honington (see page 40).

Ilmington (21-43) A most attractive stone village lying beneath Windmill Hill, the last northern bastion of the Cotswolds, and very 'Cotswold' in flavour. It spreads itself comfortably below the hill slopes, and to be properly savoured, it should be explored on foot. Here will be found a wealth of old houses and cottages, many beside small paths that stray away from the road that encircles the village. There is a fine manor house which has been lovingly restored, the beautiful gardens of which are normally open to the public at least twice a year. There are also two very pleasant inns, the Red Lion and the Howard Arms.

With luck you will first encounter the church after walking up a quiet little pathway overlooking two pools in a field in the very heart of the village. This is a largely Norman building, with Norman north and south doorways, Norman windows in the aisle, and a Norman chancel arch. Once beyond the 16th century porch, one comes upon splendid oak pews and other furnishings. These were all installed in the

Northern limits of the Cotswolds. Windmill Hill, near Ilmington.

1930s, and are the work of master-craftsman, Robert Thompson, whose descendants still produce their stout oak furniture in his original workshops in the little village of Kilburn beneath the steep slopes of the far off North York Moors. All of Robert Thompson's work, and that of his descendants too, include a unique signature, an individually carved mouse. Can you find the eleven mice that he carved upon the Ilmington oak ? However during your search for the mice, do not overlook the severely classical monument to Francis Canning and his wife, by the early-19th century sculptor, Sir Richard Westmacott, other examples of whose work will be found at Honington and Preston-on-Stour. Westmacott, much in the spirit of his times, was very fond of weeping figures and classical urns, and these features will be found in all three of the village churches concerned. The unusual lantern-like structure by the south porch is an early-19th century monument to members of the Sansom family.

Kiftsgate Court Garden (17-43) This is perhaps less well known to non-gardeners than Hidcote, but it should on no account be missed. Kiftsgate Court is situated on the very edge of the Cotswold scarp above Mickleton; a largely Victorian house with an 18th century portico which was moved, piece by piece, up from Mickleton Manor on a specially constructed light railway. Most of the garden was created in the years following the First World War, by Mrs Heather Muir, and she was no doubt helped and inspired by her neighbour and friend, Major Johnson, the creator of Hidcote (see page 39). Kiftsgate Garden's steep hillside setting is more dramatic than Hidcote's, and Mrs Muir took full advantage of this in her splendid design. Mrs Muir's daughter and grand-daughter, Mrs Binny, and Mrs Chambers have carried on the Kiftsgate tradition, and the garden continues to evolve. There are paths, flower-beds, shrubs and trees, on the terraced areas above the scarp, and a steep cliff with pine trees, and winding paths, leading to a swimming pool on a grassy terrace at its foot, with views down a wooded combe, to the Vale of Evesham. We last came here in summertime, when the air was heavy with the scent of roses, and the blue swimming pool, viewed through the pine trees from the steep hillside above, brought a hint of the Mediterranean to this lovely garden enfolded in the Cotswold hills. Teas are available here. *Tel: (038677) 777*. See also **Walk 8**.

High summer at Kiftsgate Court Garden.

The Kiftsgate Stone (13-38) This rather unexciting monolith lies half hidden in woodland just to the north-west of the road towards Broadway (see map), on the hill to the west of Chipping Campden. It marks an ancient 'moot' or meeting place, where people used to gather to organise their affairs and dispense justice (often of a very rough nature), and this was in fact the original administrative centre of the Kiftsgate Hundred. 'Hundreds' were sub-divisions of shires, a system of local government which grew up in Saxon times, and one which was so firmly established by the time of the Norman conquest, that it was absorbed into the Norman framework of administration. Traditions attached to the Kiftsgate Stone itself were indeed so strong that its use only ceased in the years following the proclamation of George III, which was celebrated here in 1760.

Kineton (33-51) First mentioned in a Saxon charter of AD 969, the large village of Kineton was for several centuries a market town of some importance. However its market square is now a quiet backwater, disturbed only once a year by its little fair. The earthworks of a medieval castle, known as King John's Castle, overlook a small bend in the Dene, the stream which flows through Kineton, but there is no proven connection with the monarch in question. There is much modern building on Kineton's fringes, but in addition to the 17th and 18th century houses lining the tranquil Market Square, there are several pleasant houses of the same period in Bridge Street. The solid Hornton

The War Memorial, Kineton.

stone church tower was completed in about 1315, but the rest is largely 19th century work. It is sad to note that the work carried out in the mid-18th century by Sanderson Miller, squire of neighbouring Radway, and amateur architect extraordinary (see page 52), was amongst that replaced by the Victorian enthusiasts. However the interior of the church was treated with more sympathy than we might have hoped for, and the Victorian architect concerned left the stone flagged floors undisturbed and did not scrape the walls down to reveal stark over-pointed stonework. Do not overlook the fine round-topped 16th century churchwardens' chest, nor the handsome 18th century monuments in the chancel.

During the Battle of Edgehill in the Civil War (see page 34), in October 1642, the baggage train of the Parliamentarian generals was quartered at Kineton, and much blood was spilt here, first when Rupert's cavalry broke through into Kineton during the battle, and two days later, when Rupert again fell upon the remnants of the Parliamentary force, their wounded and sick, and *'several wagons loaded with muskets and pikes, and all sorts of Ammunition'*.

SCALE 1:25 000 or 2½ INCHES to 1 MILE

These events appear to have struck terror into the inhabitants of this normally tranquil village, and within a few months there were reports of supernatural happenings in Kineton and the surrounding countryside.... reports of such substance that sensational pamphlets were published, and the King sent a party of officers from his headquarters at Oxford to investigate their claims. For centuries since there was talk in Kineton of wild cries and great commotion on each night of 23rd October, the anniversary of the battle; but in recent times all appears to have been quiet.

The best walk from Kineton is westwards down a lane to Brookhampton, and across the fields to Combrook.

Kings Sutton (50-36) There has been much new building in this now large village in the Cherwell valley below Banbury, but the old part remains largely unspoilt. Church, 17th century manor house, half-timbered court house, the attractive Bell Inn and several ironstone cottages are pleasantly grouped around a green on which stand the ancient village stocks. Kings Sutton church's 15th century spire is regarded by many as the finest in Northamptonshire, a county noted for the beauty of its spires, and this is surely one of the loveliest specimens in the whole of England. Tapering to 198 feet above the ground, it is a slim, elegant structure, with its base upon the equally elegant tower enriched by fine pinnacles and flying buttresses. There is a local saying, *'Bloxham for length, Adderbury for strength, Kings Sutton for beauty'*, and from the little road running out of the valley to Charlton, one can see these three splendid spires in a line stretching westwards. The interior of this largely Decorated church has a late Norman chancel, a crudely carved, six sided Norman font, and an impressive 18th century monument to T. L. Freke. Sir Gilbert Scott restored the church in 1866, and he was responsible for the large oak chancel screen.

To the immediate north of the village is the hamlet of Astrop. St Rumbald's Well, in the grounds of Astrop Park, an 18th century house, with additions by Sir John Soane, commemorates the young son of a Northumbrian king, who earned his sainthood by preaching a sermon at the age of only three, and sadly expiring soon afterwards. The well was rediscovered in the 17th century, and became a fashionable little spa, being visited by the traveller and diarist, Celia Fiennes (see Broughton, page 25), who found it, *'much frequented by the gentry'*, although she also comments that, *' the well runnes not very quick'*, *' neither is there any bason for the spring to run out of, only a dirty well full of moss's which is all changed yellow by the water'*. Despite these limitations, Astrop Wells remained in fashion until the end of the 18th century, by which time it had been visited by Horace Walpole and others, *'men given to gadding in this age'*, including, not surprisingly, many undergraduates from Oxford. The well is not accessible to the public, but there is a replica beside the road leading towards Upper Astrop. There was a Roman settlement at Blacklands, to the immediate north of Kings Sutton, which is on the probable line of the Roman road, running eastwards across the hills past Swalcliffe and Madmarston Hill (See page 35.)

Walk south from Kings Sutton, across the fields via Walton Grounds to Aynho; or turn left at Walton Grounds, and return to Kings Sutton, via Rainsborough Camp, Charlton and Newbottle. (See page 50.)

Lark Stoke and Ilmington Downs (19-43) Use **Walk 8**, or drive up the narrow, partly unfenced road, southwards from the Admington — Ilmington road on **Tour 5**. At 850 feet above sea level, this is the highest point in Warwickshire, and one of the northern bastions of the Cotswold hills. Despite the presence of a small T.V. transmitting station, this is still reasonably good walking country, and there are fine open views northwards out over the Avon valley and eastwards to the wooded silhouette of Edge Hill, and the rolling Northamptonshire uplands that lie beyond. Lark Stoke received a separate entry in the Domesday Book (1086), but there is now no trace of any ancient village on these windy hillsides, nor in the woodlands below. Walk south from here to Ebrington, south-west to Chipping Campden, or make a small circular walk by taking in Hidcote Boyce and Hidcote Bartrim, calling in of course at the splendid Hidcote Manor Garden (see page 39).

Leamington Hastings (44-67) Charming village in flat countryside just to the south of the River Leam and the massive Draycote Water reservoir. There is a row of 17th century mullioned almshouses, some half-timbered cottages and a substantial manor house. The church is surprisingly large for so modest a village, and has a red sandstone Perpendicular tower, and an elegant, Decorated style west doorway, with an ogival arch and pinnacles. Inside will be found a pulpit with late medieval panels, and a handsome monument to Sir Thomas Trevor, who was one of Charles I's Barons of the Exchequer, and one to his son, another Sir Thomas, and his wife. Walk south from here to Broadwell, and onwards to the Grand Union Canal, the towpath of which you could use to reach Napton Junction (46- 62). (See also **Walk 2.**)

Leamington Spa (See **Royal Leamington Spa**, page 54)

Lighthorne (33-55) Delightful little village in a steep sided valley to the east of the Foss Way and to the north of the great windy expanse of Gaydon airfield. This is now a motor vehicle test track, but it does not appear to disturb Lighthorne's tranquillity. There are tree-shaded greens in the valley bottom, overlooked by thatched stone houses and cottages, and a cheerful inn called the Antelope. The west tower of the church was built in 1771, by Samuel Eglinton, who was also responsible for the County Hall in Cuckoo Lane, Coventry. The rest of Eglinton's church was replaced in 1875 by a rather austere rock-faced building, the interior of which is relieved by some colourful 17th century heraldic stained glass, and two saints, also in stained glass... St Sebastian, with many arrows contributing to his painful martyrdom, and an equally suffering St Lawrence, on a grill with flames beneath. On a more cheerful note... paths radiate from Lighthorne, to Chesterton, Ashorne, Moreton Morrell, and Compton Verney. In view of the Antelope's possibilities, we would suggest that this village would make an excellent place to call in at, during a walk, or to finish in, at the end of the day.

Lighthorne.

Little Compton (26-30) Situated in a sheltered hollow between Barton Hill and the main Cotswold edge, this pleasant village, Warwickshire's southernmost, is over the watershed into the 'land of the Thames'. This great river may seem very far away, but the stream on which Little Compton lies, flows west to join the Evenlode below Moreton-in-Marsh, where it is itself near the start of its quiet journey to join the *'sweet Thames'* just above Oxford. The little church retains its 14th century tower with saddle-back roof, but the rest of the building dates from the 1860s, and is not of great interest to visitors. In the churchyard there is one gravestone carved by our favourite 20th century sculptor, Eric Gill; a simple, but fine example of his craft. The lovely 17th century manor house next to the church was the home of Bishop Juxon, who had the unenviable task of attending Charles I at his trial and subsequent execution on the scaffold outside the Banqueting Hall, Whitehall. During their walk to this place of execution, Juxon was observed by the king to be weeping, and the king is supposed to have exclaimed, *'Leave all this my Lord; we have no time for it'*. This terse comment appears at least to have stopped Juxon's tears, and eventually he received substantial consolation, for when his monarch's son, Charles II became king in 1660, Juxon was appointed Archbishop of Canterbury... a post that he held until his death, sadly only three years later.

If you pass through Little Compton during 'opening hours', call at the Red Lion. This is a cheerful inn serving Donnington Ales... beer which continued to be brewed traditionally during the dark years before the 'Campaign for Real Ale' took hold, and forced a return to 'the wood' upon many brewers who had hitherto adopted a policy of supplying only beer in pressurised kegs. Donnington Ales are brewed at a delectable little brewery in the Cotswolds a short distance to the north of Stow-on-the-Wold.

Walk northwards from Little Compton, on the quiet road over Barton Hill to Barton-on-the-Heath, or over the fields on a path parallel with the road, past Salter's Well Farm.

Little Rollright (29-30) Here, in a quiet setting beneath the hills, is a fine 17th century manor house, a modest rectory of the same period, a few cottages, and a delightful little church. This is a largely Perpendicular building, but its squat tower and south window date from the 17th century. It has a simple interior, with pleasant Perpendicular windows and two gorgeous 17th century monuments... canopied tomb chests to members of the Dixon family... still making it plain to see that the Dixons were persons of considerable substance, probably sheep graziers. Do not miss a visit to this very satisfying little building.

In Little Rollright Church.

Little Wolford (26-35) A hamlet of Victorian estate cottages and unexciting council houses, situated in gently undulating countryside, with views towards the spires of Todenham and Great Wolford out over the valley through which the little Nethercote Brook flows, on its way to join the Stour a mile or so to the north. Any dullness is relieved by tantalising glimpses of Little Wolford's delicious Tudor manor house. This is in a pleasing blend of stone and timber framing ... appropriate in an area which lies between the forest country of Warwickshire and the uplands of the Oxfordshire Cotswolds. Walk south and east, up the valley, past Pepperwell and Kings Brake farms, to Long Compton, and return via the open road across Weston Park. (See Cherington, page 27.)

Long Compton (28-32) This attractive stone village stretches out along the busy A34 for over half a mile, to the very foot of the long hill that climbs up over the Cotswold edge, across the county boundary into Oxfordshire. There is considerable modern building at its northern end, and the main road is always busy with traffic; but despite this Long Compton has much to offer. It has a cheerful inn, many trim houses and cottages, and a church whose handsome Perpendicular tower looks westwards out over a large bumpy field which is thought to have been the site of the original village. The lovely south porch is approached by a yew-lined path leading from a delightful little two storeyed lych gate, believed to be a small timber-framed cottage with its lower storey removed. The core of the church is 13th century, but externally it appears to be almost entirely Perpendicular. See the nave roof, the charming little Perpendicular south aisle chapel and the pathetically worn effigy of a lady in the porch. For a full account of life at Long Compton and in the countryside that surrounds it, read Edward Rainsberry's delightful book, *Through the Lych Gate*, published by the Roundwood Press, but now out of print.

The best walk from Long Compton leads across fields north-eastwards, skirting the southern edge of Whichford Wood, to Whichford village. There is also a good walk leading south-westwards, over a spur of the hills, and down into Little Compton.

Long Itchington (41-65) Large, widespread village in rolling blue-lias country dominated by a massive cement works, and much pock-marked by attendant quarry workings. However there are several pleasant old houses around a tree-fringed pond at the village centre, a creeper-covered inn called the Buck and Bell, and a church with 12th century origins on the banks of the Itchen, the little river from which the village takes its name. The church has a grey stone tower, with red sandstone buttresses, topped by the stumpy remains of a spire, the rest of which was blown down in 1762. Inside will be found a 14th century rood screen, a fine Easter sepulchre, and a 17th century brass beneath a stone canopy, of John Bosworth and his two wives. St Wulfstan, Bishop of Worcester, was born here early in the 11th century. He was bishop at the time of the Norman Conquest, and despite opposition from the Norman Archbishop, Lanfranc, continued to hold office during the reigns both of William the Conqueror, and William Rufus. Queen Elizabeth once visited Long Itchington, and was entertained in a tented camp, *'which for number* and shift of large and goodlye rooms might be comparable with a beautiful pallais'. For more detailed information on Long Itchington read Archibald Payne's excellent book, *Portrait of a Parish*. This is out of print, but is available in most local libraries.

Long Itchington is situated just to the north of the Grand Union Canal, and to the south-east there is a long flight of locks (the Stockton Flight), at the near end of which there is a well known inn, The Blue Lias. It is pleasant to walk from here, up the flight, especially in summertime when the locks are busy with holiday boats working through to join the Oxford Canal at Napton Junction (46-62) (see **Walk 2**).

Long Marston (15-48) Long straggling village in flat country between Welford Hill and the Cotswold edge, with a massive military store depot and an old airfield not far away. The much quoted verse attributed to William Shakespeare (see Bidford-on-Avon, page 22) refers to *'dancing Marston'*, and we suspect that this is a reference to Long Marston, rather than neighbouring Broad Marston, but like the source of the verse itself, the mystery will remain. We assume that one or other of the villages in question must have had a particularly well known troupe of Morris dancers, but here again mystery reigns.

To revert to the present day village, several pleasant farm houses and cottages stand away from the road, which is lined with uninspiring council housing at its northern end. The little 14th century church has a timber-framed bell turret which is supported by further timber within the building below. Beyond the attractive little timber-framed porch there is a pleasant interior with an old stone flagged floor and plastered walls. See the Jacobean pulpit and the monuments to members of the Tomes family. To the south of the church is Kings Lodge, where the future King Charles II is reputed to have stopped during the flight from his enemies after the Battle of Worcester in 1651. Disguised as a servant, by name Will Jackson, he was put to work in the kitchen, and is believed to have escaped detection by Roundhead troops, by receiving a beating from the cook, who was at the time quite unaware of his identity.

Lower Lemington (21-34) This is now no more than a quiet little hamlet with a farm, a few houses and a small church; all spread around an open field-cum-farmyard. However the undulating fields surrounding it conceal the remains of a larger medieval village, and on the road to its south there is a substantial 16th and 17th century manor house. The little church in its stone-walled churchyard, has a small bellcote where the nave roof meets that of the chancel, and a narrow Norman doorway within its porch. The chancel was damaged during the Civil War, but the exceptionally narrow Norman chancel arch, with minute squints on either side, has survived. There are pleasant old Commandment Boards, an early Norman tub font, an 18th century two-decker pulpit and a small 17th century brass to two brothers, Charles and Peter Greville.

Lower Shuckburgh (49-62) This is largely an estate village for nearby Shuckburgh Hall, with late Victorian estate cottages, and a church and rectory,

SCALE 1:25 000 or 2½ INCHES to 1 MILE

both built by Croft, an architect noted for his self-confident, 'High Victorian' style. The interior of the church is a perfect example of this bouncy approach, and architectural enthusiasts will enjoy a visit here. Others may prefer a walk along the towpath beside the Grand Union Canal, which passes just to the north of the village, or a walk up the hill, south-westwards across the outer edge of the beautifully wooded Shuckburgh Park.

Here is a timber-framed house, concealed behind a rather austere early Victorian front, with deer grazing not far away (**but this is not open to the public**). Upper Shuckburgh church is situated in the park, but although it is clearly visible from a path through part of the park, it is classified as a private or *'peculiar'* church, and is not normally open to the public, apart from infrequent occasions when the gardens are open. Opinions appear to be divided as to the date of the present Hornton stone church, but it is very much a family church of the Shuckburghs. The family who have been here since the beginning of the 12th century, still live in the Hall, and the monuments of their ancestors provide a fascinating picture of developing artistic fashions and changing social attitudes over the centuries. See especially (when the gardens are open) the monuments by the prolific and ever poignant John Flaxman, to Lady Shuckburgh-Evelyn (1797) and to Sir George Shuckburgh-Evelyn (1804).

Shortly before the battle of Edgehill (see page 34), Richard Shuckburgh met Charles I while out hunting on Beacon Hill, to the south of the park, and was persuaded to join his force, being knighted at the end of the battle. Soon afterwards Sir Richard was himself defeated after a skirmish on Shuckburgh Hill, and was held prisoner by the Parliamentarians at Kenilworth Castle. He eventually purchased his liberty, and returned to Shuckburgh, but sadly he died in 1656, only four years before his sovereign's son was restored to the throne. In recognition of his sufferings, his son was made a baronet by Charles II. It is a story of great honour, but one wonders how much better Richard Shuckburgh might have fared, had he not had the ill fortune to meet his king while out hunting on that fateful day in October 1642.

Loxley (25-52) Delightful village on gentle hill slopes with views northwards out over the Avon valley, these being especially fine from the road to its south-west below Long Hill. The little Fox Inn always has a warm welcome, and the church, at the other end of the village, is full of interest. Its site was given to the Bishops of Worcester, by Offa, the king of Mercia in A.D. 760, and there is herringbone work in the chancel wall, probably of Saxon origin. The tower is 13th century, but the remainder of the building is largely Georgian, and provides a white plastered interior which is full of the flavour of that most attractive period. There are box pews, an unusual wall-mounted pulpit, and a chancel window depicting St. Nicholas holding lilies.

Luddington (16-52) Minute village beside the River Avon, and almost attached to Stratford-upon-Avon by a thin ribbon of development along the road stretching beyond its race course. Here is a small green overlooked by timber framed cottages, and a little Victorian church in the local lias stone. This replaced a medieval chapel-of-ease to Stratford-upon-Avon that was burnt down in the 19th century, and incorporates a font taken from the old building. It is possible that William Shakespeare and Anne Hathaway were married here, late in 1582, the poet then being only nineteen years of age, but unfortunately the parish registers are lost to us, and it is unlikely that the truth will ever be proved. Walk from here, along the northern bank of the Avon, to Stratford, and enter the town near the parish church, or cross a footbridge near the entrance to the town, and walk along the south bank, with fine views across the river to the church and the Shakespeare Theatre.

Madmarston Hill (38-38) Site of an Iron Age hill fort, with the line of a Roman road running through Swalcliffe Lea to the south of it (see Epwell, page 35). The line of the road runs through the site of an extensive Roman settlement, and it is interesting to note that the area is known as 'The Blacklands', the same description as that for the area north of Kings Sutton, where there was also a Roman settlement (see page 43). This is probably due to a certain rich quality in the soil caused by previous human habitation. (See also **Walk 4**.)

Marston Doles (46-58) Just a few red-brick cottages mark the point where the Welsh Road (see Southam, page 59) crosses the Oxford Canal, and where this canal starts a long 'summit level', which meanders around the contours on its distant journey to the other end near Claydon (46-51). This is an enchanted countryside, its tranquillity due largely to enclosures made by sheep graziers long ago, enclosures that led to whole villages disappearing... Radbourne, Hodnell, and Stoneton... still names on the map, but now merely farmsteads in an otherwise deserted landscape. (See Wormleighton, page 76.)

Marton (40-68) Small village of half-timber and thatch, brick and slate, with a church largely re-built in the 1870s, following a calamitous fire. In Louisa Ward Close, just off the High Street, there is an interesting little Museum of Country Bygones, where there are exhibits of craftsmen's tools, used in thatching, saddlery, wheelrighting, and shepherding. There are also farm hand tools, household and dairy equipment, and wagons.

Mickleton (16-43) This busy, almost town-like village, has considerable modern development on its fringes, and is rather disturbed by traffic on the A46, which it bestrides. However it lies immediately beneath the Cotswold edge, and has several attractive stone houses and cottages in addition to those of thatch and half-timber. We especially like the little Victorian Memorial Fountain close by the Three Ways Hotel. This is an unusually restrained piece of work by William Burges, the architect of Cardiff Castle and Castle Coch, who there more typically provided two supreme examples of the High Victorian Gothic, with elaborately self-confident designs and florid colourings.

Turn up beside handsome 'Cotswold-Queen Anne' style Medford House, to visit the church, which lies on the southern edge of the village, with pleasant views up towards the wooded Cotswold edge. This has a fine 14th century tower and spire, and a most unusual 17th century two-storeyed porch. Inside will be found a 12th century crucifix or rood (over the north aisle chapel altar), some stout, late Norman arcading, and a monument to the 18th century architect, builder and quarry-owner, Thomas Woodward of Chipping Campden, erected by his grandson, Edward. There is evidence of Victorian restoration in the shape of the east window and most of the woodwork, but Mickleton church has retained an atmosphere that makes a visit here well worthwhile. There is an attractive, if challenging walk, from the church, up the hill to Kiftsgate and Hidcote Gardens (See **Walk 8**); and also one leading southwards, over the hill to Chipping Campden, passing close to the southern entrance to Campden Tunnel. (See page 25.)

Middleton Cheney (50-41) Large village on the A422, Banbury to Brackley road. It has many attractive stone cottages and farmhouses, several of which overlook a village green; but there has been much modern building here, and Middleton Cheney only just overcomes the feeling that it is a suburb of nearby Banbury. However it has a fine church, much of which was built in the 14th century by William of Edyngton, who was once rector here. William was later to become Bishop of Winchester, and it was he who built the west front of the cathedral, and who also ordained the priest who was to become Winchester's greatest Bishop, William of Wykeham, the founder of Winchester School and New College, Oxford. William of Edyngton was responsible for the wealth of Decorated detail in the church, but tower, spire and painted pulpit are Perpendicular in style, and are 15th century work. Much restoration was carried out by Sir Giles Gilbert Scott in about 1865, but Middleton Cheney's greatest treasure is its series of richly glowing pre-Raphaelite stained glass windows. These were made in the William Morris factory, and are the work of Burne-Jones, Philip Webb, Ford Madox Brown, Simeon Solomon,

Rossetti, and William Morris himself. Why so much of their work in one village church ? The rector at the time, W. C. Buckley, was a personal friend of Burne-Jones, and the last window of the series was in fact a memorial by Burne-Jones to his friend Buckley, who died in 1892. Six small lights in the west window were the original of Burne-Jones's *'Six Days of Creation'*. Spend time here, if you would like to learn at least a little about the life and works of this fascinating group of artists.

There was a small battle here in the Civil War, when in 1643, a Royalist force under Lord Northampton killed over two hundred Parliamentarian troops, some of whom are buried in the churchyard.

Mollington (44-47) Pretty ironstone village, on hill slopes below a ridge on which the Banbury to Coventry road runs, with pleasant views across to the villages of Shotteswell and Warmington and the tree-clad slopes of Edge Hill beyond. There is a lively little inn, and an early-14th century church, which was sympathetically restored in about 1855. See especially the country-style 15th century chancel screen, with Tudor roses painted on its wainscot, and the series of monuments to the Holbech family of nearby Farnborough Hall, including that of Ambrose Holbech, who built the hall in the late-17th century (see page 35). Why were the Holbech's buried here, rather than in Farnborough parish church ? We confess that we do not have the answer to this problem.

Walk south-west, across the valley to Shotteswell, and on to Hanwell and Wroxton, or north to Farnborough.

Moreton-in-Marsh (20-32) The intrepid late-17th century traveller and diarist, Celia Fiennes (see also Broughton, page 25) visited Moreton several times, as she had a widowed aunt living there. Her description of 'Morton Hindmost', as *a little neate stone built town, good Innes for traveller'* could hardly be bettered today. As Mistress Celia pointed out, it lay on the main route between London and Oxford, and the cities of Worcester and Hereford, and central Wales; and this probably accounted even more strongly for Moreton's prosperity, than for its position astride the Foss Way.

It appears that this *'little neate stone built town'* was also once called Moreton Henmarsh, the Henmarsh being low lying country much frequented by coots and moorhens; but we find Celia Fiennes's *'Morton Hindmost'* an even more endearing name. The origins of the town are somewhat obscure, but the oldest part grew up around the church, a former chapel-of-ease for nearby Bourton-on-the-Hill. The present building, lying to the east of the High Street, and south of Oxford Street, is almost entirely Victorian, and is not of great interest to visitors. However do not overlook the elegant 18th century house to its east.

Almost all of interest in Moreton-in-Marsh is situated on its broad High Street, with a series of

Shops in Moreton-in-Marsh High Street.

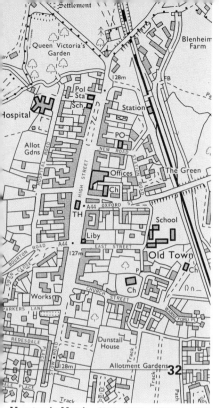

Moreton-in-Marsh. SCALE 1:10 000 or 6 INCHES to 1 MILE

Moreton, skirting to the south of Sezincote (see page 56).

Moreton Morrell (31-55) Village on high ground with occasional views west and north out over the wooded south Warwickshire countryside. It has a warm little inn, The Sea Horse, and a pleasant blend of thatched, half-timbered cottages, and mellow brick Georgian houses. The church, in its pretty churchyard, has Norman origins, with a medieval stone tower topped by Georgian brickwork. The interior is delightfully unspoilt, with old plastered walls, many clear glazed 18th century Gothic windows, and in the chancel, a fine 17th century wall monument to Richard Murden and his wife, with the two of them facing each other at prayer in separate niches, both sadly too tall to be able to see each other. Massive Moreton Hall, now an Agricultural College, was built in 1906 for an American, Mr Garland, who also had a Royal Tennis Court built almost opposite the church, but this impressive Edwardian Queen Anne style building is not open to the general public.

Napton on the Hill (46-61) Built on the southern slopes of Napton Hill, this is a delightful hotch-potch village, with several 17th century stone houses, amongst a very varied selection of later and more modest dwellings, all looking out over the almost secret countryside stretching south towards Marston Doles (see page 47). The church which is Norman in origin, sits on a fine hill-top site above the village, a long building with a west tower, the upper part of which is Georgian. The plastered interior has a Norman chancel arch and a Perpendicular east window. East from the church, and further away from the village, there is, on the edge of extensive quarries, a well restored stone tower windmill, but this is on private ground and cannot normally be visited.

Before leaving Napton, do try to visit the locks on the Oxford Canal, which lies below the village, on its south-west side. Here you will see canal-side

SCALE 1:25 000 or 2½ INCHES to 1 MILE

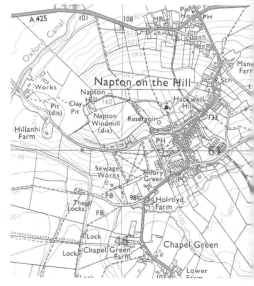

stone built shops, houses and coaching inns facing each other across the Foss Way, but divided by incessant traffic passing between the Midlands and the South-West. The Manor House Hotel and the Redesdale Arms are both pleasing buildings, and the White Hart claims the distinction of providing shelter for Charles I on 2nd July 1644. The little 16th century Curfew Tower on the corner of Oxford Street, has a bell dated 1633, which was rung each evening until as recently as 1860. On the other side of the High Street is the dominant feature of Moreton-in-Marsh, the confidently neo-Tudor Redesdale Market Hall, built in 1887 to the designs of Sir Ernest George, who was soon to carry out a similar commisssion for Lord Redesdale, in the design of a 'Cotswold-Elizabethan' style mansion at nearby Batsford Park. (See page 22.)

The coming to Moreton, in 1843, of Brunel's Oxford, Worcester and Wolverhampton Railway, brought with it a certain worldliness that some neighbouring Cotswold towns must certainly have envied at the time, and this robust quality appears to have survived here. (See also Stratford and Moreton Tramway, page 66.) So despite the traffic, do walk down both sides of Moreton's long High Street. There are several interesting and attractive shops, and the tree-lined greens at the northern end are especially delightful.

The best walk from Moreton-in-Marsh is north-westwards, up over the hills to Blockley, skirting the southern edge of Batsford Park, and possibly calling in to look round the Batsford Park Arboretum (see page 22). To make a long circular walk, move south-west from Blockley, via Dovedale and Bourton Downs, to Hinchwick (14-30), and then head east, making some use of public roads, to return to

England at its best, with views up to the windmill, and in summertime you may be fortunate enough to help a boat through the locks, on its way over the Cotswolds to Banbury and on towards the Thames near Oxford. (For Oxford Canal, see page 50.) Walk from here, along the towpath, south to Marston Doles, or north to Napton Junction, where the Oxford Canal meets the Grand Union Canal. Near to this junction is the Napton reservoir, a canal feeder, where sailing dinghies can be seen in summer and many birds may be observed in wintertime. If you prefer the field paths, try the walk south-east to Priors Marston, or eastwards to Shuckburgh, with fine views to be had from Beacon Hill (49-60).

Nether Worton (42-30) An immaculate farm, a very grand 17th century manor house, much restored in about 1920, and a little church with deserted schoolroom attached. This and a few cottages make up Nether Worton, a deliciously quiet hamlet sheltering beneath wooded Hawk Hill, in the valley of the little River Tew. The medieval church has a modest 17th century tower, and a pleasant interior, the contents of which include a Jacobean communion rail, and a wall monument by the sculptor Henry Westmacott. This gentleman was the thirteenth child (no less) of his better-known father, Sir Richard Westmacott, who was as prolific a sculptor, as he was a father.

Newbottle (52-36) Situated in remote hilly country well to the east of the Cherwell valley, Newbottle now consists only of a manor house and a church. It is probable that the old village was cleared as part of a ruthless enclosure campaign by landlords eager to aquire new wealth as sheep graziers, and signs of the vanished village are to be seen in uneven fields near the church. Newbottle church now serves the neighbouring village of Charlton (see page 27), which probably grew up as a result of Newbottle's depopulation. It is an interesting building, with a late Norman tower, but most surviving parts of the fabric are 14th and 15th century in origin. There is a monument to John and Elizabeth Cresswell (1655) by John Stone, son of Nicholas Stone, probably the finest 17th century sculptor in England; and a brass to Peter Dormer (1555), his two wives and no fewer than nineteen children. In the grounds of the Tudor manor house, there is a handsome octagonal dovecote, which is visible from the road.

Norton Lindsey (22-63) Pleasant village in high rolling country, with half-timber and thatch much in evidence, and distant views southwards to the line of wooded hills beyond the broad Avon valley. The 13th century church with its little bellcote stands on rising ground, and its rather dark interior has a pulpit incorporating Jacobean panels and a simple Norman font, its bowl being narrower than the shaft upon which it stands. The early-19th century windmill, some distance to the north-west of the church, now only has two sail arms, and looks a little sad.

Offchurch (36-65) Mellow brick and thatch village on a small hill with pleasant views out over the meandering River Leam. It has some modern development which has not added to its charm, but the Stag's Head Inn appears to be full of character. The church is largely Norman in origin, and has a

fine north doorway. The grey stone west tower is Perpendicular, and has bullet marks upon it that are claimed to have been made by Roundhead soldiers .... a good Royalist tale possibly, but now hard to disprove. The interior has unfortunately been scraped by Victorian restorers and is dark with their stained glass. However do not overlook the little serpent carved over one of the Norman windows south of the chancel. Built into the north wall are two carved stones, which are reputed to be part of the coffin lid of King Offa ... but it is little more than supposition that Offa, the Anglo-Saxon king of Mercia from A.D. 757 to 796, was even buried at Offchurch. It is likely however that the king did build both a hunting lodge and a church here.

It is possible to walk north-east from here parallel with the Leam, to the village of Hunningham, but one of the best walks from Offchurch is along the towpath of the nearby Grand Union Canal, preferably eastwards towards Bascote.

Oxford Canal (52-69)-(49-30) The Oxford Canal was one of a series of such waterways conceived by James Brindley, the pioneer canal builder, who had completed the Bridgewater Canal for the Duke of

The Oxford Canal, near Wormleighton.

Bridgewater in 1761. The Act of Parliament authorising the construction of the Oxford Canal was obtained in 1769, and work must have started very soon afterwards, from the northern end, at Hawkesbury near Coventry. However it was not until 1790 that the first load of Coventry coal was able to sail out of the canal, into the Thames at Oxford. Its length between Braunston and Napton Junction has for many years been used as part of the Grand Union Canal, but it will be noted from the map that the titling near Willoughby (52-69) is still very clearly marked 'Oxford Canal', this point being beyond Braunston. The length between Braunston and Napton soon became of key importance to the Oxford Company who levied an extortionate 'bar toll' on boats passing Napton Junction, and by so doing they obtained over a quarter of a million pounds in a mere twenty years... a great deal of money in those days.

The length of canal between Napton Junction and Oxford, much of which is in the area covered by this guide, is a delight. Brindley made great use of the contours, especially when crossing hill summits, and the meandering summit level between Marston

Doles (46-58) and Claydon (46-50) is outstandingly beautiful. From Cropredy southwards Brindley utilised the Cherwell, both as a feeder of water, and in places, for actual navigation, and this again adds to the charm of this unique waterway. In recent years the Oxford Canal has become deservedly popular with holiday boating enthusiasts, largely those hiring boats for short holidays; and this has lead to a certain crowding at times. But please do not this deter you from exploring Britain's loveliest canal. If you wish to follow it on foot, British Waterways normally have no objection, but do remember, you have no statutory right to walk their towpaths, except in exceptional cases where there is an established right-of-way for walkers. (See **Walk 3**, which uses a short length of this canal, near Cropredy.)

Oxhill (31-45) A tidy, stone village in the 'Vale of Red Horse', with views south-eastwards to the scarp face of the Oxfordshire Cotswolds, where the Red Horse itself must have once been clearly visible, on its hilly site above the straggling village of Tysoe (see page 68). Oxhill has an attractively signed, stone built inn, the Peacock, and many pleasant farmhouses and cottages; and the character of the village is not overawed by modern building on its northern edge. The interesting, largely Norman church looks out across flat country to the 'Red Horse' hills. Both north and south doorways are Norman, but the south is a much richer specimen. The tower is Perpendicular, and there is a fine 15th century roof to the nave, and a fascinating Norman font, ornamented with the rather scrawny figures of Adam and Eve, at the 'Tree of Life'. See also the fine 15th century rood screen across the tower arch, and in the south-eastern part of the churchyard, the grave of a female negro slave. She died in 1705, the property of 'Thomas Beauchamp, gent. of Nevis' who was probably a sugar plantation owner, and who almost certainly married one of the local rector's twin daughters. This has little to do with Oxhill, but Nevis was the island in the West Indies where Horatio Nelson was to marry the widow Nesbit some eighty years later.

Walks across the relatively flat countryside around Oxhill are not exceptionally interesting, but the best one runs north along the largely unfenced road to the A422, and then across fields to Pillerton Hersey. It is also possible to walk across fields to Lower Tysoe, and from thence up the scarp face to Sun Rising Hill and along the woods cladding the slopes of Edge Hill.

Pebworth (13-46) This delightful little village is the only one in our guide to lie in the county of Hereford and Worcester, and is situated on a small knoll in largely flat countryside less than two miles to the west of the point where the counties of Gloucestershire, Warwickshire and Hereford and Worcester meet. There are three streets, lined with old houses and cottages of half-timber and thatch, mellow brick and grey lias stone. Two of these streets climb up to the top of the village, where the fine old church stands in a trim, tree-shaded churchyard surrounded by a low stone wall. The church of St Peter contains much 14th century work, although the Perpendicular tower, dormered clerestory and north porch are about a century younger. Old plastered walls, stone flagged floors and much clear

glass, gives the interior a character often lacking in so many over-restored churches; and there are several features not to be missed ... a handsome Jacobean pulpit, the 17th century wall monument to Robert Marten complete with macabre skulls and delightful classical detail, and some 15th century glass in the east window.

Pebworth must have been one of the villages known to William Shakespeare, and there is a verse attributed to the poet that refers to *'Piping Pebworth'*. (See Bidford-on-Avon, page 22.) There appears to be no clue as to why Pebworth should have been noted for its piping, and its inclusion like that of one or two other villages in the verse, may have been due no more than to a poet's desire for alliteration.

Pillerton Hersey (30-48) This is centred upon a minute green with neatly tended flowers around the base of its simple war memorial. There is a large modern house beyond overlooking a tree – shaded pool. The gardens surrounding further modern housing are now so lush that nothing jars the quiet air of contentment here. There are at least three pale stone farms, a Georgian rectory faced with mellow brick, and tucked away on the north side of the village, a pleasing church with an exceptional 13th century chancel and little priest's door of the same period. See also the chancel arch, which has been charmingly distorted by age into an almost horseshoe shape, and the fine old roofs to the chancel and the nave. The north aisle is unfortunately very much of the 19th century, and is disappointing especially when compared to the chancel. The best walk from Pillerton Hersey is south-eastwards along the line of an old bridle-road, across the A422, and down a quiet partly open road, from which there are fine views south and west, ending up at Oxhill.

Preston Bagot (17-65) Scattered parish, much of it along narrow lanes, and some on a steep little knoll overlooking the valley through which the pretty Stratford-upon-Avon Canal runs. It is on this knoll that the small church stands, with a Norman nave and a neo-Norman chancel added in about 1870 by a local architect, J. A. Chatwin, who amongst many other works, was responsible for the chancel of Birmingham Cathedral.

Preston on Stour (20-49) Delightful village, with views out over the willow-bordered Stour to Alscot Park, and although less than a mile from the busy A34, with an air of tranquillity that is hard to believe. There are two large timber-framed houses, the vicarage and the Old Manor, and several smaller ones; a handsome Georgian house, and several 19th century neo-Tudor estate cottages. The church stands above a green, with its medieval tower and nave having been carefully remodelled in the Gothick manner by the Chipping Campden architect, builder and quarry-owner, Edward Woodward, for James West of Alscot Park, who was much taken by this mode. The 18th century interior is a most stylish piece of work and contains an interesting series of monuments largely to members of the West family, notably those by the sculptor Sir Richard Westmacott and by his eldest son, Richard. Do not overlook the beautiful classical sarcophagus in memory of Thomas Steavens, designed by

James 'Athenian' Stuart and sculpted by Thomas Scheemakers; nor, in contrast, the 17th century monument to Sir Nicholas Kemp, with his two wives on either side.

Walk from here, south-eastwards, beside the Stour to Wimpstone, or around a quiet road to Atherstone on Stour, and thence across the fields to Clifford Chambers. Or, if you prefer to drive, take the delightful road parallel with the Stour, south-eastwards, through Wimpstone, past Whitchurch, to Crimscote and Talton.

Priors Hardwick (47-55) Quietly situated beneath the northern end of Berry Hill, looking westwards out over the flat, secret countryside where the

Priors Hardwick ... 'an ironstone church'.

summit level of the reedy Oxford Canal meanders between Marston Doles and Fenny Compton. There were once thriving medieval villages here, depopulated in the later middle ages first by plague, and later by the rapacious enclosures of the sheep graziers (see Wormleighton, page 76). Ironstone cottages, an ironstone inn, the Butchers Arms, and an ironstone church ... all look out across the rough little village green. The church is largely 13th century in origin, and it was in this century that the fine sedilia and piscina were installed. The interior is not of consuming interest, but it is well lit by much clear glass, and has a spacious quality, quite often lacking in smaller village churches. Walk south-west from here to Wormleighton, partly using the towpath of the Oxford Canal.

Priors Marston (49-57) A pleasant village below Marston Hill, not far from the Northamptonshire border. It is situated on the Welsh Road, once used by drovers bringing their great flocks of sheep from Wales to the markets of London. No doubt that the hospitable Falcon Inn must have provided welcome relief for the hardy, dust-ridden drovers on their long journey to the south-east. This is only one of several handsome ironstone buildings in the village, most of which look out over the cross-roads at its centre from deep-set mullioned windows. The

church, standing in a churchyard surrounded by attractive stone cottages, has a Georgian west tower enriched with now mellowed Tuscan pilasters. However the rest was rebuilt in the 1860s, and is not of outstanding interest to visitors.

The countryside here lies between four and six hundred feet above sea level, but it is itself dominated by the tall radio relay tower well to the south-east of the village. This soaring concrete structure provides an impressive landmark for travellers in several parts of Warwickshire, Northamptonshire and Oxfordshire, and is a distinctive feature on many distant skylines in the area covered by this guide. Walk north from Priors Marston, over the fields to Shuckburgh, or north to Napton... and then in both cases, it is possible to return by way of the towpath on the Oxford Canal.

Quinton, Upper and Lower (18-47) There is a large army housing estate here, but most of Lower Quinton remains unspoilt, with a village green overlooked by several thatched, timber-framed cottages, a handsome mellow brick 17th century house with Cotswold stone tiles, and a well restored inn, the College Arms. This displays the arms of Magdalen College, Oxford, which still owns much land in the area. All this is overlooked by the splendid 130 foot high spire of Quinton church. This has Norman south arcading and a Norman font, and many interesting features from the centuries that followed, including a Perpendicular clerestory, an effigy of a knight that fought at Agincourt, Sir William Clopton, and a fine brass of his widow, Lady Clopton. On Sir William's death, this lady took a vow of widowhood, and is believed to have lived as an anchorite, or hermit, in a cell nearby. It is probable that it is to her that we are indebted for the clerestory and the splendid spire.

It is possible to walk across the fields to Upper Quinton, where there is an early timber-framed manor house with very close vertical timbers, visible from the road. To the south of Upper Quinton, is Meon Hill, one of the northern outliers of the Cotswolds. There are memories here of suspected witchcraft in comparatively recent times, and its summit is crowned by the ramparts of an Iron Age hill fort.

Radway (37-48) Delightful Hornton stone village beneath the partly wooded slopes of Edge Hill. Many of the houses and cottages here are thatched, and at the far end of the village there is a small green enriched by a tree-shaded pool, and overlooked by further cottages and a little 19th century chapel. The small spired church was built on a new site in 1866, to replace a brick building at the other end of the village. Its contents are not of great interest, apart from a monument brought here from the old church, to Captain Kingswell, a Royalist officer, killed at the battle of Edgehill in 1642 (see page 34), and a plain wall monument to Sanderson Miller, who died in 1780.

Sanderson Miller was squire of Radway, and owner of Radway Grange, the handsome stone building in its own park, not far from the church. He was an outstanding 'gentleman architect', and one of the pioneers of the Gothick style, being at least three years ahead of the better known Horace Walpole, who was soon to begin his famous improvements to Strawberry Hill. Miller was responsible for a fascinating series of architectural works, from Wiltshire to East Anglia, including the Shire Hall at Warwick, and Hagley Hall in Worcestershire. He made considerable alterations to his own home, the Elizabethan Radway Grange, and built the Edgehill Tower on the ridge above his park, marking the spot where the Royal Standard was raised at the Battle of Edgehill. He also planted the hanging woods above the park, and the large statue of Caractacus, which now stands in the garden of Radway Grange, originally intended for the Edgehill Tower but found to be too large for its niche. Radway Grange was, in Sanderson Miller's time, a centre of fashion and intellect, and Fielding read the manuscript of his novel *Tom Jones* to Miller and his friends Lord North, the Earl of Chatham and Sir George Lyttleton in the dining room. It is sad to relate however that Miller spent the last years of his life confined in the house of a doctor in Lincolnshire, on account of his insanity.

Do not miss a visit to Radway, and if possible, walk up the hill, using at least part of **Walk 6**. It is unfortunately not possible to walk north-westwards over the Edgehill battlefield site, as this is occupied by the military authorities.

Ratley (38-47) Small stone village just over the watershed between Thames and Severn, with enviable south facing views towards the softer country of the Thames, rather than north to the Midland plain, the more sombre prospect from the woods above neighbouring Radway. A sunken road leads down the village, to a grey stone church, almost entirely Decorated in style. Squire of Radway, Sanderson Miller, would have probably ridden this way to visit his friend Lord North of Wroxton Abbey, and it seems likely that the pretty ogival-shaped arches of medieval Ratley church played some part in influencing the Gothick style for which he was to become so noted. While here, do not miss the medieval churchyard cross.

Walks from Ratley include one south across the fields to Hornton, east to Warmington, or south-west past Uplands Farm, south along the Oxfordshire boundary, and round to the south of Upton House parklands. It is also possible to walk to Radway via Edgehill village.

The Rollright Stones (29-30) These consist of three separate features... *The King's Men*, a Bronze Age stone circle, about a hundred feet in diameter, and dated between 2000 and 1800 BC. This is situated to the immediate south of a road between the A34 and the A44. *The Whispering Knights*, the remains of a Bronze Age burial chamber, four hundred yards to the east of the circle, and finally *The King Stone*, an isolated 'standing stone', nearly opposite *The King's Men*, and almost certainly associated with them, although its exact purpose is not known. These features all lie in fine upland country, and there are splendid views, especially northwards from *The King Stone*. The ridge on which these stones are situated is believed to have carried one of Britain's earliest and most important tracks... the so called Jurassic Way, leading south and west along the limestone belt, from the shores of the Humber, to Salisbury Plain and the coast beyond. For further reading on the subject of trackways in this area, may we suggest G. R. Crosher's excellent book, *Along the Cotswold Ways*.

The 18th century antiquary, William Stukeley,

The King Stone ... one of the Rollright Stones.

referred to the Rollright Stones as being, *'corroded like wormeaten wood by the harsh jaws of time'*, but despite their exposed upland setting they still survive. In earlier times they were the subject of a legend relating to a king intent on the conquest of England, who was confronted by a witch who spoke thus:

> *If Long Compton thou canst see,*
> *King of England thou shalt be.*

Unfortunately for the king and his followers this proved to be impossible at the time, and the witch continued...

> *As Long Compton thou canst not see*
> *King of England thou shalt not be.*
> *Rise up stick, and stand still, stone,*
> *For King of England thou shalt be none.*
> *Thou and thy men hoar stones shalt be,*
> *And I shall be an eldern tree.*

And so, the king, his men and his knights were all turned into stone, and the witch into an elder tree.

Rowington (20-69) An unspoilt little village in quiet countryside through which the Grand Union Canal winds, on a long lock-less level, with a tunnel at Shrewley Common well to the south-east (21-67). This has small access tunnels for the horses, which had to plod away from the canal and over the hill, leaving the bargees to 'leg' their boats through unaided. Rowington church stands on a small hill to the south of the village, and has a complicated architectural history, leaving us with a wide, clear glazed Perpendicular west window, a fine wagon roof to the nave of the same period, a 15th century stone pulpit, and a prettily restored chancel. Shakespeare Hall, a stout timber-framed 16th century building was the home of Thomas Shakespeare, a possible relative of the playwright. There is some doubt about this, but his son was certainly apprenticed to the printer and publisher William Jaggard, who in 1623 published *Mr William Shakespeare's Comedies, Histories, and Tragedies*, the well known 'First Folio'.

The best walks from Rowington are along the

towpath of the nearby Grand Union Canal, or along that of the Stratford-upon-Avon Canal, which is not far distant.

Royal Leamington Spa (31-65) The 16th century antiquary William Camden referred to a well at Leamington in his famous survey of the British Isles, *Britannia*, first published in 1586. However it was not until 1786, that a certain William Abbots built Leamington's first Spa Bath, no doubt to meet the rapidly expanding demand for more spas, following, along with Matlock and Buxton, the trend set by the well established and highly fashionable town of Bath. The Pump Room was built in 1814, and in September 1819, the Prince Regent visited Leamington, and granted the new hotel there the right to use his name and coat of arms.

However it was Dr Henry Jephson who was largely responsible for the town's fame, and it was he who secured Queen Victoria's authority to add the titles 'Royal' and 'Spa' to that of Leamington in 1838. Many of Leamington's public buildings are of a more recent date than this, but almost all of its really elegant terraces, squares, crescents and private villas were built by the middle of the 19th century. Lansdowne Crescent, Newbold Terrace, and Clarendon Square are amongst the most handsome of Leamington's buildings, but there are many quiet corners worth exploring, and many delightfully detailed features to be observed, especially the finely fretted ironwork verandahs, some of which can still be seen suspended above the waters of the Grand Union Canal, and the little River Leam. Leamington has several 19th century churches, but these are not of great interest to the visitor.

Royal Leamington Spa.

SCALE 1:10 000 or 6 INCHES to 1 MILE

Bridge over the Avon, and the Royal Pump Room, Royal Leamington Spa.

The Jephson Gardens, between Newbold Terrace and the banks of the Leam, are well worth visiting, ... thirteen acres of beautifully laid out gardens, with bordered walks and shaded arbours. There is an aviary with tropical birds, and wild ducks use the lake. Sited at Southgate Lodge, the entrance to the Gardens from the lower end of the Parade, is a very helpful Tourist Information Centre. At Newbold Comyn Park, to the east of Jephson Gardens, there is a Childrens Play Area, and various sports facilities. There are also two nature trails which incorporate riverside walks, pools, and extensive views from an adjoining hillside. Details of these trails may be obtained from the Tourist Information Centre or the Art Gallery and Museum in Avenue Road, the contents of which include paintings by Dutch and Flemish masters, and some 20th century paintings and watercolours, mainly by English artists.

There has of course been much new building in Leamington, and it is a lively modern town. There are pleasant shops in the town, many of which are on the Parade, the town's main street, and several retain a flavour of Leamington's past elegance. There are some industrial features that would preferably have been sited further from its centre, but much of Leamington still has an enviable feeling of quiet prosperity, a flavour that owes much to the work of Jephson and all those who helped to establish 'Royal Leamington Spa', in the early days of Victoria's reign.

Ryknild Street (13-31) This Roman road only traverses a small section of the area covered by this guide, but it was an important route running northwards from the Foss Way near Bourton-on-the-Water, and down the Cotswold edge between Saintbury and Weston Subedge. From here it ran across the Midland plain, past Birmingham and Derby, ending up at Templeborough near Sheffield. Its line across Bourton Downs is not easy to spot on the ground, although slight humps where it crosses two roads at Ref. 13-33, provide a fascinating clue which has been substantiated by excavation at Bourton Far Hill Farm, a short distance to the south. Good walking country north from Hinchwick.

Sezincote (17-30) In medieval times there was a small village here, but its church was destroyed by Cromwell's forces, apparently due to the estate

Sezincote ... 'Moghul splendour in an English rural setting'.

having been in the hands of ardent royalists. In 1795 Sezincote was purchased by Colonel John Cockerell, a 'nabob' recently returned from Bengal. He died only three years later, leaving the estate to his younger brother Charles, who had served with him in the East India Company. Charles, who became a Baronet in 1809, and a Member of Parliament for Evesham, built a new house, employing another brother, Samuel Pepys Cockerell (the family were distantly related to the diarist Pepys), as his architect.

S. P. Cockerell, who was also Surveyor to the East India Company, worked closely with Thomas Daniel, an artist who had also recently returned from India, and together they created a house in the Indian manner. This creation was inspired by the work of the 16th century Moghul emperor, Akbar,

SCALE 1:25 000 or 2½ INCHES to 1 MILE

who had deliberately mixed Islamic and Hindu styles in an attempt to integrate the diverse cultures of the two races. The result achieved at Sezincote is unique; a grand house in the authentic Moghul style in a rural English setting, the beauty of which was further enhanced by the outstanding landscape artist, Humphrey Repton, who helped to create the delightful water gardens and lakes on the descending hillside that gives birth to the River Evenlode. To add to these delights, Sezincote offers a highly elegant, classical interior, which has been beautifully restored in the mid-20th century, and a visit here should certainly not be missed. *Tel: (0386) 700444.*

Sezincote was visited in 1806 by the Prince Regent who was staying with the Marquess of Hertford at Ragley, and it appears that he was so impressed by Sezincote's style that he advanced his plans for the Indianisation of his Pavilion at Brighton, although the Prince's favourite architect John Nash, was given the commission, rather than Cockerell.

Shenington (37-42) Large stone and thatch village, grouped around a wide green, standing over five hundred feet above sea level, and looking across the valley of the Sor Brook to the smaller village of Alkerton. It has an attractive little inn, the Bell, which is noted for its mouth-watering bar meals. The church has a Perpendicular west tower, and a porch of the same period, but it is otherwise largely in the Decorated style. It was heavily restored in 1879 by an architect, who was not always so ruthless, J. L. Pearson, the builder of Truro cathedral. Here are shiny tiles, pitch pine pews and scraped walls, but we like Pearson's 13th century style chancel arch, the medieval ornamentation of the south aisle arcade capitals, and the

The Bell Inn, Shenington.

sculptured figures of a man and his ox on the outside of the south wall.

Walk north up the valley of the Sor Brook from here, beside Upton House's Temple Pool, and on to Upton House and Edge Hill, partly using the roads. Alternatively walk down the valley to Shutford, and on to Tadmarton or Swalcliffe. This countryside is the Oxfordshire Cotswolds at its best, high rolling countryside, intersected by deep valleys running south towards the distant Thames.

Sherbourne (26-61) A delightful estate village in mellow brick, with woodlands close by and the little Sherbourne Brook flowing past to join the Avon just to its south. Sherbourne Park estate with its handsome 18th century house looking out over the fields to Barford's bridge over the River Avon, was purchased by the Birmingham wire manufacturer, Samuel Ryland in 1837. It was his daughter, Louisa Anne, who in the 1860's had the splendid Decorated style church built by the prolific and highly successful architect, George Gilbert Scott, who must have only recently completed his work on the chancel at nearby Hampton Lucy church for the Lucy family. Was Louisa inspired by this very high calibre work ? It would appear very likely, and there is little doubt that the interior of elegantly spired Sherbourne, when completed, was even more splendid than Hampton Lucy, with richly carved detail at every turn, and fine proportions to the whole. Do not miss a visit here.

There is a quiet road running west and south from Sherbourne towards Hampton Lucy, and it is possible to spot the earthworks of long vanished Fulbroke Castle, to the west of the road, about a mile from Sherbourne (25-60). Fulbrook had an unusually short life, having probably been built by Henry VI in the 1430's, and being already in ruins by 1478. The remains were given by Henry VIII to Sir William Compton, and it is believed that much of the surviving fabric was used by Sir William in the building of his magnificent new house at Compton Wynyates (see page 32).

Shipston-on-Stour (25-40) *'Sheepstown'* was once an outstandingly important market for sheep, and its variety of delightful houses from the 17th, 18th and 19th centuries bear witness to a prosperity lasting for many hundreds of years. That it continued to thrive in the 19th century must have been due in part to the enterprise of the local canal promoter William James of Henley-in-Arden, who completed a tramway between the canal wharfs of

Shipston-on-Stour. SCALE 1:10 000 or 6 INCHES to 1 MILE

The Horseshoe Inn, Shipston-on-Stour.

Stratford-upon-Avon and Moreton-in-Marsh in 1826, with a later branch line to Shipston, opening in 1836 (see page 66). Eventually in 1889, many years after the Oxford, Worcester and Wolverhampton line came through Moreton-in-Marsh, part of the tramway was converted into a railway branch-line between there and Shipston. Another factor contributing to Shipston's continuing prosperity, was its position astride a busy north-south coaching route, and a number of the old coaching inns survive to this day, amongst which are those in the delightful High Street, Shipston's little market square. This is just far enough away from the busy traffic of the A34, Stratford — Oxford road, but those living or working on the line of the A34 itself must look forward eagerly to relief from the long promised and much disputed M40 motorway. But despite this, Shipston is today a busy little shopping town, with many shops attractive enough to tempt customers from far and wide.

The church has a 15th century west tower, but is otherwise the creation of Victorian architect, G. E. Street. The interior is not of outstanding interest, but do not miss the very unusual conversion of a sounding-board from an earlier pulpit, into an octagonal table. There is also a handsome little monument to another person to whom Shipston must have owed some of its prosperity... John Hart, who died in 1747... *'A considerable Improver and Promoter of Manufacture in this his native Town'*. There is an attractive walk, partly beside the River Stour, to Barcheston, and on to Willington, and also one south-westwards across the fields to Todenham.

Shottery (18-54) This rather over-developed village lies to the immediate west of Stratford-upon-Avon, and is today almost swallowed up by it. It is renowned for the thatched and timber-framed farmhouse, known as **Anne Hathaway's Cottage**, once the home of Shakespeare's wife, and scene of William's youthful courtship. Anne, daughter of Richard Hathaway, a member of a long established yeoman family, was born in 1556. She married the young poet in 1582, and was destined to outlive him by seven years. The 'cottage' is situated on the west side of the village beyond a little brook, and stands in a delightful old world garden with clipped box hedges, roses, herbs and many other plants known to the Elizabethans. There

SCALE 1:25 000 or 2½ INCHES to 1 MILE

Anne Hathaway's Cottage, Shottery.

is a small orchard beyond, with wild flowers in the greensward beneath blossoming fruit trees.

The oldest part of the house, which incorporates a pair of curved oak timbers pegged together at their apex in the 'cruck' method of constuction, dates back to the 15th century, but most of the fabric is 16th and 17th century work. The beautiful interior is full of interest, being furnished as it would have been in Shakespeare's day, with splendid oak pieces, most of which belonged to the Hathaway family and their heirs, including the famous Hathaway bedstead. *Tel: (0789) 292100.*

The rest of the village is very much a residential area of Stratford-upon-Avon, but it does have a fine manor house dating back to the 14th century, which is now part of a large girl's school, and which has a fine square dovecote in its grounds. The church was built as late as 1870, and apart from its carved pulpit and screen, is not of great interest to visitors. In the centre of the village, there is a lively inn, the Bell, serving excellent bar meals.

Shutford (38-40) Quiet village on steep slopes amidst small bumpy hills. The prettily signed George and Dragon inn is comfortably sited almost beneath the church. This has a miniature pinnacled tower, Perpendicular in period, Norman arcading, a pleasant oak screen, also Perpendicular, and early-19th century box pews. The largely 16th century manor house has an unusually tall, projecting staircase tower, and local legend claims that the upper storey of the house once had an eighty foot gallery (not an uncommon feature in houses of this period), where Lord Saye and Sele, of nearby Broughton Castle, used to drill local troops before the outbreak of the Civil War. There is a bridle-road south from here, beside Madmarston Hill, to Swalcliffe, and on beyond, south-west to Hook Norton. Alternatively there is a path up the valley of the little Sor Brook to Shenington, and beyond to Upton House. There is also an attractive, partly unfenced road east and south-east to Broughton, with its beautiful moated castle.

Sibford Ferris and Sibford Gower (35-37) These two together with Burdrop, a minute hamlet sandwiched between them, make up a large village, with Ferris to the south, and Gower to the north, of a quiet valley running south-westwards to the Stour. Burdrop has a colourful little inn called the Bishop's Blaize, looking out over the valley. Ferris has a large Quaker boarding school including one or two elegant 18th century houses, and a short unfenced road with fine views, leading south-westwards, past Woodway Farm. Gower has a largely unremarkable Victorian church, which is however worth visiting on account of the charming little monument to Mrs Isabelle Stevens (1907) by her son Frank Lascelles, who lived at the manor house and who was in his day well known for the great pageants that he used to organise. Gower also has a wealth of Hornton stone and thatched cottages, and a hospitable inn called the Wykeham Arms, which is noted for its cold buffets and bar meals generally. It is possible to walk westwards from here, across the fields to Ditchedge Lane, an old 'green road', which forms the border between Warwickshire and Oxfordshire, following it southwards to the point where it crosses the Stour at Traitor's Ford (see page 67), or north to the hills above Compton Wynyates. For much of its length

Ditchedge Lane is on a ridge and there are far reaching views on every side (See also **Walk 3**).

Snitterfield (21-59) Large village on high ground to the north of the ridge on which a lonely war memorial stands, looking southwards out over the Avon valley to the wooded hills beyond Loxley and Wellesbourne. There are some timber-framed and thatched cottages, mellow brick farm houses, and several Tudor style 19th century houses, almost all with pretty flower filled gardens. The manor house of the Hales family, and then the Earls of Coventry is now no more, apart from a high garden wall, and the attractive Park House cottages. The church, at the eastern end of the village, has a 14th and 15th century tower, and its interior is full of interest. See especially the great Decorated font beneath the tower arch, the 16th century carved pew fronts and pew ends, and the early-18th century pulpit with its oval panels. In the chancel there are five monuments to members of the Philips family, the builders of Welcombe – the great Victorian mansion between Snitterfield and Stratford-upon-Avon, which is now a hotel. The tall obelisk, known as the Welcombe Monument can be seen from many parts of south Warwickshire and was erected in 1876 in memory of Mark Philips, by his brother Robert.

Richard Shakespeare, the playwright's grandfather, farmed land near Snitterfield in the vicinity of Marraway, (Map Ref. 23-60), and it is believed that he lies in Snitterfield churchyard. It appears that his son John, left for Stratford in 1551, and married Mary Arden daughter of a prosperous Wilmcote farmer, at Aston Cantlow six years later, their son William being born in 1564.

A distant ancestor of Lady Diana, the Princess of Wales, once lived at Snitterfield. He was an enterprising farmer named John Spencer, who moved as a young man to Wormleighton, and founded one of England's most powerful families on wealth made from sheep grazing. (See Wormleighton, page 76.)

King's Lane, a small road between Snitterfield and Bishopton (19-56), is thought to have been used by Charles II, when as a fugitive after the Battle of Worcester, he rode pillion to Miss Jane Lane, disguised as her servant, Will Jackson. Charles II's own account, dictated many years later to the diarist Samuel Pepys, mentions Wootton and Stratford-upon-Avon; and Snitterfield would appear to be rather far to the east of his route. However with Cromwell's troops very much in evidence during those difficult days in September 1651, diversions may have been very necessary.

As a pedestrian route Charles II's way is now too busy with motor traffic, but there is a good walk, through Welcombe Park, past the obelisk, to Stratford-upon-Avon, after some use of the public road in the early stages.

Southam (41-62) Busy little town, which had a thriving market from the time of Henry III, who granted a charter for this purpose in 1227. This survived until comparatively recent years, and Southam's prosperity has been due both to the market trade and to the great number of hungry and thirsty cattle drovers passing along the Welsh Road, which ran through Southam. Several of the inns that they must have used have survived, and amongst them, the Craven Arms, the Old Mint, and the Black Dog still bring a touch of character to the

Southam Church.

town. But the really dominant feature of Southam is the 120 foot high, 15th century red sandstone spire of its church, a handsome, largely silver-grey lias building. Its lofty interior is well lit by clerestory windows, beneath a fine low pitched roof, with carved angels and Tudor roses. The Jacobean pulpit, which is well worth looking at, is believed to have been re-discovered in a barn at Wormleighton after being 'lost' for many years.

There is a small zoo on the A425 Daventry road, about a mile to the east of the town *(Tel: (092681) 2431)*. The best walk from Southam is westwards, close to a Holy Well, then to the north of Stoney Thorpe Hall, and beside Ufton Wood, to the village of Ufton.

South Newington (40-33) Situated in the valley of the little River Swere, this delightful village has an inn on the A361 road called the Wykeham Arms. Much of the rest of the village lies beyond a small trim green which is overlooked by South Newington's exceptionally interesting church. This has a handsome Perpendicular porch with canopied niche, a cylindrical Norman font with a zigzag band, a Jacobean pulpit, and a series of box pews (all as originally numbered, which is an unusual survival in this area). There are also a number of interesting medieval stained glass windows. However most

South Newington Church.

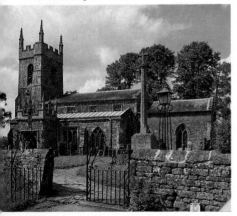

visitors come here to see the splendid series of wall paintings, especially the 14th century specimens in the north aisle and elsewhere. These are regarded by Professor Tristram, the great expert on wall paintings, as quite outstanding, and they must have been the work of an artist far more sophisticated in style than those normally working at the time on most small parish churches. See especially the *Martyrdom of St Thomas à Becket* over the north doorway, and to the east of it, the *Martyrdom of Thomas, Earl of Lancaster*. This Thomas was beheaded at Pontefract in 1322 for leading a rebellion against Edward II, and was probably featured on South Newington's walls due to his friendship with a local family, the Giffards, one of whom perished with him at Pontefract. The whole series of paintings must have been a wonderful picture-book bible for the medieval peasants of this parish, and they are fascinating in every detail. Do not overlook the framed documents relating to compulsory burial in woollen shrouds; a popular measure in this sheep country, but one that was probably to the advantage of the sheep graziers rather than the peasants. ·

It is possible to walk up the Swere valley to Wigginton and on to Swerford, or down to Barford St Michael and St John. There is also a bridle road northwards over hill country to Milcombe and Lower Tadmarton.

Stockton (43-63) This village grew in size in the 19th century due to the great blue-lias quarry workings around it, and from then until the present day, great quantities of cement have been produced here; the villagers still being proud of the fact that London's Victoria Embankment was constructed of Stockton cement. The village is well isolated from the cement workings and lies below the ridge on which the main A426 runs, with occasional glimpses south-eastwards to Napton windmill.. There is a little green, on the southern side, overlooked by the attractive Barley Mow Inn (which has a restaurant), and beyond it there is a church with a Perpendicular, red sandstone tower; the rest being built in the mid-19th century in a mixture of sandstone and the local blue-lias stone. The interior is not of great interest to visitors, but it does incorporate a Perpendicular chancel arch, which like the tower is of sandstone. To the north and east, beyond the quarry workings, is the Grand Union Canal, and the best walk from Stockton is north-east along a minor road to the canal, and then south-east along the towpath towards Napton Junction, where the Grand Union joins the older and more rural Oxford Canal. There are two lively canal-side inns near Stockton; the Blue Lias on the minor road to Long Itchington, and the Boat Inn on the A426, well to the north of the village **(See Walk 2)**.

Stourton (29-36) This is virtually a continuation of Cherington (see page 27), but it lies closer to the Stour than its neighbour. There are several pleasant old houses, including two mills on the Stour. Walk north-east from here beside the banks of a small tributary of the Stour, to Lower Brailes.

Stratford-upon-Avon (19-55) A still-thriving market town and busy route centre, which grew up on the west bank of the river Avon, at a crossing point

Shakespeare's Birthplace, Stratford-upon-Avon.

used since earliest times. There is evidence of prehistoric settlement nearby, and the Roman road between Worcester and Kings Sutton (just to the south of Banbury) forded the river here. There was a monastery here in Anglo-Saxon times, possibly on the site of the present parish church, and in the 12th century Stratford was granted the right of holding a weekly market, by the Bishop of Worcester. In the century that followed, a group of prosperous citizens achieved virtual independence from manorial control by the establishment of the Guild of the Holy Cross, a powerful body that controlled almost all that happened in the town, and whose members included the Duke of Clarence, Lord Warwick, and Stratford's own Sir Hugh Clopton, who re-built much of the Guild Chapel, and who also built the stone bridge over the Avon that still bears his name. The Guild continued to grow ever more powerful, and came to own considerable properties until its suppression, in 1547, in a process which had been started by Henry VIII some eight years earlier.

In place of the Guild, a self-governing body was established, consisting of a bailiff, later designated by the title of Mayor, 14 aldermen and 14 burgesses; and in 1568, the bailiff was none other than John Shakespeare, father of the man who was to have so much influence upon the story of his town, the poet and playwright, William Shakespeare. (For an account of *'The Shakespeare Connection'*, see page 10.) A considerable number of half-timbered houses that stood in Shakespeare's time, including his own birthplace, have survived to this day, and Stratford's medieval street plan has remained largely unchanged. However, the town's continuing prosperity in the centuries that followed, led to the erection of many handsome new buildings, especially during the Georgian period. It is for this reason

that we find such a delightful selection of mellow-brick houses and public buildings amongst the timbered houses of Shakespeare's day. It is sad to relate that modern shop-fronts have not always been sympathetically designed, but let us hope that the good example set by at least one recent development will be widely followed in the future.

There is a wealth of places to be visited in Stratford-upon-Avon, and a walk, or series of walks, around the town is essential. Cross reference numbers will be found on the Stratford Town Plan, and preceding each place listed below. To set the scene, a visit to the house where Shakespeare was born, should come first on your list. This is now entered via...

(1) The Shakespeare Centre, Henley Street. *(Tel: (0789) 204016.)* The first stage of this fascinating modern building was opened in 1964, and the extension was completed in 1981. It is primarily a place for study and research based on the Shakespeare Birthplace Trust's very extensive library and archive collections, but it also houses the Trust's administrative offices, and has facilities for lectures and displays. The Centre incorporates works by many leading contemporary artists and craftsmen, including glass panels engraved by John Hutton, lettered plaques by John Skelton and Richard Kindersley, a wooden panel carved by Nicolete Gray and bronze Shakespeare medallions by Paul Vincze.

For this reason alone, the Centre is worth visiting in its own right, but it also serves as the entrance to the poet's Birthplace, and visitors follow a paved walk past a fountain, and through a delightful garden containing trees, herbs and flowers mentioned by Shakespeare to arrive at:

(2) Shakespeare's Birthplace, Henley Street. *(Tel: (0789) 204016.)* A beautiful oak timbered and

gabled, early 16th century building, which of necessity has been much restored over the centuries. The house where Shakespeare was born is the western part, and the adjoining part, now an interesting museum, was used by his father, John, for his business as a glover and wool-dealer. In the Birthplace itself, there is an attractive series of rooms furnished in Elizabethan and Jacobean style, including the birthroom in which William is believed to have been born.

(3) The Motor Museum, Shakespeare Street. *(Tel: (0789) 69413.)* Here only a short distance to the north-west, is a complete contrast to the world of William Shakespeare. A well laid out museum which sets out to re-create the 'Golden Age of Motoring' , with a collection of elegant Rolls-Royces, Bugattis and Lagondas.

(4) The Jubilee Memorial Fountain, Rother Street. This was built in 1887 in memory of Shakespeare; the gift of an American enthusiast, George Washington Childs of Philadelphia, and is an elaborate neo-Gothic 'market-cross-cum-spire', which has been rather unkindly described as 'Disneyland' in one recent guide book. It may not be beautiful, but Stratford would be duller without it.... Thank you Mr Childs.

(5) Judith Quiney's House (on the corner of Bridge Street and High Street at the very centre of the town). This timbered building was originally the 'Cage' or town prison, and later became the house of Thomas Quiney, a vintner, who married Shakespeare's daughter Judith. It now houses Stratford-upon-Avon's busy **Tourist Information Centre** *(Tel: (0789) 293127.)*

(6) Harvard House, High Street. *(Tel: (0789) 204507.)* This richly carved, timber-framed house, was built in 1596 by Thomas Rogers, whose daughter married Robert Harvard of Southwark in 1605. Their son John, emigrated to America, but died in 1637 when only thirty, and left a will which led to the founding of Harvard University. In 1909 Edward Morris of Chicago bought the house and gave it to Harvard. It is attractively furnished in Elizabethan style, and contains interesting displays relating to the life and times of the Harvard family. Do not overlook the lively Garrick Inn, next door, which must have been built at about the same time as Harvard House.

(7) The Town Hall, Chapel Street. This was built in Cotswold stone in 1767 in a handsome Palladian style. The impressive statue of Shakespeare which looks out over the High Street from its niche on the north front, was given by the actor David Garrick, on the occasion of the famous Shakespeare Jubilee (see page 10 or 11). Like so many town halls, its ground floor was originally open, and used for market trading, but this was filled in many years ago. Do not miss the proud Georgian lettering still visible on the Chapel Street frontage, proclaiming 'God Save the King'.

(8) The Arms and Armour Museum, Poet's Arbour, Sheep Street. *(Tel: (0789) 293453.)* Here up a narrow alley off Sheep Street (by the Cobweb Restaurant), is a fascinating and extensive collection of arms, armour and accoutrements dating from about 1400 to the first world war... guns, swords, suits of armour, helmets, cross-bows, bows and arrows, and even cannons.

(9) The Shrieve's House, Sheep Street. This beautifully timbered, largely 16th century house is almost opposite the entry to Poet's Arbour, and was the home of William Rogers, Serjeant- of-the-Mace, a borough officer of some considerable standing, and thought to be the original of Shakespeare's 'Sergeant' in the Comedy of Errors. The house is not open to the public, but the fine,

The Knott Garden and the Guild Chapel, Stratford-upon-Avon.

recently restored barn behind it, houses an interior-decorating business and is well worth visiting.

(10) New Place and Nash's House, Chapel Street. (Shakespeare Birthplace Trust) *(Tel: (0789) 292325.)* New Place was one of the largest houses in Stratford in Shakespeare's day, and by 1597 the poet was prosperous enough to purchase it. Later he returned to live here permanently, and he died at New Place in 1616, on his birthday, April 23rd, at the age of fifty two. The house was unfortunately pulled down in 1759 by its owner, Reverend Francis Gastrell, following a quarrel with the Borough authorities, but its foundations can still be seen together with the Knott Garden, which is a replica of an enclosed Elizabethan garden, based on gardening books of the time. Beyond the Knott Garden is the Great Garden, originally the orchard and kitchen garden of New Place, which is now a formal garden with hedges of box and yew enclosing colourful flower borders, all in a framework of paths and lawns. New Place garden is reached by way of Nash's House, a richly timbered building, which belonged to Thomas Nash, the first husband of Shakespeare's granddaughter Elizabeth Hall. Furniture and other exhibits illustrate life in Elizabethan England, the times in which Shakespeare lived and worked. This is also Stratford's local museum, which accommodates a collection of local archaeological and historical material, including two small, but delightful panels of tapestry produced at the Sheldon 'tapestry factory', at Barcheston (see page 21).

(11) The Guild Chapel, Chapel Street and Chapel Lane. It is known that the powerful Guild of the Holy Cross was founded in 1269, but its chapel dates largely from the 15th century, the beautiful nave, with its Perpendicular windows and disturbing 'doom' painting. above the chancel arch, having been re-built by prosperous Sir Hugh Clopton in 1496 (Sir Hugh later became Lord Mayor of London). Light floods in through Sir Hugh's fine windows upon pleasant light-oak stalls, but this does not entirely dispel the unease no doubt orchestrated with such careful deliberation by the medieval artist who created the horrors of the 'doom' painting above the chancel arch.

(12) The Grammar School, Church Street. The 15th century half-timbered building adjoining the Guild Chapel was once the Guild Hall, and council meetings continued to be held here until the 19th century. But part of the building has in fact been used as the Grammar School since the dissolution of the Guild. The ground floor consists of the 'Rood Hall' and an 'armoury'. and the Over Hall on the first floor is believed to have been the room in which Shakespeare studied. The 'Pedagogue's House', in the little courtyard visible through an archway below the Over Hall, was probably the original school house.

(13) The Almshouses, Church Street. These are in the same range of buildings as the old Grammar School (see above),and they are also fine examples of 15th century timbering. Built by the Guild, they still house local aged people, and although not open to the public, they look most attractive from the pathway in front of them.

(14) Hall's Croft, Old Town. (Shakespeare Birthplace Trust) *(Tel: (0789) 292107.)* Another beautifully timbered building, with its origins in the early 16th century, this was the home of Dr John Hall, who started his medical practice at Stratford-upon-Avon in about 1600. He married Shakes-

The Tramway Bridge and Clopton Bridge, Stratford-upon-Avon.

peare's daughter Susanna in 1607, and their only daughter, Elizabeth, was born here in the following year. On the death of her father in 1616, Elizabeth and her husband moved to New Place, and after their death both were buried in Stratford's parish church. The interior has now been restored, and the rooms on view to the public have been tastefully furnished in Elizabethan style, including one room, which has been equipped as an early 17th century dispensary, complete with an assortment of original apothecary's jars and other appropriate items. The charming walled garden with its mulberry tree, poplars, and herbaceous borders is an ideal antidote to the rigours of Stratford's busy tourist round.

(15) Holy Trinity Church. This is beautifully sited on the southern fringes of the town, on the banks of the river Avon, in a churchyard shaded by tall limes. Although it was probably built on the site of an Anglo-Saxon monastery, the present building appears to have its origins in the Early-English period (about 1200 AD). The aisles belong to the Decorated period, but the finest work in this building was carried out in the 15th century; the chancel, with its magnificent east window, the clerestory windows bringing new light to the tall nave, and the north porch, now at the end of a long avenue of lime trees. The central tower is part of the 'Early English' church, but the present tall spire was re-built as recently as 1763, and is an outstanding landmark in the lush countryside around Stratford.

The interior of the church is full of interest, and in the search for the tombs of Shakespeare and his relations, do not overlook such items as the elaborately sculpted sedilia and piscina in the chancel, nor the amusingly carved misericords beneath the choir stall seats, the latter providing a rich harvest of late-medieval imagery. See also the tombs of the Cloptons in their family chapel, and of course the stones marking the tombs of William Shakespeare and his wife Anne in the chancel, also that of Thomas Nash, Dr John Hall, and that of his wife Susanna, all nearby. Upon the north wall of the chancel is a monument to the poet with a bust which is thought to be the best remaining likeness of him. It was erected shortly after his death, and was the work of a Southwark mason.

This is the southernmost extent of our walk, and

although there is much more still to be seen, you might wish to stray from our track awhile. If so, walk on past the church, down Mill Lane, and cross the Avon by a concrete foot bridge. From the far side of this bridge you can return northwards along the far bank of the river, through the 'Recreation Ground' a wide meadow with ample space for children to run, from where there are fine views of Holy Trinity Church, and the Royal Shakespeare Theatre, and you can cross back over the Avon on the old Tramway Bridge, and return to the town through the Bancroft Gardens. However if you wish to continue our recommended walk, turn back from Holy Trinity Church, and after a few yards, turn right through a small gate into:

(16) The Avonbank Garden. This has a quiet tree-lined path beside the river, and is a beautifully cool place to relax in after the hot pavements of the town. At its far end, in a 19th century summerhouse, will be found an interesting Brass Rubbing Centre. *(Tel: (0789) 297671.)*

(17) The Theatre Garden. This stretches from a point opposite the picturesque Black Swan Inn (known as the Dirty Duck to more than one generation of Shakespearian actors, and other visitors to the town), as far as the Theatre itself.

(18) The Royal Shakespeare Theatre Picture Gallery and Museum, Waterside. *(Tel: (0789) 296655.)* This is housed in the surviving old part of the Theatre (see below), and contains portraits of Shakespeare himself, and of many famous Shakespearian actors and stage scenes, together with a fascinating collection of theatrical mementoes.

(19) The Royal Shakespeare Theatre, Waterside. *(Tel: (0789) 295623.)* The original theatre was built in 1879, but this ambitious neo-Gothic structure was largely burnt down in 1926, and only that section now containing the Picture Gallery and Museum has survived to give us a hint of what we have missed. The 'new' red brick theatre was opened in 1932, and although much criticised at the time, the passing of the years has mellowed both its

Stratford-upon-Avon.

SCALE 1:10 000 or 6 INCHES to 1 MILE

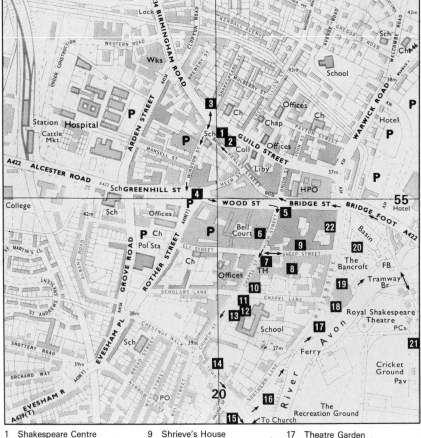

1 Shakespeare Centre	9 Shrieve's House	17 Theatre Garden
2 Shakespeare's Birthplace	10 New Place & Nash's House	18 R.S.T. Picture Gallery & Museum
3 Motor Museum	11 Guild Chapel	19 Royal Shakespeare Theatre
4 Jubilee Memorial Fountain	12 Grammar School	20 Bancroft Gardens
5 Judith Quiney's House	13 Almshouses	21 Stratford Butterfly Farm (provisional)
6 Harvard House	14 Hall's Croft	22 World of Shakespeare
7 Town Hall	15 Holy Trinity Church	
8 Arms & Armour Museum	16 Avonbank Garden	

The Royal Shakespeare Theatre, Stratford-upon-Avon.

brickwork and the prejudice of its critics. It stands amongst-flower filled gardens on the banks of the Avon, and its terraces and balconies overlooking the water are almost as attractive as the frequently up-dated facilities for actor and visitor alike within the theatre itself.

(20) The Bancroft Gardens. These extensive gardens stretch from the theatre to the main road at Bridge Foot. They incorporate a large canal basin, which was once a busy canal port, with wharves and sheds, and tramway lines. This was not only the point where the Stratford Canal entered the River Avon, but it was also a trans-shipping point between the river, the canal and the Stratford and Moreton Tramway... the hub of William James's short-lived vision of Stratford as the centre of the south Midland's transport system, with its own railway line to London. (See Stratford and Moreton Tramway, page 66.)

Canal barges have returned, but these are now pleasure craft, and the old wharves are now edged by lawns, flower filled borders and blossoming trees. And during the summer months, barges may be seen using the lock down into the Avon, which also borders these delightful gardens. Overlooking the gardens is the Gower Memorial Statue of Shakespeare, surrounded by the figures of Hamlet, Prince Hal, Falstaff and Lady Macbeth. This was given to the town in 1888 by Lord Gower, who had devoted no less than twelve years to its design. Just beyond this memorial, on the pathway leading towards the old Tramway Bridge, there is a restored tramway wagon on display. Cross the mellow-brick Tramway Bridge if you wish to visit the far-flung Recreation Ground with its putting green, its children's playground, and its pleasant path beside the river, southwards to the footbridge beyond Holy Trinity Church. From the Tramway Bridge, there are good views of the grey stone Clopton Bridge, built by Sir Hugh Clopton in the late 15th century, and still Stratford's only road bridge across the Avon.

(21) Stratford Butterfly Farm. This was not yet

open at the time of printing, but it is hoped that it will be located on the edge of the Recreation Ground, near the southern end of the Tramway Bridge, in a large and specially built glass-house. And now back towards the town...

(22) The World of Shakespeare, Waterside. *(Tel: (0789) 69190.)* This is a spectacular audio-visual presentation which gives an unusual insight into the life of the young William Shakespeare and the times in which he lived. Shows last for twenty five minutes, and should appeal to all ages and all nationalities.

From this point, it is a relatively short walk to return to Shakespeare's Birthplace, the start of our exploration around Stratford-upon-Avon. Walk up Bridge Street, noting the very effective way that Marks and Spencer have adapted the Georgian frontage of what was once the Red Horse Hotel, for their new store. Then move into Henley Street, keeping the impressive Barclay's Bank on your left, to return to the Birthplace, completing your walk round Stratford-upon-Avon.

If you wish for more walking from Stratford-upon-Avon, there is a pleasant path, partly across open fields, to the little village of Shottery (to visit Anne Hathaway's Cottage, see page 58). This is well signed, and starts from Evesham Place, beyond the far (southern) end of Rother Street. It is also possible to walk northwards from Welcombe Road, which lies to the north-east of the Warwick Road, to the Welcombe Monument in the Welcombe Hills (20-57) (marked 'obelisk' on map). (See Snitterfield, page 59.) There is a 'Welcombe Hills Nature Trail', and for details *Tel: (0926) 496848.* For lovers of river walks, it is possible, after crossing the foot bridge beyond the end of Mill Lane, to walk along the south bank of the Avon, as far as Milcote and Welford-on-Avon (14-52).

The Stratford-upon-Avon Canal (20-54)-(18-69)
The building of this canal started in 1793, and it ran

from Kings Norton on the Worcester and Birmingham Canal to Kingswood where there was eventually to be a junction with a canal which was to become the Grand Union. However it was not until 1816 that the canal finally reached Stratford. This southern section between Kingswood and Stratford, most of which is on the map covered by this guide, is at present in the care of the National Trust; a thirteen mile stretch through quiet, unspoilt country, which is a delight either to walk along, or to navigate by boat. Do not miss a visit to the fine aqueduct near Bearley Cross (16-60).

The story of this canal is a complex and most interesting one, and it is told in the fascinating book, *Waterways to Stratford*, by Charles Hadfield and John Norris. Here one can read of the larger-than-life character, William James of Henley-in-Arden, who was owner of the Upper Avon Navigation between Evesham and Stratford, who was much involved with the Stratford-upon-Avon Canal, and largely responsible for a further transportation project which was planned to link in with the other two, at the canal basin in what is now Stratford's Bancroft Gardens. For details of this project, 'The Stratford and Moreton Tramway', please see below.

The Stratford and Moreton Tramway (20-54)-
(20-32) This was the brainchild of William James of Henley-in-Arden (see above), part of an ambitious scheme to link his other transport and mining interests to London, by a line entitled the Central Junction Railway. However James was only able to gain local support for a line as far as Moreton and a branch to Shipston, but an Act of Incorporation for this scheme was passed on 18th May 1821, surprisingly only six weeks earlier than the Act of Incorporation for that world pioneer line, the Stockton and Darlington. One wonders what would have happened to Stratford-upon-Avon if James's scheme for the Central Junction had been accepted in full. As it was, the local scheme soon ran into difficulties, both with civil engineering problems, and with the prevention by the authorities of the use of steam trains on at least the first six miles south of Stratford-upon-Avon. The line to Moreton was finally opened in 1826, but by then James had been declared bankrupt, and all passenger and goods traffic was restricted to horse drawn waggons provided not by the company, but by toll-paying local traders.

In 1836 a branch line was opened to Shipston-on-Stour, and when Brunel's main railway line was built in 1853, the tramway provided a useful link to it at Moreton-in-Marsh. The Moreton-Shipston section was eventually converted to take steam trains, as a branch of the Great Western Railway, an arrangement that lasted until its final closure in 1960. The most enduring monument to the tramway is its mellow brick bridge over the Avon at Stratford, and on the town side of the bridge there is an old tramway wagon on display, between the gardens and the timber yard. The line of the tramway may be followed in several places, especially beside the Shipston road out of Stratford, but its total disappearance in others is a reflection of the problems often facing archaeologists looking for signs of civilization many hundreds, or even thousands of years older. Read the most interesting story of this tramway in Hadfield and Norris's *Waterways to Stratford*.

Sutton-under-Brailes (29-37) Most of this village is spread around a delightful green, once shaded by great trees, but now having to 'start all over again', due to the ravages of Dutch elm disease in the late 1970's. The church of St Thomas à Becket has a well proportioned Perpendicular south tower, but the austere interior appears to have never recovered from the harsh treatment inflicted upon it almost a hundred years before the coming of the elm disease, and it is all pitchpine pews and thoroughly scraped walls.

Walk north-west from here, over the side of Brailes Hill, to Shipston-on-Stour, or north-east up beside a small stream to Lower Brailes.

Swalcliffe (37-37) Small stone village astride the Banbury-Shipston road, with a massive tithe barn at its western end... a fine specimen said to have been built by William of Wykeham, the founder of New College, Oxford. New College also used to own the large manor house to the west of the house, a building which retains many of its medieval features. At the centre of the village is a pleasantly thatched inn called the Stag's Head, which is overlooked from the other side of the road by a most interesting church. This has a handsome 17th century door within a Decorated style south doorway, and an old roof looking down on pleasing 17th century seating, pulpit and lectern. These last two items were given to the church in 1639 by Anne Wykeham and there is a colourful monument to Anne and her husband Richard, with their kneeling figures in a wall frame. See also the monuments to John Hawten, John Duncombe and to an 18th century Richard Wykeham. There is a 14th century wall painting of St Michael in the south aisle, and also two figures on the west wall of the same aisle.

The small mansion of Swalcliffe Park is on the south-west side of the village, and there is a pleasant road southwards just beyond it, leading past Swalcliffe Grange, towards Tadmarton Heath. This is a largely open road, from which there are fine views westwards to the distant line of the Cotswolds above Chipping Campden and Blockley, with the outline of Broadway Tower just visible on a clear day. Walk northwards from Swalcliffe to Shutford, passing close to Madmarston Hill (see page 47), or southwards beyond Swalcliffe Grange to Hook Norton. It's all good walking country hereabout. (See also **Walk 4**.).

Swerford (37-31) This is situated near the head of the quiet valley of the Swere, a stream which flows east from here to join the Cherwell near Dedd-

SCALE 1:25 000 or 2½ INCHES to 1 MILE

ington. Swerford has a pleasant green by the church, which is set in a neat churchyard overlooking the earthworks of a long vanished Norman 'motte and bailey' castle. The church has a dumpy spire and a 13th century porch enriched with a series of earthy gargoyles, but the interior is not very exciting. Swerford Park is an 18th century mansion, with elegant early-19th century alterations by a pupil of Sir John Soane, and is beautifully sited on slopes above the little River Swere. It is not open to the public.

There is a delightful, but all too short, field road over towards Wigginton, with glimpses of the Swere to its immediate south. The best walks from Swerford are north-eastwards down the Swere valley to South Newington, or north-westwards, up over wold country to Hook Norton.

Tadmarton (39-37) Modest village of stone and thatch strung out along the Banbury to Shipston-on-Stour road, with a handsome manor house opposite a church, which is of Norman origin. The fine 14th century font is richly ornamented, and in the nave there are some well carved bench-ends about a century younger. Do not miss the little doorway to the original rood loft, behind the pulpit.

Temple Grafton (Map 150) (12-54) This village lies to the west of the main area covered by our guide, but it may be located on the Key Map on page 4, six miles west of Stratford-upon-Avon. We have included it here as it features in a little verse which was possibly written by William Shakespeare (see Bidford-on-Avon, page 22). The verse refers to 'Hungry Grafton', and it is possible that this was an oblique comment on the quality of the soil hereabouts.

At least we know for certain why the village is called Temple Grafton, for in the reign of Henry III the Knights Templar had a church here. The Knights Templar were a military-religious order founded in 1118, to protect pilgrims to the Holy Land. But when the Holy Land eventually fell to the Saracens, the Templars returned to Europe, where, in the words of one history book, 'their pride and licentiousness excited considerable odium'. They were eventually suppressed with great cruelty in France, and later, in 1308, in England too; but without the barbaric excesses practiced on the other side of the Channel.

The village of Temple Grafton is situated in a countryside of orchards and gentle little hills, with the views northwards to Exhall and Oversley Wood being especially good from its westward extension, Ardens Grafton. There are many grey-lias cottages, several thatched, and some timbered, and almost all have pretty flower-filled gardens. The old church was replaced in 1875, by a brown and grey stone building in the Early English style and is not of great interest to visitors.

Tidmington (25-38) This consists of a 17th century bridge over the River Stour, crossed here by the ever busy A34, and overlooked by an old water mill. Well to the north, beside the garden of Tidmington House, a largely 17th century building with a handsome 18th century front, is one of Warwickshire's smallest churches. This has a late-12th century tower with pyramid roof, a 16th century chancel, the rest being a rebuild of about 1875.

However the early Norman font has an interesting carving of Christ upon it, and makes a visit here well worthwhile.

Todenham (24-36) An attractive and unspoilt village, with views out across quiet countryside to the low wooded hills around Cherington and Stourton. It has a handsome late Georgian manor house, and next to the church, a little mellow brick 18th century inn, the Farrier's Arms. Writing of this nearly twenty years ago, we noted that 'this inn has so far escaped the attention of the brewery restorers', and that 'it still had a really rural flavour'. Happily by some miracle, this still appears to be the case, although we must confess that we have not recently been through Todenham during opening hours.

The church of St Thomas of Canterbury is largely 14th century in origin and has a fine tower and octagonal, broached spire. There are many pleasing items in the Decorated style here, including the east window, the sedilia, and the little priest's door on the south side. On the north side of the chancel will be found Perpendicular style windows added by the Greville family in the course of building a north chapel and north aisle in the early 16th century. Victorian restoration was carried out here with a very much lighter hand than at neighbouring Lower Lemington (see page 46) and the interior of Todenham church is well worth a visit. See especially the 13th century font, with the names of the churchwardens of 1773 inscribed upon it, the brass to William Molton and his wife (1614), and outside, the memorial tablet on the south wall complete with skull and crossed bones.

Walk north-west, over the fields, to Stretton-on-Fosse, or eastwards to Little Wolford, in both cases, back from Gloucestershire into Warwickshire.

Traitor's Ford (33-36) A beautifully cool place in the lightly wooded valley of the infant Stour. A normally tranquil spot, it could become crowded on a summer Sunday afternoon. Who was, or who

The Infant Stour at Traitor's Ford.

were the traitor(s) ? We have still to solve this mystery, but like to imagine some small, but inevitably violent encounter in medieval times, perhaps during the Wars of the Roses. Traitor's Ford lies on the border between Warwickshire and Oxfordshire, and there is an ancient trackway leading north from here, along the line of this boundary, called Ditchedge Lane. Walk up the hill, and along the lane, from which there are fine views on both sides, towards the hill country above Compton Wynyates and Tysoe. The road south towards Great Rollright leads over high, open hill country, and here again there are splendid views especially westwards out over the Stour valley to the distant line of the Cotswolds above Blockley and Chipping Campden.

Tredington (25-43) An elegantly beautiful village in the valley of the Stour, with wide, well mown grass verges and several interesting old houses. However everything has been so polished and tidied up that Tredington's real character has all but vanished, and to the west of the busy A34 there is also considerable modern housing development. But do not let this description deter you from exploring Tredington; it is still very pleasant to walk along its small roads leading to a church, which is well worth visiting. This has a tall tower topped by a noble 15th century spire, which is a landmark from many points of the delightful south Warwickshire countryside. It has a Norman south doorway and a Perpendicular two-storey north porch, and inside will be found old stone floors, beautiful old benches, a handsome Jacobean pulpit, a Perpendicular rood screen, lovely roofs of the same period in nave and transepts, and several interesting brasses. Architectural enthusiasts will note evidence of Anglo- Saxon origins, but everyone who comes here will be delighted by the atmosphere of the past that lingers in this fine building.

Tysoe (33-43) A long straggle of a village, consisting of Lower, Middle, and Upper Tysoe, all beneath the scarp face on which the Red Horse was carved (see below), and on the edge of wide valley country, the Vale of Red Horse, through which a series of little streams flow lazily north and west towards the River Stour. There is much modern development, but the little 'old' fire station, with its thatched roof, still stands next to the Peacock Inn, which ironically was largely destroyed by fire some years ago. The handsomely pinnacled church has a Norman south doorway and a fine 14th century font with sculptured figures of the Virgin and saints. The interior is unfortunately rather cold in feeling, with walls scraped and pointed by over enthusiastic Victorian 'restorers'. However do not miss the medieval and Jacobean seating nor the three interesting brasses.

Upper Tysoe is overlooked by a well restored stone tower windmill, which stands on a hill to its south, part of the Compton Wynyates estate. For many generations this mill was worked by the Styles family of Tysoe, and in the mid nineteenth century, there were no less than three windmills in the district, at Tysoe itself, and also at Burton Dassett and Hornton, which were being worked by three Styles brothers. Sadly the last milling Styles was killed during the 1914-18 war. For a wonderfully evocative account of life in Tysoe in the latter half of the 19th century, and the early years of the 20th,

read *Joseph Ashby of Tysoe*, by his daughter, Miss M. K. Ashby. In his youth, Joseph was much influenced by Joseph Arch, the founder of the National Union of Agricultural Workers, who lived at Barford (see page 21).

The giant hill figure, the Red Horse, has long since disappeared, a victim of the enclosure of the village's open fields. It was originally cut into the red soil on the hillside above Tysoe (*'opposite the end of the church'*), probably in medieval times and possibly by Richard Neville, Earl of Warwick, known as the 'kingmaker', in memory of the horse that he killed at the Battle of Towton, on Palm Sunday 1461, in an attempt to assure his wavering troops that he had no intention of retreating from the field. At first sight this seems an unlikely story, but it is interesting to note that the Red Horse was in fact preserved for centuries by an annual scouring ceremony that took place on each Palm Sunday, the very anniversary of the battle where Neville killed his horse.

Walks from Tysoe are numerous: from Middle Tysoe, north-east across the fields and up to the woods near Sun Rising Hill; from Lower Tysoe, up past Old Lodge Farm, over the scarp, and down a valley south-eastwards to Alkerton; from Upper Tysoe, up the hill to the south, past the windmill, and on to Winderton, skirting well to the west of Compton Wynyates.

Upton House (36-45) Given to the National Trust by the 2nd Viscount Bearsted, this fine, William and Mary mansion built of local Hornton stone, stands at the end of a straight driveway, off the main A 422, Stratford-upon-Avon to Banbury road. It is situated less than half a mile behind the Edge Hill scarp, and from its south front, there are pleasant views out over wide grassy terraces and beautiful, steep sloping gardens, to its Temple Pool, enhanced by a little temple in the Tuscan style at the far end. This is said to have been designed by Sanderson Miller, squire of nearby Radway, and architect extraordinary. (See Radway, page 52.) Miller may also have carried out improvements to the house in the 1730's, but about this there appears to be some doubt.

The interior of the present house is largely the work of 20th century architect, Morley Horder, who created a series of fine neo-Georgian rooms in about 1927. These provide a perfect setting for the oustanding collection of works of art presented by Lord Bearsted to the National Trust in 1948. This includes 18th century furniture, Brussels tapestries, and 18th century porcelain, both English and European. But of outstanding interest is the superb collection of pictures, with works by Bosch, the Breughels, Holbein, Rembrandt, Van Dyck, Canaletto, Goya, El Greco, Tiepolo, Tintoretto, Constable, Hogarth, Reynolds, Romney, Sartorious and Stubbs. On no account should you miss a visit here for it provides, in the heart of the English countryside, a sparkling insight into the rich diversity of European civilization... an experience that many think, quite wrongly, can only be achieved by visits to one of the great cities of the world. *Tel: (029587) 266.* (Upton House may be reached on **Walk 6**).

Walton (28-53) Here, in the wooded valley of the little River Dene, is a massive stone mansion built in the Decorated style by Sir George Gilbert Scott in the 1850s for Sir Charles Mordaunt. There is also a smaller, more elegant building, an 18th century chapel, with Tuscan porch and a Venetian window; and memories at least, of a 'bath house', in the 'cyclopean' style, which was probably designed by Sanderson Miller. (See Radway, page 52.) There is a lake formed by a small dam across the River Dene, and a tidy little estate village in brick, contemporary with the Hall, well to its north. A small footbridge crosses the Dene, to the north of the village, and it is possible to cross this and walk north to Wellesbourne.

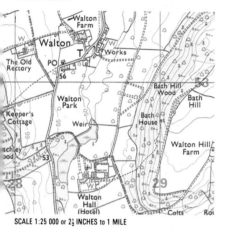

SCALE 1:25 000 or 2½ INCHES to 1 MILE

For a full account of the Mordaunt family and their life at Walton, read Lady Elizabeth Hamilton's excellent book, *The Mordaunts*.

Wappenbury (37-69) Minute village on a bend in the River Leam, with a modest red sandstone church which has 'Early English' origins and which was heavily 'restored' in the 1880's. This was a time when money for this type of work was readily available, but regrettably it was a few years too early for the philosophies of William Morris and his Society for the Protection of Ancient Buildings to have had any great impact. (See Burton Dassett, page 25.) On the banks of the Leam, to the south of the church, is a small Roman Catholic chapel, built in brick in about 1849, possibly by the architect A. W. N. Pugin, best known for his work on the House of Commons, for Sir Charles Barry.

Wappenbury, as its name, which includes the word *'bury'*, would lead us to suspect, is on the site of an extensive Iron Age encampment, although the earthworks surrounding it are now almost ploughed out. The south rampart runs parallel with the River Leam, which is here forded by stepping stones; this crossing being a probable reason for the original siting of the camp. It was inhabited in late Iron Age times, and probably during at least the early years of the Roman occupation.

Wardington (49-46) Long and pleasing stone village, the northern part of which is largely astride the A361, Banbury to Daventry road, and the southern part of which is known as Upper Wardington. This has a beautiful Jacobean manor house, which has been sensitively altered and restored in the present century, much of this work being carried out by Clough Williams Ellis, the creator of that magical village on the Welsh coast, Portmeir-

ion. Glimpses of this delightful building may be had through its lovely wrought-iron gates. There are two lively inns at Upper Wardington, the Plough and the Red Lion, the latter overlooking a small green at the far end of the village, where there is a pleasant Caravan Club site close by.

The large church, in the lower part of the village, but well away from the main road, stands in a sloping churchyard close to the village school, with massive yew trees overhanging one of the paths. The chancel is 12th century, and the north and south doorways are about a hundred years younger. The architectural history of the rest of the building is complex in the extreme, but we are indebted to 15th century builders for the fine tower and the clerestory, with its line of windows flooding the nave ceiling with light. The interior was over-restored by the Victorians but visitors should not overlook the 14th century slab in the floor of the south aisle, with a cross and the top of a man's head with his hands clasped in prayer, nor the quaint little octagonal 17th century font, dated 1666.

There is a pleasant road south-east and then south, over the fields to Thenford, and one north-eastwards to Edgcote. It is possible to walk westward over the fields to Cropredy (See **Walk 3**), or south to Chacombe.

Warkworth (48-40) Now consisting of only a church, a few houses and two farms, Warkworth was of considerable importance in medieval times. There was a fine castle with large gatehouse and a series of semi-circular towers. Much altered in the 17th century, it was sadly demolished in 1805. No sign of the castle remains, but the heavily restored church, situated in fields and only approached by a grassy track leading eastwards from the road south from Overthorpe, is well worth visiting. There are fine views, especially westwards out over the Cherwell valley, in which Banbury lies, and it is easy to appreciate the strategic reasons for the great castle here. The trim, surprisingly well maintained church contains a series of memorials to members of the families that owned Warkworth. The mid-14th century effigy of Sir John de Lyons, clad in armour, and lying on a thin tomb chest, is an outstanding example of sculpture in clunch, a type of hard chalk. The sculptured detail is still remarkably crisp and the work as a whole, most elegant. The parents of this handsome knight, another Sir John de Lyons and his wife Margaret, lie in effigy in two arched recesses nearby, while the memorials to various members of the Chetwode family are in brass, together with a brass to one of their descendants, William Ludsthorp, who died in 1454. See also the finely carved heads on the north arcade capitals, and the attractive 14th century font with sculptured arches around it.

Warmington (41-47) Herbert Evans, the author of that most delightful early guide book, *Highways and Byways in Oxford and the Cotswolds*, found that this village, *'nestles umbrageously at the foot of the hill'*, and we must assume that, travelling by bicycle, he came here on a hot summer day, and found many shady trees in its cool churchyard, perched high above the village. Since Evans came here in about 1900, Warmington has happily changed little. The main Warwick to Banbury road now runs a little further to the west of the village in an even deeper cutting than it did in Evan's day, and the village still has its lovely little sloping green complete with pond and sheep dip, and overlooked by a series of charming Hornton stone houses and cottages, including an early-17th century manor house, and an elegant little Georgian rectory.

The church is approached up a long flight of steps, and in its steeply sloping churchyard there are a series of table tombs beneath pines, probably the very trees that inspired Evans's use of the delightful word *'umbraceous'*. Despite his possible fatigue, Evans was able to note a gravestone in memory of a Captain Alexander Gaudin, dated October 1642; no doubt one of the many who fell on Edgehill Field, or died from their wounds soon after. Like the rest of the village, the church is of toffee-coloured Hornton stone, and its Norman origins are revealed by the substantial north and south arcading within. There is much Decorated work, and the priest's door, the sedilia and the piscina are all headed with delightful little ogival arches. The

vestry is two-storeyed and the upper storey must have been the priest's room, and is still complete with fireplace and little window looking down into the chancel.

Warwick (28-65) This is surely one of England's loveliest county towns, situated on the River Avon, with the rich south Warwickshire countryside never far away. It lies at the meeting point of several main roads, but is now happily shielded from the worst effects of traffic, by a large by-pass to its west. The crossing of the River Avon gave Warwick a strategic significance very early in our history, and Ethelfleda, one of the daughters of Alfred the Great, built a fortress here in the early years of the tenth century. This was part of a plan made in conjunction with her brother, King Edward the Elder, to defend the English from attacks by the Danes, who had already secured all England north and east of the Watling Street, the Roman road which here ran

Warwick. SCALE 1:10 000 or 6 INCHES to 1 MILE

1 Warwick Castle	5 Court House	9 St John's House
2 Lord Leycester's Hospital	6 Shire Hall	10 Friends Meeting House
3 Warwick Doll Museum	7 Northgate House	11 St Nicholas Park
4 Church of St Mary	8 Warwickshire Museum	

Warwick Castle and the River Avon, from Castle Bridge.

only twenty miles to the east of Warwick.

Warwick had become a royal borough by the time of the Norman conquest, and it was given to Henry de Newburgh soon after the death of William the Conqueror. Henry began the building of the present castle and was created 1st Earl of Warwick. His descendants, the Beauchamps, held the title for four centuries, and after they became extinct the earldom was revived by Queen Elizabeth who gave it to Robert, Earl of Dudley . The ownership of the castle was granted to Sir Fulke Greville (the first Lord Brooke, and a descendant of the famous woolstapler of Chipping Campden, William Grevel) by James I, although the Earldom did not pass with it, only doing so in 1759, when Francis Greville, a descendant in the female line from the Beau-champs, was created Earl of Warwick. The castle is now no longer owned by the Earl of Warwick, having been sold to a leisure group.

Survivors of Warwick's great fire of 1694 include only the castle itself, some of the town walls, the East and West Gates and a few other small buildings. However within only three years much rebuilding had already taken place, and the diarist and traveller, Celia Fiennes (see Broughton, page 25), who passed through Warwick on one of her journeys in 1797, wrote thus: *'the town of Warwick by means of a sad fire about 4 or 5 year since that laid the greatest part in ashes, its most now new buildings which is with brick and coyn'd with stone and the windows the same; there still remains some few houses of the old town which are all built of stone; the streetes are very handsome and the buildings regular and fine, not very lofty being limited by act of parliament to such pitch and size to build the town'*

This extensive reconstruction went on well into the 18th century, and most of the delightful results have survived intact, bringing a very special charm to this small county town upon a hill. When walking round the town, ensure that you include the Market Place, Northgate Street, Church Street, High Street and Jury Street in your itinerary; but here is a brief account of Warwick's outstanding buildings to help you in your exploration of this fascinating town. *(Cross reference numbers will be found on the Warwick Town Plan and preceding each place listed below:)*

(1) Warwick Castle. *(Tel: (0926) 45421)* Drama-tically sited on a great cliff above the River Avon and the ruins of the 14th century 'Great Bridge', this is one of the finest castles in the whole of Europe. Although none of the existing buildings are earlier than the 13th century, the Norman walls having been destroyed by the forces of Simon de Montfort in 1264; the form of the original motte and bailey earthworks is still apparent, the motte being known as Ethelfleda's Mound. It was in the mid-14th century that Thomas Beauchamp built the Clock Tower (gatehouse), Caesar's Tower and the curtain walls connecting them; and his son added the massive Guy's Tower nearly fifty years later. Warwick Castle is now owned by a company specialising in the provision of leisure facilities and a visit here is well worthwhile. The 'attractions' include the State Rooms and Great Hall, the Armoury, Dungeons, 'Torture Chamber', Clock Tower and Barbican, Rampart Walk, the Conservatory Spectacle *'The Bear's Quest for the Ragged Staff'* and a waxwork tableau entitled *'A Royal Weekend Party — 1898'*. The sixty acre grounds, much of which were laid out by Capability Brown, incorporate picnic areas, woodland walks, and of course the River Avon.

(2) Lord Leycester's Hospital. *(Tel: (0926) 492797)* A delightful group of 15th century buildings by the West Gate, which were originally owned by the Guild of St George. After Henry VIII dissolved the guilds, there was considerable rebuilding, and in 1571 Robert Dudley, Earl of Leicester, transformed them into almshouses for 'old brethren', usually soldiers, and they still serve that purpose today, with twelve 'Brethren' and a Master in residence. The chapel stands above the West Gate, close to the beautifully timbered frontage of the 'Hospital'. The chapel, the courtyard, the kitchen and the great hall are all in regular use, and on special occasions

Preston Cottages, Warwick

the Brethren still wear their traditional Elizabethan dress. The Chaplain's dining Hall now houses the Regimental Museum of the Queen's Own Hussars.

(3) The Warwick Doll Museum. *(Tel: (0926) 495546)* This is to be found in the beautifully restored Oken's House, in Castle Street, a timbered building, one of the few to survive the fire of 1694. It houses a fine collection of dolls, toys and other bygones.

(4) The Church of St Mary. This is on the site of an early Norman church, but the crypt, with its massive circular piers, is the only survivor from this early period of St Mary's history. The tower, the nave and the transepts were burnt down in the great fire of 1694, and in 1697 Celia Fiennes noted that *'the ruines of the church still remaines the repairing of which is the next worke design'd'*. She was correct in her assumption, for by 1704, only seven years later, the fine neo-Gothic tower was complete. It was probably built in this style, not popular at the time, to blend in with the splendid Perpendicular chancel, which had happily survived the fire. The interior of this church is full of interest, but its outstanding treasure is the exquisite Beauchamp Chapel, built in 1443-64 in accordance with the will of Richard Beauchamp, Earl of Warwick, who had died at Rouen in 1439. This is, in our opinion, the most beautiful chantry chapel ever built, one of the high points of Gothic art, and a superb example of the Perpendicular style. However do not allow the Beauchamp Chapel to blind

you to the many other features of interest in St Mary's, and before leaving, do try to climb to the top of the 174 foot high tower, for its fine views out over Warwick and the surrounding countryside.

(5) The Court House, Jury Street. This was completed in 1728, the work of the local architect who was responsible for much of Warwick's splendid early-18th century re-birth, Francis Smith. It is built in an Italianate style with a colonnaded facade of rusticated stone, and parts of the interior, including the Mayor's parlour and the ballroom, are open to the public. The Court House, Jury Street, is the site of the very helpful Warwick Tourist Information Centre. Also housed here are the interesting Warwickshire Yeomanry Museum and the Warwick Town Museum.

(6) The Shire Hall. This was built in 1753, in delightful Northgate Street, to the design of Sanderson Miller, squire of Radway, and gentleman architect extraordinary (see page 52). It is a handsome red sandstone building with a classical front. The County Dungeon is all that remains of the 17th century County Gaol, and consists of an octagonal underground room where prisoners were chained in depressingly close confinement. The Shire Hall is open for viewing by arrangement. Apply to the County Secretary, Warwickshire County Council, Shire Hall, Warwick.

(7) Northgate House. Facing the end of Northgate Street, this lovely mellow brick William and Mary style house was completed in 1698, and is open to the public by written appointment only to Mr R. E. Phillips.

(8) The Warwickshire Museum. *(Tel: (0926) 493431)* In the Town Hall which is situated in the broad Market Place. Exhibits include geology, wildlife, the history of Warwickshire, and the great Sheldon tapestry map of Warwickshire (see Barcheston, page 21).

(9) St John's House. *(Tel: (0926) 493431)* To be found at Coten End on the road towards Leamington Spa. This is another branch of the Warwickshire County Museum, and its collections include bygones, period costume and musical instruments, and a Victorian classroom. The Museum of the Royal Warwickshire Regiment is on the first floor.

(10) The *Friends Meeting House.* Situated in the High Street, this was built in 1695, only a year after the fire and still as originally furnished.

(11) St Nicholas Park. This large park can be found near the bridge over the Avon. It has extensive leisure facilities including boating on the Avon, fishing by day permit, an indoor swimming pool, and many children's amusements including a model village. Myton Fields, on the opposite bank of the Avon, provide an informal park and picnic ground.

Do not allow this rather long catalogue to deter you from your own exploration of the delightful, largely 18th century streets of Warwick. If you wander at will, you will find many other small gems of architecture, and a fine flavour of 18th century England. There are pleasant hotels and restaurants, lively inns, and several shops of great character, including a well stocked and individually run bookshop in the High Street.

Welford-on-Avon (14-51) A picturesque village with many half-timbered, thatched cottages, several elegant houses, and a tall maypole on the village green. There are lush glimpses of the River

Avon from the long narrow bridges over the Avon by the Four Alls Inn, and distant but equally attractive views out over the river from the top of Cress Hill on the small road running westwards from the village. Walk down Boat Lane, from the Bell Inn, past a series of almost too perfect, black and white thatched cottages to look at the little blue-lias church. This has Norman origins, and although much restored by the energetic George Gilbert Scott in the 1860's, it retains a pleasant flavour of the past. The timber-framed lych gate is a much photographed feature and it is worth walking beyond the church to look at Cleavers, an elegant 18th century house in mellow brick. Ask locally for exact directions to the path leading beside the river from the vicinity of the mill and weir, to Cress Hill.

Boat Lane, Welford-on-Avon.

Wellesbourne (27-55) Busy, ever growing village, with its two halves, once known as Wellesbourne Hastings (to the north-east), and Wellesbourne Mountford (to the south-west), on either bank of the little River Dene. Traffic thunders through on the A429, while oft repeated hopes for a by-pass continue to be unfulfilled. There is also an industrial

estate on the edge of a wartime airfield, itself now revived for the use of light aircraft. But despite all this Wellesbourne does have its attractions... Chestnut Square, where Joseph Arch of Barford (see page 21) addressed his first audience of agricultural workers, advocating a rise of 6d a day, a reduction in the working hours to nine per day, and the formation of a union. In the words of the Trade Union song (to be sung to the tune of *'Auld Lang Syne'*)...

> *When Arch beneath the Wellesbourne tree*
> *His glorious work began,*
> *A thrill of hope and energy*
> *Through all the country ran.*

Apart from the busy traffic this is a pleasant square overlooked by the half-timbered 'Stag's Head' and several handsome 18th century houses. The other quieter corner is behind the King's Head, where a road leads to the church. This is largely Victorian, but it has retained its grey stone Perpendicular tower and its sturdy Norman chancel arch. Do not miss the fine, small brass of a knight in armour, Sir Thomas le Straunge (1426), who was once Constable of Ireland. Walk south from the churchyard, crossing the River Dene by a little footbridge, and then walk north-westwards beside the Dene, to Charlecote. The path passes a sewage works, but it does not dominate the scene for more than a few minutes. The other attractive walk from Wellesbourne is up beside the Dene to Walton (see page 68), and for those not wishing to forsake their cars, the road to Walton, and up the valley of the Dene, to the Foss Way, is pleasantly relaxing.

Westington (14-38) This is the quiet and rather over-trim south-western part of Chipping Campden, with some bewilderingly beautiful houses and cottages, many of which are thatched. On Westington Hill, on the B4081, south of the village, there is a little stone conduit by the roadside, built by Sir Baptist Hicks in 1612, to supply water to his almshouses by Chipping Campden church. (see page 29.)

Weston-on-Avon (15-51) A minute and enviously quiet village tucked away at the end of a little cul-de-sac road, and not far from the reedy banks of the River Avon. There are thatched cottages and a few other houses, some rather less beautiful. The small church is almost entirely late 15th century, with a low tower, a fine range of straight headed, Perpendicular style north windows, and an unspoilt interior containing several items of interest. See especially the medieval floor tiles set in a circle near the pulpit, the 17th century wall panelling, and the two 16th century brasses, to Sir John Grevill, and to his son, Sir Edward, who fought at the Battle of the Spurs in 1513.

Whatcote (29-44) A remarkably remote little village in the Vale of Red Horse (see Tysoe, page 68), flat farming country between the Stour valley and the scarp face of the Oxfordshire Cotswolds. John Leland, the 16th century antiquary wrote of the area, *'Corn is the cheapest commodity grown in the county, whereof the Vale of Red Horse yieldeth most abundantly'.*

The church tower is Perpendicular, but a Norman doorway and two windows are evidence of its much earlier origins. The south porch and part of the nave

73

wall were damaged by a bomb in the 39-45 War, but all has been made good and the interior is well worth visiting. See especially the three finely carved 15th century benches; the brass to William Auldyngton, a fifteen inch long, headless figure in mass vestments dated 1511; and the shaft of a medieval cross in the churchyard, crowned by an 18th century sundial. See also the tablet in the church in memory of William Sanderson Miller, at one time rector of Whatcote, and the last Squire Miller of Radway, a descendant of the 18th century architect, Sanderson Miller. (See Radway, page 52.) There is a much visited inn here, the warm and lively Royal Oak, which is renowned for its bar meals.

Whichford (31-34) Here is a wide green surrounded by houses and cottages of almost every age; not outstandingly beautiful, but one of the most comfortable villages in southern Warwickshire. It is enfolded in beautifully wooded hill country, not far from the Oxfordshire border, but well sheltered from the winds that blow around Great Rollright, on the hills to its south. The 18th century rectory in mellow stone is one of the most elegant country buildings one could wish to encounter, and the church close by, is equally attractive. This has a Norman south doorway, a rugged early-14th century tower, and in contrast, a finely built Perpendicular clerestory. The white painted interior was restored in 1845, when neo-Gothic pews were installed, and these now blend in well with their surroundings. Do not miss the medieval stained glass in some of the window heads, nor the coffin lid, thought to be that of Sir John de Mohun, who fought at the Battle of Boroughbridge in 1322, and who died shortly afterwards. See also the alabaster relief of John Merton, and the tomb chest with brass, of Nicholas Asheton, both rectors of Whichford in the 16th century.

The best walk from Whichford is along the southern edge of Whichford Wood, and southwest, down over the fields to Long Compton. It is also possible to walk eastwards round the flank of Whichford Hill, to Hook Norton; or northwards to Brailes, past Whichford Mill and New Barn Farm.

Whichford Church.

Whitchurch (22-48) Here is a small church surrounded by trees, in broad meadowland not far from the River Stour. It is believed that the monks of Deerhurst, (a priory near Tewkesbury, which was itself a cell of the Abbey of St Denis at the northern gate of Paris), built a wooden church here in Saxon times, and that this was rebuilt in stone in about 1020. Its subsequent architectural history is a complex one, but the herringbone masonry in the north wall is almost certainly Saxon work. There is a Norman south doorway, a 13th century chancel and a Perpendicular east window; and its contents include an incised alabaster slab, a monument to a 15th century rector, William Smith, who was also chaplain to the powerful Guild of the Holy Cross in Stratford-upon-Avon. A much later parish priest here, was J. Harvey Bloom, the father of novelist Ursula Bloom, who makes reference to him in her rather gossipy book *Rosemary for Stratford-on-Avon*. At one time this apparently harmless and friendly man appears to have crossed the path of Stratford's other novelist, the formidable Marie Corelli, who once referred to him as *'that awful fat Mr Bloom'*. Bloom was in fact, a great collector of antiquarian detail, and it was he who discovered the tale of the 17th century vicar of Whitchurch, who *'to the great discomfort of the parishioners sitting near by it'*, used to store cheese in the font during the whole winter.

Wigginton (38-33) Quiet village above the little River Swere, with pleasing views out over the valley to the wooded ridge along which the Banbury to Chipping Norton road runs. There are a variety of Banbury stone houses and cottages, including a handsome 18th century house at its centre, which was the Dolphin Inn until a few years ago. The church has a late-13th century nave, and a Perpendicular tower. In the 14th century chancel will be found a stone seat with a swan on the arch above it, and also two 14th century effigies, one of a knight and one of a civilian complete with minute effigies of a wife and child. Do not miss the lovely 15th century roof to the nave, well lit by the accompanying clerestory.

Wilmcote (16-58) Large village with a creeper covered inn, the Mason's Arms, and a small hotel, the Swan, which looks across its principal road junction to the beautifully timbered 16th century **Mary Arden's House** which has a gabled wing with herringbone strutting. This was the childhood home of William Shakespeare's mother, the youngest of eight daughters of Robert Arden, by his first wife, and it was probably from here that she left to marry John Shakespeare at neighbouring Aston Cantlow church in 1557. This delightfully furnished house, in the care of the Shakespeare Birthplace Trust, is well worth visiting and it is now linked with the adjoining Glebe Farm to form a Shakespeare Countryside Museum, comprising farming and rural life exhibits, which bridge the period from Shakespeare's time to the present day. An ancient dovecote has nesting places for over six hundred birds. *Tel: (0789) 293455.*

Most of Wilmcote's old buildings are constructed of blue-lias stone, for there were extensive quarries in the parish. Wilmcote church, built in 1841, is no exception, and the adjoining school and vicarage are also of the same material. There is a good circular walk from Wilmcote, northwards over the

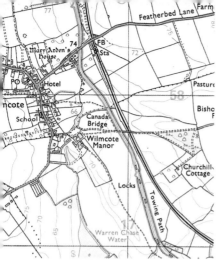

fields to the attractive hamlet of Newnham, and returning to the village on the towpath of the Stratford-upon-Avon Canal. This towpath may be used for a walk southwards to Stratford-upon-Avon, or north towards Wootton Wawen, passing over the interesting Bearley Aqueduct (16-60).

Mary Arden's House, Wilmcote.

Winderton (32-40) Beautifully sited on the steep southern slopes of a hill, with views out over the tree lined fields of the Feldon countryside to the tower of Brailes church. Here are farmhouses and cottages, some thatched, and all on different levels. The handsome Victorian church, built in 1878 by a certain Canon Thoyts, stands just above the village, and its slender spire is a well known local landmark. It has a very grand apsidal chancel enriched with alternative bands of red and white stone, and lancet windows with deep coloured glass. This is Victorian architecture at its best, and should on no account be missed... non-enthusiasts will at the very least enjoy the splendid views from the churchyard. Walk south-westwards over the fields to Lower Brailes, returning via Upper Brailes, with its castle earthworks.

Wixford (Map 150) (09-54) This small village lies to the west of the main area covered by our guide, but it may be located on the Key Map on page 4, 9 miles due west of Stratford-upon-Avon, on the B4085, north of Bidford-on-Avon. We have included it here, as it features in a little verse which is attributed to William Shakespeare. (See Bidford-on-Avon, page 22.) The verse refers to 'papist

Wixford', and we assume that the village's connection with the Roman Catholic Throckmorton family, of Coughton Court about four miles to the north, may have been the reason for this rather sly dig.

Wixford is situated just to the east of the little River Arrow, here crossed by a pleasant single arch, mellow brick bridge. Close by the bridge is the attractive Fish Inn, and a row of pretty half-timbered almshouses, built long ago by Sir William Throckmorton. The church sits on a small rise, with views out over the Arrow valley from its church-yard. It has Norman doorways, and a narrow nave, which is largely Early English in style. However the best feature is the Perpendicular south chapel, which contains the outstandingly beautiful 15th century brass of Thomas de Cruwe and his wife, with the two finely engraved figures beneath elaborately crocketed ogival canopies. Do not miss this.

Wolfhampcote (52-65) A mysterious little place, best approached over the long, often open road which heads north through Flecknoe and Nether-cote, and best visited in summertime. It lies in flat country through which the infant Leam flows, and was once disturbed by two railway lines, now both dismantled. The Grand Union Canal runs just to its north, but in the days when it was first built, as part of the Oxford Canal, it wound in a wide loop through the hamlet. This loop, along with many other contoured meanderings was eliminated in the 'modernisation' that took place between 1827 and 1834, although certain traces are still visible at the entry, especially to the right of the road, where there is a delightful willow-shaded stretch, still full of water. Read the fascinating book, *Lost Canals and Waterways of Britain*, by Ronald Russell, if you wish to explore this and other lost sections of our beautiful waterways. The large church, with its low, squat 13th century tower, is normally locked, but the key's location is given on the notice-board in the churchyard. Its contents include a 14th century chancel screen and a good 17th century commu-nion rail, but most visitors will more appreciate its peaceful setting and its pastoral views across the county border to the spire of Braunston church in Northamptonshire. The best walks here are, in-evitably, along the canal towpath, east to the lively 'canal port' of Braunston (outside the scope of this guide), or south-west to Shuckburgh and Napton.

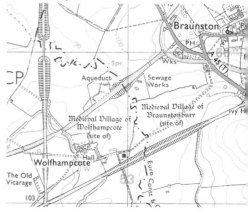

Wootton Wawen (15-63) A village of considerable character, unfortunately overawed by excessive traffic on the A34, Birmingham to Oxford road. It is situated in the valley of the little River Alne, parallel to which runs the Stratford-upon-Avon Canal. This crosses the A34 on an aqueduct built in 1813, on piers of mellow brick that look frighteningly vulnerable to the heavy traffic that thunders past. Beyond the aqueduct there is a beautiful late-18th century mill, which was once powered by water from the Alne, stored in Wootton Pool, a quarter of a mile to

Wootton Wawen Church ... 'A story in stone'.

the north, and visible from the small road running north from here to Preston Bagot. The A34 then crosses the Alne, which is here dammed again, this time to form an ornamental weir and lake known as the Serpentine, in front of Wootton Hall.

This elegantly fronted, late-17th century mansion, now the centre of a residential caravan park, was the childhood home of the unfortunate Mrs Fitzherbert, a Roman Catholic widow whom the Prince of Wales, afterwards George IV, secretly married in 1785, and who after a stormy relationship, was finally dropped by this totally ruthless prince in 1803.

Beyond the Hall lies Wootton Wawen church, once described by the architect, Sir George Gilbert Scott, as *an epitome in stone of the history of the Church of England*. It does indeed have a long and most complex history, and the site appears to have been first used by monks who were given land by Aethelbald, King of Mercia in the early years of the 8th century. Origins of a pre-Norman Conquest, Anglo-Danish church, are to be found in the stonework of the lower half of the fine central tower, and as Scott implied, there is evidence of work from almost every medieval style of architectural in the fabric of the church that remains today. The interior of the church is full of interest and has a strong flavour of the past. Light floods in from the tall Perpendicular clerestory, and the large east window.

The south chapel is delightfully paved with old pale bricks, and there is a fascinating collection of monuments. See especially the effigy of a 15th century knight in alabaster, the early-16th century brasses of John Harewell and his wife and children on a tomb chest, and the handsome monument to Francis Smith (1605), showing him lying on his side beneath his coat of arms.

The best walks from Wootton are along the canal towpath, south to the large Bearley aqueduct, and on to Wilmcote; or north to Preston Bagot and Lowsonford. Otherwise use the road north towards

Preston Bagot, and head off north-east across the fields beside the River Alne, past Blackford Mill Farm, to Henley-in-Arden.

Wormleighton (44-53) Many medieval villages in this area (see Marston Doles, page 47) were ruthlessly cleared and depopulated by landlords building up great flocks of highly profitable sheep. In the year 1498 the medieval village of Wormleighton suffered a similar fate, and its site including that of an old moated manor is now only marked by slight mounds to the north-west of the present village. However in 1508, the estate was purchased by John Spencer, a prosperous flockmaster from Snitterfield, near Stratford-upon-Avon, and he built a large manor house on the hill just above and to the south-east of the depopulated village. This became the centre of a vast estate, and he established great flocks of sheep over a wide area to its north and west, depopulating the medieval villages of Hodnell and Stoneton in the process.

In the same year that he purchased Wormleighton, John Spencer had also acquired an estate at Althorp in Northamptonshire, but his descendants continued to live at Wormleighton, and even acted as host to Prince Rupert on the eve of the Battle of Edgehill in 1642. By this time, the Spencers were one of England's great families and the third Baron Spencer became the Earl of Sunderland in 1643. But towards the end of the Civil War, Prince Rupert had Wormleighton Manor partly destroyed, to prevent it falling into Cromwell's hands, and although the Earl of Sunderland was killed at the Battle of Newbury, his young heir moved to Althorp, and eventually panelling and other items from Wormleighton was installed there. In the 18th century the Fifth Earl inherited the Marlborough dukedom by marrying Anne, the second daughter of John Churchill, the famous first Duke. He moved to Blenheim as a Spencer-Churchill, while his younger brother continued to live at Althorp, the ancestor of the Earls Spencer, and of our present Princess of Wales, Lady Diana Spencer. It must also be reported that the Wormleighton Parish Registers include members of George Washington's family as early as 1595, and a Robert Washington was married in the church here.

All that remains of the great Spencer manor house is a range of mellow brick buildings, now a farmhouse and not easily viewable, and a fine stone gatehouse built by Baron Robert Spencer in 1613. The rest of the village consists of farms and a few estate cottages. However before leaving Wormleighton, walk down through the gatehouse archway to visit the 13th century Hornton stone church. Here will be found a fine carved oak, Perpendicular rood screen and loft, brought here from Southam in the Civil War; also Jacobean panelling, stalls with poppy heads, and a wall monument to a John Spencer dated 1610.

This minute village therefore has many memories of things past, and is a delightfully quiet place, on its small hill overlooking the still sparsely populated countryside through which the Oxford Canal runs. Walk north-east from here past Stoneton, the site of one of the depopulated villages to which we have previously referred, turn north-west, and then follow the towpath of the Oxford Canal around its long contour hugging bends, to return to Wormleighton, up a choice of three different pathways across the fields.

Wroxton (41-41) This is a delightful village, much of it around a sloping green with a pretty pond usually lively with ducks. Here are many thatched stone cottages so typical of the Oxfordshire Cotswolds, where the local ironstone is less suitable for splitting into tiles than the true Cotswold stone further to the south and west. Each roofing method has its own merits, but how pleasant these cottages look with their climbing roses and small trim gardens. There are two lively inns here, the White Horse, and the Lord North; and a pleasant hotel and restaurant, the Wroxton House Hotel.

SCALE 1:25 000 or 2½ INCHES to 1 MILE

An Augustinian priory was founded here in the early-13th century, but only fragments of this remain in the present Wroxton Abbey, a fine 17th century mansion with 18th and 19th century modifications. The 17th century house was built by Sir William Pope, but it passed to the North family soon after. Many improvements were made in the 18th century by Lord North, Prime Minister during the time England lost her North American colonies. He appears to have been not only a client, but also a great friend of Sanderson Miller, the architect-squire of Radway (see page 52), and Miller carried out work for him not only on the house, the chapel and the park, but also on the village church. Wroxton Abbey is now a college for students of Farleigh Dickinson University, New Jersey, and is only open to the public infrequently. (Tel: (029573) 551.) However the delightful gardens and park, with their sweeping lawns, rich woodlands and series of lakes, are now once again open regularly, having been extensively renovated in recent years. Do not miss a visit to the early-18th century ice-house and the octagonal dovecote, nor the distant views of the Gothic arch on a wooded ridge to the east . These features are probably all the work of Sanderson Miller.

The largely 14th century church has a west tower designed by Sanderson Miller, and built in 1748. See the series of elaborate tombs to various inhabitants of Wroxton Abbey, especially the beautifully canopied tomb of the builder of Wroxton, William Pope, Earl of Downe and his wife; and the handsome monument to George III's Prime Minister, Lord North, by the brilliant sculptor, John Flaxman. Thomas Coutts, the founder of the famous private bank is also buried here.

Do not miss the quaint 17th century guide post, put up by Francis White in 1686. A Hornton stone pillar topped by an urn and ball, standing by the A422 road at the western end of the village.

Duckpond at Wroxton.

Motor and Cycle Tours

Tour 1
The Heart of the Shakespeare Country

39 miles. Reasonable for Cyclists.

Our route first runs south-westward, parallel with Shakespeare's Avon, and then heads north, across the Avon, through quiet villages of blue-lias stone and thatch to Aston Cantlow, the village where the poet's mother and father were almost certainly married, and then to the delightful Mary Arden's House, the home of Shakespeare's mother at Wilmcote. And now into gently wooded countryside, the southern fringes of what was once the Forest of Arden, to Snitterfield, where Shakespeare's grandfather farmed, and where he is probably buried. We then head into the lovely old county town of Warwick, with its magnificent castle poised above the Avon, and its wealth of late 17th and early 18th century buildings. From Warwick we head south across the Avon and move down the valley, returning towards Stratford-upon-Avon, passing two fine Victorian churches, and the splendid National Trust property, Charlecote Park, where the young Shakespeare is believed to have been caught poaching deer.

Leave **Stratford-upon-Avon** by crossing bridge over River Avon and bearing right at roundabout just beyond, on to the A34

Deer in Charlecote Park.

(Oxford road). Embankment of old **Stratford-and-Moreton Tramway** soon visible on right, beyond end of houses. Fork right on to A46 (Broadway road). Over River Stour and fork right off A46. (But go ahead and turn first left if you wish to visit pretty cul-de-sac village of **Clifford Chambers**.) Cross line of old railway and bear right at Y-junction near council houses. Straight, not right at next T-junction (unless you wish to visit **Weston-on-Avon** church).

Turn right at entry to **Welford-on-Avon**, then straight through village (but walk down left at T-junction by Bell Inn to look at attractive half-timbered and thatched cottages in Boat Lane, and church just beyond). Over bridges crossing River Avon beyond Four Alls Inn. Turn right with care on to A439, and almost immediately turn left off A439 (Sign — Binton). Keep left at sunken road junction below Binton church, and up through **Binton** village.

Turn right at X-rds by lively Blue Boar Inn (excellent bar meals and restaurant). Over offset X-rds with great care, crossing A422, a Roman road. Fine views back right, out over Avon valley to the Cotswolds. Pass hamlet of Billesley ... lush Billesley Manor Hotel, simple 17th century church. Fork left at Y-junction, woodlands up to left, wide grass verges to road (picnic possibilities). Turn right at X-rds (Sign — Aston Cantlow).

Turn left at T-junction, and enter **Aston Cantlow** village, to visit church where parents of William Shakespeare were probably married, and the beautifully timbered King's Head Inn. Turnabout and then turn left at end of village. After one mile, turn left at T-junction by Aston Holdings Farm (fresh farm produce on sale here). Up hill and into **Wilmcote**. Creeper-covered Mason's Arms Inn on left. Turn left opposite Swan Hotel. Mary Arden's House on left (lovely half-timbered, childhood home of Shakespeare's mother. Owned by Shakespeare Birthplace Trust. Open to the public).

Leave village, and over Stratford-upon-Avon Canal and railway. Turn right with great care, on to A34 beyond bungalows at Pathlow. After short distance, turn left, off A34 by Dun Cow Inn (good bar meals). Up curving little hill, and along pleasant tree-shaded road. Radio masts to left. Turn first left and enter **Snitterfield**. Turn right at first X-rds in village, then turn left. Churchyard on right is probable burial place of Snitterfield farmer, Richard Shakespeare, Will's grandfather. Distant Spencer ancestors of Lady Diana, Princess of Wales also came from here. Now straight, not right, leaving village.

Bear left at Y-junction by Luscombe Farm. Fork right in **Norton Lindsey**, near Old New Inn, and turn right at X-rds beyond village. Go straight, not right, and straight, not left,

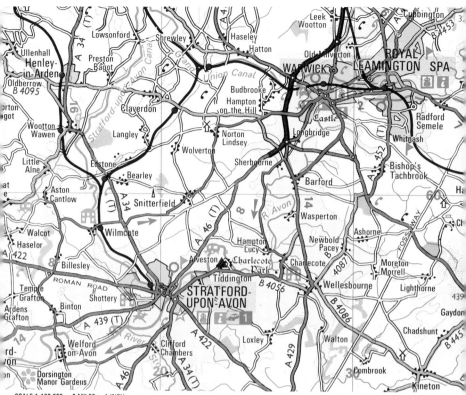

SCALE 1:190 080 or 3 MILES to 1 INCH

joining B4095 (Signs — Warwick). Keep on B4095 into **Warwick**, with race course on left. In Warwick, turn left with care on to A429, up past West Gate and beautifully timbered Lord Leycester's Hospital, and along High Street. St Mary's church up to left, Court House and Tourist Information Centre on right. Keep straight into Jury Street (a continuation of High Street), and turn right at traffic lights by the East Gate.

Keep straight at roundabout (but go right round and take first left to go to car park for Warwick Castle). Entrance to St Nicholas Park on left. Over bridge crossing River Avon. Fine views of castle above river, up to right. Keep straight at small roundabout, on to A425 (Sign — Banbury). After one mile, fork right with care, on to B4462. Drop into valley with small pool to left, and enter **Barford**.

Barford church on left. Turn right with care, on to A429. Over bridge crossing River Avon. Good views of handsome Sherbourne Park (house) and church over to left. Bear sharp left with care, off A429, and keep straight in delightful **Sherbourne**. (But turn left if you wish to visit exceptionally elegant Victorian church.) After about one mile, earthworks of long vanished Fulbroke Castle visible to right (near Court Farm). (See

Sherbourne, page 57.) Now on long, pleasant road, with occasional glimpses of River Avon over to left.

Straight, not right at T-junction (Sign — Hampton Lucy), and into **Hampton Lucy**. Bear left in village, (unless you wish to visit handsome Victorian church and/or Boar's Head Inn). Over bridge crossing River Avon, restored water-mill on left (sometimes open at week-ends, parking probably in meadow beyond on left). Boundary of **Charlecote Park** soon on right, deer usually visible. Turn right at T-junction in **Charlecote** village, keeping park fence on right. Fine views out over park. Straight, not left by church on right, and Charlecote Pheasant restaurant on left. Car Park for Charlecote Park just beyond on left. Do not miss a visit here.

Over attractive stone bridge crossing little River Dene, and turn right at X-rds on to B4086 (Sign — Stratford). Through series of dangerous bends, with views of Charlecote Park to right (for passengers only!), please do not park here. Avon water-meadows over to right. Pass three turns to right, keeping on B4086 (but take first right if you wish to divert through **Alveston**, and visit the Ferry Inn). Keep straight through village of Tiddington, and into **Stratford-upon-Avon**, completing Tour 1.

Tour 2
Arden Forest Country
28 miles. Reasonable for Cyclists.

Our route first heads north from Stratford-upon-Avon on the busy Birmingham road, but we soon turn into quiet lanes, following the approximate course of the lovely Stratford-upon-Avon Canal, through a lightly wooded countryside of small bumpy hills and narrow lanes, as far as Lowsonford village. Here we cut across to Rowington, only a mile or so away, and turn eastwards to follow the course of the wider but still very pleasant Grand Union Canal, as far as Hatton, where there is a long flight of locks carrying this waterway down into the Avon valley to Warwick. And now, after calling at an

interesting craft centre near Hatton, we head south, through leafy countryside, with an occasional distant view out over the Avon valley, through the villages of Wolverton, and Snitterfield, with its connections not only with Shakespeare, but also with our Princess of Wales, Lady Diana.

Leave **Stratford-upon-Avon**, northwards on the A34, (Birmingham road). After four miles, turn left at X-rds by Golden Cross Inn, off A34. Pass under railway bridge, and fine aqueduct carrying the Stratford-upon-Avon Canal. Straight, not left twice, joining B4089 (sign Wootton Wawen). Also good walk along towpath, south to Wilmcote, or north to Wootton Wawen. Follow B4089 into **Wootton Wawen**, and bear right with great care on to A34. Wootton Wawen church on left , once described by Sir George Gilbert

Wootton Hall ... the elegant south front.

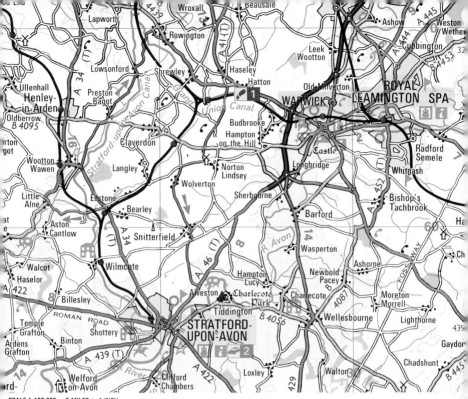

SCALE 1:190 080 or 3 MILES to 1 INCH

Scott as *'an epitome in stone of the history of the Church of England'*, and well worth visiting. Elegant 17th century Wootton Hall in park just beyond. Over River Alne by attractive waterfall to left, and turn left with care, just beyond mellow brick mill, and **before** reaching aqueduct.

Views to left of Wootton Pool (once used to power the watermill). Bear right on to B4095, and turn left off B4095 just beyond the Crab Mill Inn on left (sign — Preston Bagot). Good canal walks from here, south to Wootton Wawen, north to Lowsonford. Thirst-quenching pubs abound. Turn right in **Preston Bagot**, up steep hill. Small church with Norman nave to left. Fork right in Preston Fields, and over X-rds in Lowsonford, near canal bridge, but not crossing it. Pass the Fleur de Lys Inn, and then turn right, cross the Stratford-upon-Avon Canal, and up steep hill through Finwood hamlet. Under railway bridge, and then over **Grand Union Canal** near entry to **Rowington**. Walk on canal towpath, south-eastwards to tunnel near Shrewley Common (Ref: 21-67), and on to **Hatton** Flight (Ref:24-66).

Turn right at T-junction, and through **Rowington**. Bear right with care on to B4439. Rowington church on left. After two and a half miles, turn right at third X-rds. Over canal and railway. Walk down towpath to left to look at **Hatton** flight of locks **(linking on to Walk 1)**, and possibly visit the

popular Waterman Inn (this can also be reached on the A41, ref: 24-66). **Hatton** craft centre down farm drive to left (marked Hatton Farm on Map 151). A variety of craftsmen normally at work here. Coffee, teas, and light meals. Straight, not right, and straight, not left, in wooded area. Over offset X-rds, crossing B4095 at Gannaway. Turn right at T-junction near entry to **Norton Lindsey** (but turn left if you wish to visit village).

Turn left at X-rds, and through Wolverton, with little church well up to right, with timbered bell-turret and delightful colour-washed interior. Walk up here to visit church and for pleasant views. Clough Williams-Ellis, of Portmeirion fame, built part of Wolverton Court... on left at end of village, not open to the public. After two miles, enter **Snitterfield**. Straight, not right and turn right at next T-junction, unless you wish to visit church... Richard Shakespeare, the poet's grandfather reputed to be buried here. Distant ancestors of Lady Diana, the Princess of Wales, also came from Snitterfield (see page 59). Now turn left at next T-junction, and leave village, by turning right by war memorial (from which there are fine views out over the Avon valley. Fork left, down hill, and eventually turn right with very great care on to A46. Pass entrance to Welcombe Hotel and Golf Course, and into **Stratford-upon-Avon**, completing Tour 2.

Tour 3
Edge Hill Country

38 miles. Hilly.

Our route passes through quiet, gently undulating, and lightly wooded countryside between Stratford-upon-Avon and the steep escarpment of Edge Hill, heading up through the valley of the little River Dene, then along part of the Roman Foss Way, and also beyond Kineton, passing the site of the first great battle of the Civil War, Edgehill. It then runs parallel with and just above this tree-clad scarp-face, passing Upton House, with its fabulous collection of pictures and porcelain, and through an area of small bumpy hills, along the Warwickshire-Oxfordshire border. Near Compton Wynyates, sadly no longer open to the public, it descends once again into the 'plain', and moves across quiet farming country, on its way westwards, to return to Stratford-upon-Avon.

Leave **Stratford-upon-Avon** by crossing bridge over the Avon, and turning left on to B4086 (Tiddington Road). Turn right almost immediately, up Loxley Road. Follow signs over open country to **Loxley**, pleasant little village on gentle slopes, with small orchards amongst its varied houses and a welcoming inn, The Fox. Church has medieval tower, the rest is delightful 18th century work, with box pews still intact. Straight not right by sloping green, then turn right beyond church, and eventually left with care, on to A429. Turn right at entry to **Wellesbourne**, and up valley of River Dene to **Walton**, a small mellow-brick 'estate village' for Walton Hall, which is on left beyond village. This was built by Sir George Gilbert Scott in the 1850's, a massive but not unduly beautiful mansion in wooded parkland (FP through grounds). Turn sharp left with care on to the **Foss Way** (Roman road stretching from Lincoln to Exeter). Turn first right off Foss Way, and into **Combrook**, a delightful village in a hollow, with a Victorian church built by Lord Willoughby de Broke, of **Compton Verney**, in whose estate Combrook lay. (**Link to Walk 7.**)

Through Combrook, and eventually turn right on to B4086 (**but turn left to link with Walk 7**). Into **Kineton**, large village with church mostly rebuilt in 1880s, but with good medieval tower. Character houses, especially in Bridge Street and the little tucked-away Market Square. Leave Kineton on the Banbury Road (B4086). Modern monument on right of road (Ref: 35-50) commemorates Battle of Edgehill, 23rd October 1642 (see page 34) ... first major battle of Civil War ... result inconclusive ... actual site of battle to south (right) of road, now occupied by the Ministry of Defence. Turn first right, off B4086, into **Radway**, pretty Hornton

Upton House. A fine William and Mary mansion containing a wealth of art treasures.

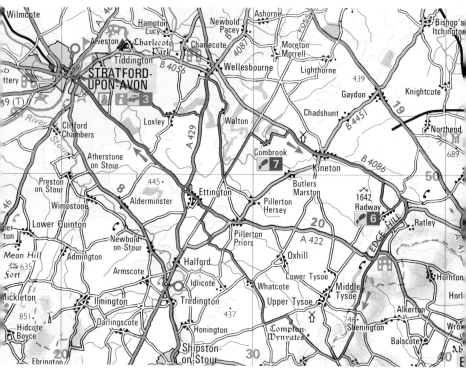

SCALE 1:190 080 or 3 MILES to 1 INCH

stone (ironstone) village beneath Edge Hill. Elizabethan Radway Grange, much altered about 1745 by Sanderson Miller, squire and gentleman architect (see page 52). Miller also planted woods on slopes above village. (**Link to Walk 6**.)

Turn left in **Radway**, and then turn right to rejoin B4086. Up pleasantly wooded hill, and at top keep right, leaving B4086. Into **Edge-hill** village **(Link to Walk 6)**. Edgehill 'castle', built by Sanderson Miller about 1746, to mark site of royal standard raising at start of Battle of Edgehill ... now the Castle Inn. Turn left beyond Castle Inn, then right, leaving village. Turn right with care, on to A422. Entrance to **Upton House** on left. This National Trust property is a William and Mary mansion with very attractive terraced gardens and lakes, and a quite outstanding collection of porcelain and pictures, including works by Bosch, the Brueghels, Holbein, Rembrandt, Van Dyke, Canaletto, Goya, El Greco, Tiepolo, Tintoretto, Constable, Stubbs, Hogarth, Reynolds, Romney and Sartorious. Do not miss this.

Bear left at first bend beyond **Upton House**, keeping on A422, heading towards Stratford, but only briefly, going straight at second bend, leaving A422. Keep straight over X-rds beyond old airfield on left. Straight, at next T-junction, then over X-rds by stone cottage called White House (Ref: 34-40). Straight at next T-junction. Compton Pike just visible up to left, and lovely mellow-brick mansion of **Compton Wynyates** (not open to the public) in hollow down to right, with windmill on hill beyond (see page 32). FP to windmill to right a quarter of a mile beyond house entrance gates. FP continues past mill, down to Tysoe. Good walk with fine views.

Go straight, joining wider road, and then almost immediately left at next bend, on to unfenced road. Turn right at X-rds, (sign — Whatcote). Final stretch of road into Whatcote follows course of Roman road running from Kings Sutton to Worcester (see Epwell, page 35). Bear left in **Whatcote** by the Royal Oak, pleasant inn serving good bar meals. Surprisingly, the church was damaged by a bomb in 2nd World War .. now well restored and with Norman features, good woodwork and 16th century brass, and is worth visiting. Straight at T-junction, over X-rds in hamlet of Fulready, and turn right on to B4451. Almost immediately turn left, off B4451. Then right with care, on to **Foss Way**, and left with care, on to A422 into Ettington, long straggling village strung out along A422, with early-20th century church and remains of 18th century church tower overlooking monster roundabout at end of village. Return to **Stratford-upon-Avon** on A422, completing Tour 3.

83

Tour 4
The Stour Valley

30 miles. Reasonable for Cyclists.

Our route first heads southwards along the busy A34, Oxford road, running parallel with the little River Stour. Beyond Newbold-on-Stour, we loop away to the pretty stone village of Armscote, before crossing the A34, and the Stour near Tredington. Now south again, but on the quieter eastern side of the valley, through exquisite Honington, and past a hamlet where beautiful tapestry maps were made. Beyond Burmington, we again cross the Stour, and head north to Shipston-on-Stour. Once through this pleasant little market town, we head away from the valley, and into quieter countryside lying below the northern bastions of the Cotswolds. Through sleepy Darlingscott, and Ilmington, one of the loveliest villages we know. And now, back down into the Stour valley, along quiet roads through pretty hamlets and small villages, only re-joining the dreaded A34 for the last two miles into Stratford-upon-Avon.

Leave **Stratford-upon-Avon** by crossing bridge over River Avon, and bearing right at roundabout just beyond, on to the A34 (the Oxford Road). Embankment of **Stratford and Moreton Tramway** soon visible on right, beyond end of houses. Keep on A34 for six miles, passing **Alscot Park** on right. 18th century early Gothic mansion in fine deer park. Through **Alderminster** village, lively Bell Inn and church with Norman origins, stout 13th century tower and views of Stour from churchyard. After one mile, cross Stour, and views of 19th century Gothic mansion of **Ettington Park** to left. Not surprisingly, this has been used for location work on a horror film.

Into Newbold-on-Stour, grey stone and mellow brick village, mostly astride the A34, with welcoming White Hart Inn, offering good bar and restaurant meals. Church not of outstanding interest. At end of village, turn right with care, off busy A34 with some relief.

Ilmington, below the Cotswolds' far northern slopes.

At entrance to **Armscote**, first village on route with 'Cotswold' flavour, bear right, and turn right, beyond modest driveway entrance to fine Jacobean manor house. Turn sharp left beyond Wagon Wheel Inn on right, and over small X-rds near pond, at end of village.

Turn left with great care, on to the busy A429, the **Foss Way**, a Roman road running from Lincoln to Exeter. Bear round to right at roundabout, on to the A34, (sign — Oxford). Into beautifully polished, Cotswold stone village of **Tredington**. Turn down left to explore village. Handsomely spired church with Norman origins is well worth visiting (see page 68). After one mile turn left with care off A34, at small T-junction, between stone pillars (sign — Honington). Over pretty stone bridge, crossing Stour, with views over to left of handsome 17th century mansion of Honington Hall (for details, see page 40). Through delightful **Honington**, with tree-shaded green overlooked by enviably beautiful houses. Visit church and Hall, if open.

Fork right at end of village, and go southwards, parallel with the Stour. Straight, not left, by Fell Mill Farm. Over X-rds, crossing B4035. Then straight, not right unless you wish to visit **Barcheston**. Church has interesting medieval interior, hamlet has memories of Sheldon tapestry maps. (See page 21). FP to Shipston beside Stour. Through Willington hamlet. Fork right well beyond, and then turn right at X-rds, into Burmington. Bear right with care, back on to A34. Over Stour in **Tidmington** hamlet, on right is minute church with 12th century tower, beside handsomely fronted Tidmington House. Into **Shipston-on-Stour** on A34. Attractive little market town with excellent shops and welcoming hotels and inns. Church not outstanding.

In Shipston, turn left, off A34, on to B4035. After short distance, turn right in town, off B4035 (sign — Darlingscott). Leave town, and cross A429 (The Foss Way) with great care. Over X-rds in small Cotswold stone village of Darlingscott. Victorian church not exceptionally interesting. Fork right beyond end of village, and head directly to Ilmington, following signs. Junction of long vanished **Stratford and Moreton Tramway** was in fields to left, but now difficult to spot. Turn left at entry to **Ilmington** and then turn left again beyond bungalows on left. This beautiful village at the northern tip of the Cotswolds is well worth exploring on foot. Howard Arms on right. Red Lion Inn on right. Bear right twice, keeping sloping green up to your left, and eventually come to church, visible to right. Visit church to find mice (see page 42), and other features of interest. Be sure to walk beyond to look at pools, and to explore the 'inner village' on foot.

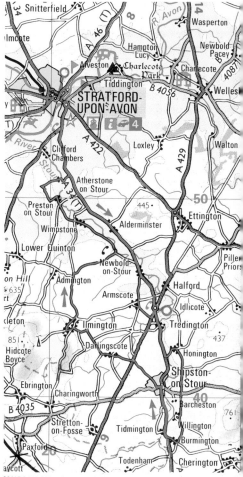

SCALE 1:190 080 or 3 MILES to 1 INCH

Bear right well beyond church, and then turn left, (sign — Stratford). Straight, not left at next T-junction, and almost immediately turn right at next T-junction. Over pleasantly quiet road, with open views, to hamlet of Crimscote, back in the Stour valley. Bear left in Crimscote, and over partly open road, with views of little **Whitchurch**, church in water-meadows to right. Keep left at entry to pretty Wimpstone hamlet, and over X-rds beyond. Over diagonal X-rds, and into delightfully quiet village of **Preston on Stour**. Church has elegant 18th century interior, with fine monuments to the Wests of nearby **Alscot Park**. Views of Alscot Park across Stour from east (right) of village. Bear left beyond church, turn right twice, and descend into valley, through Atherstone on Stour. Victorian church with spire. FP parallel with Stour, to **Clifford Chambers** and **Stratford-upon-Avon**. Turn left, with great care, back on to the over-busy A34, and return to **Stratford-upon-Avon**, completing Tour 4.

Tour 5
The Cotswold Fringes

39 miles. Hilly.

Our route heads south from Stratford-upon-Avon, along the A46, Broadway road, for a few miles before passing through quieter farming country beyond Quinton. After Admington we take a fine road south, up over Ilmington Downs, the highest point in Warwickshire, and a northern bastion of the Cotswolds. Beyond stone and thatch Ebrington, we drop down into orchard country, and move on to the charming hillside village of Blockley. Now heading northwards, we pass through one of the loveliest small market towns in England, Chipping Campden, before climbing up to look out over the Avon valley from the super viewpoint of Dover's Hill. We now run parallel with, and just above, the steep Cotswold scarp, visiting two very special gardens, Hidcote and Kiftsgate, before dropping down into the vale, for a run home across rich market-garden country. We cross the Avon beyond pretty Welford-on-Avon and then head east along the busy A439, to return to Stratford-upon-Avon.

Leave **Stratford-upon-Avon** by crossing bridge over River Avon, and bear right at roundabout just beyond, on to the A34 (Oxford road). Embankment of **Stratford and Moreton Tramway** soon visible on right, beyond end of houses. Fork right on to A46 (Broadway road). Follow A46 for nearly five miles, and then turn left (sign — Quinton). Through **Lower Quinton**, attractive College Arms Inn on left, splendidly spired church on right. Interior should not be missed. Bear left beyond end of village, and straight, not left at next T-junction. Turn right at next T-junction, into Admington.

Glimpses of handsome Admington Hall on right, at end of hamlet. Bear left, just before passing under power lines. Turn right, off wider road, just beyond next houses on right. Not signed, this road looks almost like a track and could easily be missed, but it will all be worthwhile. Up steep hill, along partly unfenced road through an area known as **Lark Stoke**. Best views back, northwards, from a point before the 'summit' is reached. Small TV transmitter to right, FP down track to right, to Hidcote and Kiftsgate Gardens, and on down to **Mickleton. (This is part of Walk 8.)** Straight, not left, joining wider (fenced) road.

Start to drop down off so-called 'Ilmington Downs'. Straight road points to tower of Chipping Campden dead ahead. Bear left at T-junction, continuing down hill. Turn left at X-rds and enter stone and thatch village of

Ebrington. Straight, not right, joining B4035. Visit church to see Keyte and Fortescue family monuments. Keep straight, by Ebrington Arms, leaving B4035 (sign — Paxford). Drop down into valley, and over X-rds. Turn right, joining B4479 at entry to Paxford. Small Victorian church not of great interest to visitors. Stone-built Churchill Inn looks friendly. Keep through village on B4479. Over level-crossing by brickworks, and head straight into Blockley.

Blockley is a charming hillside village in Cotswold stone, once thriving with silk mills feeding the Coventry ribbon industry, and now a delightfully undisturbed place in which to wander . . . but on foot please. See the interesting church, visit an inn, and if possible, walk up the wooded Dovedale, using **Walk 5**, starting from south-western end of the village (see page 108). Coming in from Paxford, turn right and right again, and take the road northwards, much of it pleasantly tree lined, to Broad Campden. Pause awhile at the top of the hill before dropping down into Broad Campden, for fine views ahead to Chipping Campden. Turn left at entry to **Broad Campden**, a quiet village tucked away in a small valley, with an hospitable inn, the Baker's Arms, and an excellent guest house, called the Malt House.

Enter **Chipping Campden** by turning right in the attractive Westington area, and then turn right into the High Street. If possible park, and explore this outstandingly beautiful, small Cotswold town at the leisurely pace it deserves. But however much time you have, do stop for at least an hour or so. (For details, see page 29). Pass Market Hall on left, and then keep out of town on the B4035 (sign — Evesham). Shortly after leaving town, turn left, off B4035, and climb hill with fine views out over Chipping Campden to left. Turn right at X-rds, and then right again into the car park for **Dover's Hill**, a large crescent shaped field in the care of the National Trust, which is the site of Dover's Games and from which there are splendid views.

Now **turnabout** from **Dover's Hill**, retrace route for a short time, by turning left at X-rds, and then turn left, on to B4035, at the point where you left it. Sounds complicated? It will become more than clear once you are

Chipping Campden.

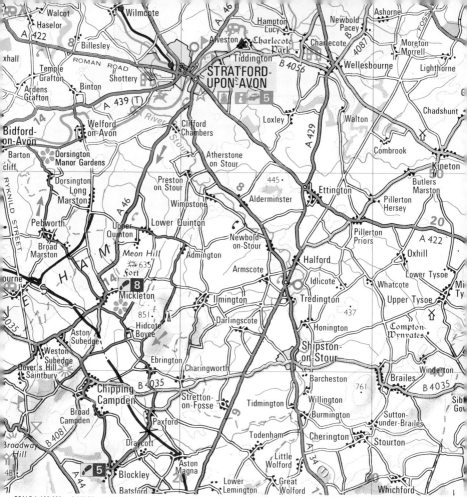

SCALE 1:190 080 or 3 MILES to 1 INCH

on the ground. Now almost immediately fork right, off B4035, on to B4081, and after a quarter of a mile, fork right again (sign — Hidcote Gardens). After half a mile, pass a tree-clad embankment, the spoil heaps created in about 1850 by the builders of **Campden Railway Tunnel**. (See page 25 for a brief account of the so-called *'Battle of Mickleton'*.) Turn left at X-rds, straight, not right at edge of **Hidcote Boyce**, pass beautiful 17th century Hidcote House on right, and turn left at T-junction (sign — Mickleton) **(But go straight ahead to visit Hidcote Manor Garden and or Kiftsgate Court Garden...see pages 39 and 42 respectively. Do not miss these.)**

Go down hill into **Mickleton**, large village with mixture of stone and half-timbering. Church with spire and interesting interior. Butcher's Arms and Three Ways Hotel make this a good place to stop awhile. Pleasant walk up hill to **Kifstgate** and **Hidcote (using Walk 8)**. Turn right at entry to village, on to A46, and take first left, off A46 (sign — Pebworth). Leave village, and after two

miles, turn left and go under railway bridge, then through Broad Marston. Now enter **Pebworth**, head for church up small street. Attractive village on little knoll in otherwise flat country, with full-of-character church. Take Dorsington road northwards from almost opposite church (now off Map 151 for short distance).

Bear left by Dorsington church, leave village, and **Dorsington Manor Gardens** soon on right (see page 33). (Now off Map 151 again for short distance.) Turn sharp right at next T-junction, and go straight to Welford-on-Avon. Fine views of River Avon down left from hill before entering village. Turn left by village green with maypole in **Welford-on-Avon**. Then straight through village (but walk down left at T-junction by the Bell Inn, to look at attractive half-timbered and thatched cottages in Boat Lane, and church). Over bridges crossing River Avon beyond Four Alls Inn. Turn right with great care on to A439, and return on this road to **Stratford-upon-Avon**, completing Tour 5.

Tour 6
Four Shires Country and the Rollright Stones

39 miles. Hilly.

Our route heads westwards from attractive Moreton-in-Marsh, along the A44, passing entrances to two places well worth visiting ... Batsford Park Arboretum, and Sezincote. Now up steep hillside Bourton-on-the-Hill, and off the busy A44, for the delightful village of Blockley. From here we drop into valley country, through a series of quiet villages totally unspoiled by tourism. We cross the A34 beyond Little Wolford, and at Cherington we are again in the Stour valley (see Tour 4). Beyond here the countryside becomes hilly, with Whichford enfolded in wooded hills, and Great Rollright, on the windy uplands above. Now heading westwards again, along a ridge road, on the boundary between Warwickshire and Oxfordshire, with fine views especially to the north. We pass the mysterious Rollright Stones, and soon drop down again into lower country, passing two villages with an interesting past, Little Compton and Barton-on-the-Heath, before passing the handsome Four Shire Stone on the A44, back into Moreton-in-Marsh.

Leave **Moreton-in-Marsh** westwards on A44. After one and a half miles, turning to **Batsford Park Arboretum** on right, and turning for **Sezincote** on left. Both places should be visited if possible. **Batsford Park Arboretum** has fifty acres of splendid woodlands, while **Sezincote** is a beautifully sited mansion in the highly exotic Moghul style, with an elegantly classical interior. Continue up A44 through hillside village of **Bourton-on-the-Hill**, with its small terraces of stone cottages beside the road, and its interesting church. (Have you ever seen a Winchester bushel and peck?)

At top of hill, beyond **Bourton-on-the-Hill**, turn right, off A44, and on to B4479 (sign — Blockley). Go through most of **Blockley** on B4479 (for details, see Tour 5, , as this is one of the few places visited on more than one route). **(Link here with Walk 5.)** Towards end of village, well beyond Great Western Arms, fork right, off B4479 (sign — Draycott). Keep straight through Draycott hamlet, and on to hillside village of **Aston Magna**. Church not of great interest, but do not miss the Bygones Museum at Bank Farm (on right, just before first T-junction). Keep right by church at end of village. Turn left with great care on to A429 , the **Foss Way** (Roman road running from Lincoln to Exeter.)

Turn first right, off A429 (sign — Todenham). Over the little Knee Brook, and just beyond, the line of the long vanished **Stratford and Moreton Railway**. Turn right and almost immediately left at entry to **Todenham**. (But turn left to visit village ... 14th century church with fine spire and interesting interior, plus an inn of considerable character.) Turn right at entry to **Great Wolford**, and over small X-rds near church with tall spire. Bear left at T-junction beyond village, and head for **Little Wolford**, where the fine Tudor manor house is visible on left near the

At Batsford Park Arboretum.

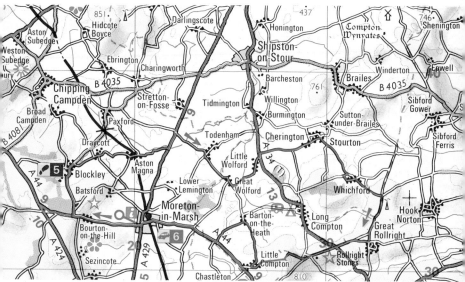

SCALE 1:190 080 or 3 MILES to 1 INCH

entry to this otherwise undistinguished hamlet.

Over off-set X-rds with great care, crossing A34. Straight, not right at first T-junction (Small road to right leads through Weston Park and is partly unfenced . . . this makes good winter walk (see **Cherington**)). Bear right twice in delightful village of **Cherington**. Do not miss the largely 13th century church, the contents of which includes a beautiful 14th century tomb chest. Bear right in Stourton which is almost part of Cherington, and beyond here, go straight, not right, heading over hilly country to **Whichford**.

In **Whichford**, go straight not right twice, and then bear right at the far end. The 18th century rectory, and the medieval church close by, complement each other excellently, and a visit to the latter should not be missed. FP from near the church, south-westwards over the fields, and beside Whichford Wood, to **Long Compton**. Drive slowly hereabouts, the wooded, hilly countryside is much too good to be rushed. Now climb out of **Whichford**, and at very top of long hill, turn right at X-rds on to a road that forms the border between Warwickshire (on right) and Oxfordshire (on left).

Fork left, and then turn right at X-rds at entry to **Great Rollright**. (But turn left if you wish to visit the interesting Norman church.) If the wind is blowing hard up here . . . and it often does . . . you may not wish to stay too long. Bear left, and then straight, not right, keeping on the high ridge road, from which there are fine views. Now over A34 with very great care (unless you wish to visit **Long Compton**, when you will divert to the right, down a long hill). Our road now on the county border again. After less than half a mile, the first of the **Rollright Stones**, are visible well over to left . . . these are the Whispering Knights, the remains of a Bronze Age burial chamber. Next, on the right . . . the King Stone, an isolated standing stone, almost opposite which, on the left of the road, is the King's Men, a Bronze Age stone circle. Come here if possible on a clear day in winter, to walk round the stones, and to savour the magnificent views, especially those northwards from the King Stone . . . and perhaps you will experience some of the atmosphere from the distant past that seems to linger here still.

Over next X-rds (but turn down left if you wish to visit **Little Rollright** church, with its beautiful canopied 17th century monuments). After short distance, fork right (sign — Little Compton), and then straight, not right, soon afterwards. Now go down long hill into **Little Compton**, with its simple church, lovely manor house, and reminders of Charles I's execution on the scaffold at Whitehall. Bear right twice in village (but not before visiting church, and taking a glimpse at the manor). Over rolling hilly country to **Barton-on-the-Heath**, where there is an interesting little church with Anglo-Danish origins, and a pleasant green. Turn left opposite church, just beyond entry to Barton. Turn right with care, on to A44, in Kitebrook hamlet. Over next off-set X-rds, keeping on A44, but do not miss the **Four Shire Stone**, at junction with road to right. Now pass large Fire Service Training College, and keep into **Moreton-in-Marsh** on A44, completing Tour 6.

Tour 7
The Oxfordshire Cotswolds

38 miles. Hilly.

Our route heads westwards from Banbury on the B4035 Shipston road, turning off it near outstandingly beautiful Broughton Castle. Now heading into hilly upland country of the Oxfordshire Cotswolds, through a series of rich, toffee-coloured ironstone villages, untouched by fame and pleasing in the extreme. At Swerford, with its Norman castle earthworks and handsome mansion in a deep valley, we change direction, and head northwards, first to the full-of-character town of Hook Norton, and then to the charming Sibfords. Beyond here we cross into Warwickshire at dark, tree-shaded Traitor's Ford, and head down to Brailes, with its fine church tower and dramatic castle earthworks. We now climb back into the Oxfordshire hills near Epwell, and go through delightful Shenington and its small neighbour Alkerton, finally returning on the A422 through Wroxton, to visit Wroxton Abbey, with its splendid gardens and park, before returning to Banbury.

Leave **Banbury** from Banbury Cross, westwards on B4035. After less than three miles, turn right with care, off B4035, by the Wykeham Arms, **Broughton**. Entrance to **Broughton Castle** on left. Beautiful, moated Tudor mansion with fine panelling, fireplaces, and good period furniture. Interesting Civil War connections. Try not to miss a visit here, but not open every day. Bear left at small T-junction, narrow road with old parkland to left, road later becomes unfenced, with gates, but worthwhile for fine open views. FP's to left and right .. good walking opportunities. Turn left, beyond Broughton Grounds Farm, on to wider road. Over five-way X-rds, and into **Shutford**.

Keep straight through **Shutford**, quiet village on valley slopes, with attractively signed George and Dragon Inn, manor house with tall tower, and a small church with Norman origins. Turn left at T-junction beyond end of village. In less than one mile, cross course of Roman road that ran from Worcester to Kings Sutton (see **Epwell**). Can be identified by track leading to left. Good walk along here, to Swalcliffe Lea, beneath **Madmarston Hill**, Iron Age hill fort. Turn left, with care, on to B4035, and move to **Swalcliffe (Link with Walk 4)**. At entry to village turn right, down small wooded road (but go straight ahead for fine tithe barn, visible to left, interesting church with monuments and medieval wall paint-ings, and thatched inn called the Stag).

After leaving **Swalcliffe** on small road, wooded at start, bear left at T-junction by Swalcliffe Grange (farm), on to largely open road running over fine rolling country with splendid views to right towards the Cotswolds above Blockley and Chipping Campden. Broadway Tower visible on skyline on clear day. Source of River Stour near to barn on right in slight dip. Was marked as 'Stour Well' on previous editions of map. Straight, not left, at T-junction, and over X-rds at Wigginton Heath. Down steep little hill with bends, and over X-rds with care, just beyond remains of the long vanished Banbury and Cheltenham Direct Railway.

Straight, not left by Swan Inn, **Wigginton**. (But turn left if you wish to visit village, a quiet place with attractive stone houses, interesting church, and pleasant views out over the Swere valley.) Straight, not left in valley, and straight, not left at top of small hill just beyond. Now on delightfully quiet little road, later beside the Swere stream, before turning sharp left beyond gate, into **Swerford**. Turn sharp right, and earthworks of a Norman castle on right, just before church. This has small spire and 13th century porch, but interior is not of great interest. Beyond village, glimpses of Swerford Park, elegant 18th century mansion, over to right.

Turn right at T-junction, down into Swere valley, cross line of old Banbury and Cheltenham Direct Railway. Right at T-junction, left at T-junction, bear left at Y-junction, and into **Hook Norton**. Explore this large, flavour-packed village on foot, including the church with its finely pinnacled tower and its fascinating Norman font, and the delightful Victorian brewery (not open to the public. . . but be sure to have a glass of 'Hooky' in one of the inns serving this delectable local brew). Try to find time to walk eastwards to look at the great stone piers that once supported a long viaduct carrying the Banbury and Cheltenham Direct Railway across the valley here. From centre of **Hook Norton**, head north, first keeping church on immediate left. Keep straight out, and bear to left at edge of village. Over X-rds by the Gate Inn, and eventually enter **Sibford Ferris**, pleasant stone village, with large Quaker boarding school, and several elegant Georgian houses **(Link with Walk 4)**. Bear right at T-junction, and then left, down into valley, into Burdrop hamlet. Bishop's Blaize Inn up to right. Bear left beyond valley, and turn left in **Sibford Gower**, another attractive stone village, with an hospitable inn, the Wykeham Arms (noted for its cold buffets). Now drop down into deep valley of the infant Stour, and go straight, not left beyond farm.

Climb out of valley, and turn right at T-junction. Turn right at second T-junction,

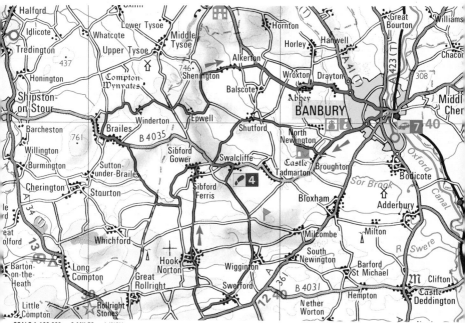

SCALE 1:190 080 or 3 MILES to 1 INCH

joining road that follows boundary between Warwickshire and Oxfordshire. Back into valley, crossing Stour again, at tree-shaded 'Traitor's Ford'. Bear left beyond ford, track heading straight up hill is Ditchedge Lane, continuing along county boundary, and making a fine walk, with views to left and right from ridge. After one mile fork right, leaving valley.

Turn left, with care, on to B4035. Keep through Lower Brailes on B4035, church with fine tower, known locally as the 'Cathedral of the Feldon', the Feldon being this richly agricultural part of south Warwickshire. **Brailes** was important market town in medieval times, and size of church bears this out. 'The George' on left. Turn right at T-junction before entering Upper Brailes. Impressive earthworks of long vanished castle up to left, another clue to Brailes's past importance (FP allows access to this). Turn right at X-rds, and then right again, at T-junction.

Enter minute hillside village of **Winderton**, with spired Victorian church up to left. Good views over to right of the 'Cathedral of the Feldon' (see Brailes above). FP's to Upper and Lower Brailes from here. Straight, not right, in **Winderton**. After half mile, turn right at T-junction. Up hill, good views over to right of Cotswolds beyond Stour valley. Over X-rds by the White House (ref: 34-40). Turn right at T-junction in valley (sign — Epwell). Enter tucked-away, stone and thatch village of **Epwell**, with Chandler's Arms serving Hook Norton ales. Turn left at T-junction by church. Bear right, and

through small ford, and turn left at T-junction at end of village.

Turn left at T-junction, and through countryside of small bumpy hills. Turn right at T-junction. Old airfield on left (noisy go-karts on some week-ends). Enter attractive village of **Shenington**, interesting church, wide green, and friendly inn, the Bell, noted for its bar meals. Good walks up valley to Temple Pool and **Upton House**. Into valley and through small neighbour, **Alkerton**. Fascinating sculptures on church. Over X-rds, signs of ironstone quarrying here. Bear right with care on to A422. Countryside to left , and later on both sides, lower than normal due to extensive ironstone quarrying.

Straight, not right by 17th century stone guide post on right, at entry to attractive Hornton stone and thatch village of **Wroxton**, and bear right just beyond. Go straight by duck-pond, keeping gates to Wroxton Abbey on immediate right, and Lord North Inn on left. Wroxton Abbey is fine 17th century mansion, enhanced by restored gardens and parkland. Bear up to left, pass church, which has elegant interior and go straight, not left, re-joining A422. Wroxton House Hotel and White Horse Inn back to left. Leave village on A422, keep on this through Drayton, neat village on outskirts of Banbury, with interesting little church (the contents of which includes the effigies of two 15th century knights), and an inn called the Roebuck. Return to **Banbury** on A422, turning right on to A41 at entry, thus completing Tour 7.

Tour 8
Banbury Villages and the Cherwell Valley

36 miles. Hilly.

Our route leads north from Banbury up the busy A41, and then across country to Cropredy in the Cherwell valley. Climbing out of the valley at Chipping Warden, the route then heads southwards, keeping mostly to high ground to the east of the Cherwell valley, and largely in the county of Northamptonshire. This is unspoilt country, despite its proximity to the busy modern town of Banbury, and several of the villages have considerable flavour. Through Kings Sutton with its glorious spire, and on southwards to trim and colourful Aynho, where we change direction again, heading across the Cherwell valley to Deddington, with its castle earthworks, and distant memories of market-town prosperity. Then through the Barfords, and north to Bloxham, another village with a fine spire, and so, northwards along the A361, to return to Banbury.

Leave **Banbury** northwards on A41 (the Warwick road). At one mile beyond end of houses, turn right at X-rds, off A41 (sign — Hanwell), and into **Hanwell**. This is a pretty ironstone village, with remains of large castle tucked away, to right of our road near church which has fascinating series of 14th century carvings. Valley beyond threatened by M40

King's Sutton ... 'one of the finest spires in all England'.

extension at time of writing. Turn left, with great care, on to A423, and soon turn right, off A423, to Great Bourton, small village on slopes of Cherwell valley, church largely Victorian. Good walk from here, down to **Oxford Canal**, and along towpath to **Cropredy**.

Keep straight down, through Great Bourton, to valley. Enter the full-of-character, canal-side village of **Cropredy (Link with Walk 3)**. Its bridge was site of Royalist victory during Civil War battle. Interesting Perpendicular church. At least two lively inns, and pretty towpath walks. Head north out of village (sign — Claydon), but after half mile, bear right at T-junction, and soon cross **Oxford Canal**. Stop here if possible, either to stand and stare, or to take a towpath walk. Gentle, haunted country beyond. Turn right twice in Appletree hamlet, and then for contrast, industrial estate on old airfield to left.

Turn left with great care, on to A361, in **Chipping Warden**, and almost immediately go straight, not left, leaving A361, and leaving village (but cross A361 to explore first). This is a pretty ironstone and thatch village, and has an interesting church looking out over its green. Walk from here, across the little Cherwell valley to **Edgcote**, where your 'driver' could pick you up later (see below). Leave village, and after one mile turn right at T-junction. Over bridge crossing the infant Cherwell, and immediately turn right. Bear left near handsome 18th century Edgcote House. But turn down right if you wish to visit church, with its fine selection of family monuments (see page 34). Bear left with great care, on to A361, by the Hare and Hounds Inn, **Wardington**. Elegant gateway on right, and turn left, with care, off A361 into quieter part of **Wardington (Link with Walk 3)**. This is a most attractive stone village, with a large church, and a series of lovely houses culminating in the superb manor house, restored partly by Clough Williams-Ellis, of Portmeirion fame. Turn left at end of 'Lower' Wardington, and manor house is then on left. Bear right in Upper Wardington. Plough Inn on left. Red Lion beyond on right. Caravan Club site at farm almost opposite. Now **turnabout** and beyond manor house, go straight, not right (sign — Chacombe), leaving village.

Bear left at Y-junction, straight not right at next Y-junction, and enter **Chacombe**, compact village with much modern building, a 17th and 18th century house called Chacombe Priory, an over-restored church, and an attractively signed inn, called the George and Dragon, serving good food. Turn left at T-junction (Priory over to right), and then bear right near George and Dragon **(Link to Walk 3)**, up to left, keeping most of village

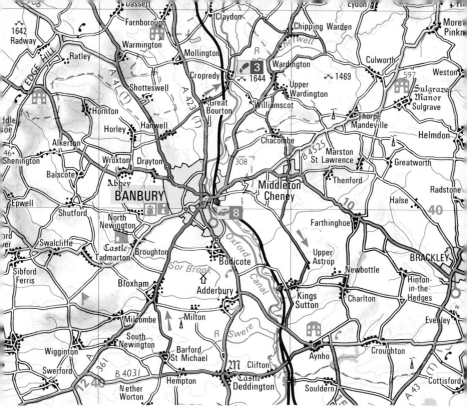

SCALE 1:190 080 or 3 MILES to 1 INCH

over to left. Bear right, and leave village. Cherwell Edge Golf Course on left. Over X-rds, crossing B4525, and enter **Middleton Cheney**, a large village with much modern building, but with a character of its own in the little streets close to its handsomely spired 14th and 15th century church. Do not miss the splendid series of pre-Raphaelite stained glass windows in the church.

Over X-rds with care in **Middleton Cheney**, crossing A422. After two miles, over disused railway line, and turn left at T-junction along straight road. Bear right at entry to Astrop (see **Kings Sutton**). Astrop House in park over to left. Pass replica of St Rumbald's Well. Bear right near entry to **Kings Sutton**, large village with much modern building. However there is a series of pleasant cottages and houses grouped around a little green near the church, which has one of the finest medieval spires in the country. Before reaching church, bear left, and then over small X-rds, heading south out of village.

Turn left with care, on to A41, and up hill into the beautifully neat village of **Aynho**, with its grass verges and flowering trees, its handsome mansion, its elegantly 18th century church interior, and its warm and welcoming Cartwright Arms. Turn right at top of hill in **Aynho**, on to B4031. Down into Cherwell valley, under railway bridge, over

second railway bridge and over canal. Through Clifton hamlet, and bear left into **Deddington**, busy village, with the earthworks of what was once a great medieval castle on our left. It was from here, in June 1312, that the unfortunate Piers Gaveston was abducted by the Earl of Warwick. (See page 37 for details of Gaveston's eventual demise.) Keep on B4031, past church on right, and over X-rds at traffic lights, crossing A423.

Keep on B4031, out of **Deddington**. Over X-rds at far end of stone and thatch hamlet of Hempton, keeping on B4031. Then turn right at next X-rds, off B4031, and drop down into **Barford St Michael**. Bear left in village to pass church, which has outstandingly fine Norman north doorway, and other items of interest. Bear left near end of village, and over little River Swere, into smaller village of Barford St John. Climb out of valley and try to ignore monster aerial array to right (after all, it is there for our protection). Beyond on right, entry to carpet factory, which has interesting retail shop usually open. Now bear right on to A361, into large village of **Bloxham**, and pass church, which has a splendid 14th century spire, fascinating carvings of about the same date, and a pre-Raphaelite east window. Go straight through village on a A361 and continue on this into **Banbury**, thus completing Tour 8.

Tour 9
Hornton Stone Country

35 miles. Hilly.

Our route heads north from Banbury on the A41 Warwick road for a short distance, and then leads off into hill country which has in its time provided both iron ore for the blast furnaces of South Wales, and building stone for great projects like Liverpool Cathedral. One of the attractive villages we pass has given its name to the toffee-coloured local building stone ... Hornton. Beyond Edge Hill, we drop down into lower country, but stone is still the predominant material in the villages here. Across this low country to the little Burton Dassett hills, with an unspoilt Country Park providing simple pleasures, and a fascinating church nearby. Then to Fenny Compton, and on to Wormleighton with its memories of the wealthy graziers who were to become the ancestors of Lady Diana, the Princess of Wales. Now briefly into Northamptonshire, and turning southwards across quiet canal countryside to Claydon , before visiting the National Trust's Farnborough Hall, and the delightful village of Warmington, beneath steep Deddington Hill. Returning through Shotteswell, we then head home to Banbury on the A41.

Leave **Banbury** on the A41 (Warwick road). After one mile beyond end of houses, turn left at small X-rds, leaving A41. Turn right at T-junction, and down steep hill into valley, with views of Horley ahead. Enter **Horley**, typical Hornton stone village, with Norman towered church poised at top of single street. Don't miss medieval wall painting of St Christopher in church. Bear left at top of village, and follow out on to ridge between two valleys. Route goes straight at next T-junction. (But turn left if you wish to explore **Hornton** village, site of the great quarries that gave their name to the local stone. Also see the medieval 'doom' wall painting in the church.)

Turn right on to A422 with great care. After short distance, turn right, off A422. But keep on A422 for a few yards if you wish to visit **Upton House**, entrance to which is on left **(link with Walk 6)**. This National Trust property is a William and Mary mansion with very attractive terraced gardens and lakes and a quite outstanding collection of porcelain and pictures, including works by Bosch, the Breughels, Holbein, Rembrandt, Van Dyke, Canaletto, Goya, El Greco, Tiepolo, Tintoretto, Constable, Stubbs, Hogarth, Reynolds, Romney and Sartorius. The inclusion of **Upton House** in both Tour 3 and

Tour 9 is evidence of its importance. Please do not pass it by.

Having turned right off A422, head towards **Edgehill** village, but go straight, not left at entry. Now pass stone quarry on left, and turn left at T-junction at entry to **Ratley**. (But turn right if you wish to explore **Ratley**, a pleasantly situated village in a south-facing hollow, with a largely Decorated style church.) Turn right at T-junction beyond our entry to **Ratley**, keeping Edge Hill woods on left **(link with Walk 6)**. FP down to **Radway** from this point. Bear left, down wooded hill, joining B4086. Just beyond wood, but while still on hill, turn sharp right, on to narrower road. Pass remains of light railway line (not very obvious), and through Arlescote hamlet. Handsome 17th century manor house, with little corner pavilions, on left. Several FP's lead from here. Nadbury Camp, a large prehistoric fort on hill well up to right, but on private ground.

Now on pleasant, partly open road, with good views of hill slopes to right. Over X-rds, crossing A41 with great care. Turn left at entry to pretty village of **Avon Dassett**. Victorian church contains interesting 13th century tomb. Area to south and east threatened by M40 extension, but until it comes, good FP to **Burton Dassett**. Up through village, and left at X-rds well beyond. Along ridge road with good views to right. Into

Wormleighton ... the gatehouse of Princess Diana's ancestors.

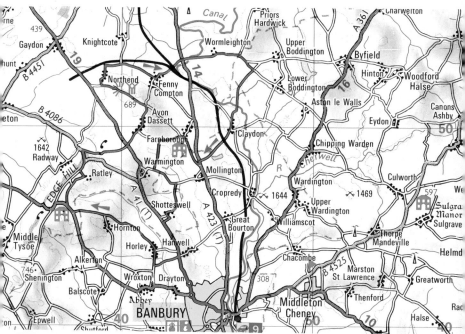

SCALE 1:190 080 or 3 MILES to 1 INCH

Burton Dassett Country Park area. Kite flying, walking, or simply relaxing. Best on winter weekdays. Don't miss **Burton Dassett** church, delightful setting, atmospheric medieval interior. Turn right beyond bottom of hill, and into Northend. Not of great interest. Bear right beyond end of village. Quiet road to left leads to Gaydon. Makes good winter walk, when fields too muddy.

Straight, not right, and straight not left, at T-junctions, and on to **Fenny Compton**, scattered Hornton stone village beneath the Burton Dassett hills. Bear left in village, unless you wish to visit church. Pass factory on right. Under railway line, then marina up to right (excellent shop at marina with good stock of canal and railway books). This is on the **Oxford Canal**. George and Dragon Inn up to right. Over off-set X-rds, crossing A423 with great care (sign — Wormleighton). Over bridge crossing Oxford Canal. Pleasant canal views down to left. Through **Wormleighton** village. But turn down left to look at church and old manor gatehouse. Ancestors of Lady Diana, the Princess of Wales, lived here. Interesting church, walks down across fields to canal.

Straight, not left at next T-junction. Then fork right, and soon turn right at X-rds (sign — Claydon). Pass 'Three Shires' on right. Meeting of Northamptonshire, Oxfordshire and Warwickshire over to right. Over course of old railway line (the East & West... once linked Towcester with Stratford-upon-Avon ... used largely for transport of ironstone to

South Wales). Now over **Oxford Canal**. Pleasant walks on towpath from here, especially south towards **Cropredy**. Keep straight into **Claydon**, and bear right beyond little church. After two miles, turn left with great care, on to A423, and almost immediately turn sharp right, off A423.

Straight, not right in delightful Hornton stone and thatch village of **Farnborough**, unless you wish to visit church and inn. Entrance to Farnborough Hall (N.T.) to left ... do not miss this ... elegant interiors, fine terrace walk. Bear left just beyond Hall entrance. Views of Hall to left, lake to right. Beyond lake and woods, turn left at T-junction, and along largely unfenced road (but beware, this is threatened by plans for M40 motorway extension). Slight views of temples and obelisk on terrace up to left.

Turn right at T-junction, and then bear left, up into charming village of **Warmington**. Large green with pond, overlooked by lovely Hornton stone houses. Interesting church poised above and beyond. Now re-trace route, bearing right, out of Warmington, back as far as T-junction, and go straight, not left. Turn right at next T-junction (sign — Shotteswell). Climb up to hillside village of Shotteswell. Fine wooden furnishings in church make visit here worthwhile. Good views out over valley. Motorway here still not certain at time of printing. Keep up through village, and turn left with great care, on to A41. Now head south to **Banbury** on A41, completing Tour 9.

95

Tour 10
Northamptonshire Border Country

28 miles. Reasonable for cyclists.

Our route heads eastwards from the little market town of Southam to Napton on the Hill, with its windmill and canal-side walks; then south-east, through Priors Marston and across the border into hilly Northamptonshire countryside, here dominated by the slender Post Office Tower. At Byfield we turn westwards, passing Boddington Reservoir nestling in its quiet pastoral valley, and through Upper Boddington before moving back into Warwickshire. Here we look westwards across secret countryside, depopulated by sheep graziers in the 16th century, and still largely deserted. Beyond Priors Hardwick, we cross the lovely Oxford Canal, heading home to Southam, along the lonely Welsh Road, once used by Welsh cattle drovers on their long haul to the London meat markets.

Start from **Southam** (41-62), small town to east of **Leamington Spa**. Leave **Southam** eastwards on the A425, Daventry road. Southam Zoo on left beyond end of town. After one and a half miles turn right, off A425. Over canal bridge by old brickworks. Napton windmill on hill to left. Enter the full-of- character village of **Napton on the Hill**.

Pleasant inns, good views from churchyard. To visit canal locks, turn right and right again, but otherwise keep straight through village, bearing left until reaching A425, when you turn right (sign — Daventry).

Along A425, crossing **Grand Union Canal** twice, and at entrance to **Lower Shuckburgh** turn right with care, on to gated road. (But go beyond and take first turn left if you wish to visit 'high-Victorian' church, or take a quieter look at the **Grand Union Canal**, which runs just to north of village.) Good walk south-eastwards along edge of Shuckburgh Park, and then south-westwards over Beacon Hill, scene of historic meeting before **Battle of Edgehill** (see page 34), to **Napton**. Now back on route, climbing gently away from A425, on gated road, with trees to right. Bear left at T-junction, and after two miles enter **Priors Marston**, attractive, largely unspoilt ironstone village. Into village centre, keeping church to left. Turn left by small stone monument on green, and up hill with 17th century Falcon Inn on left.

Turn left at X-rds (sign — Hellidon), then turn left at T-junction, and enter **Hellidon**, small stone village, where the River Leam rises. Church ruthlessly 'restored' by the Victorians. Leave village northwards on attractive gated road, and go through hamlets of **Lower Catesby** and **Upper Catesby**, but bear right at entry to **Upper Catesby**, and return through **Hellidon**. Note spoil heap and air shafts of large tunnel that carried the long vanished Great Central Railway beneath these quiet hills. Leave

SCALE 1:190 080 or 3 MILES to 1 INCH

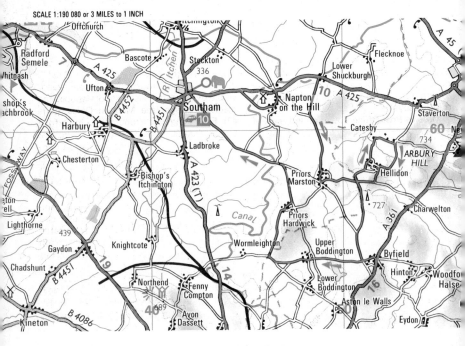

'Canal-side England at its best' ... the Oxford Canal at Napton on the Hill.

Hellidon southwards, keeping windmill to left. At T-junction (marked 179 on map), turn right, and then turn left at X-rds (completing the small circle that has taken in Hellidon and the Catesbys).

Massive Post Office Tower on left, part of a chain of microwave radio communication towers linking Britain's major cities, and a major landmark in this area. Bear left at Y-junction on to wider road (marked 'Iron Cross' on map, but no cross visible). Turn right at X-rds at entry to **Byfield**. (But turn left if you wish to visit large village of **Byfield**, with its fine assortment of old stone houses, and little tree-shaded greens.) Into valley, with attractive **Boddington Reservoir** to left. This feeder for the **Oxford Canal** is especially colourful at weekends, with sailing dinghies much in evidence.

Keep straight through pretty hillside village of **Upper Boddington** on wider road, but bear left by Plough Inn if you wish to visit church. Well beyond village, bear right twice, and then turn right at T-junction beyond wood on right (sign — Priors Hardwick). After one mile, moated Stoneton Manor visible over to left. This is site of depopulated medieval village (see Marston Doles, page 47). FP leading past Stoneton, on to **Oxford Canal**, leaves road diagonally left, quarter mile beyond. Beyond entry to **Priors Hardwick**, straight, not right, and pass small green, with attractive Butcher's Arms to left and church to right. Good walks from here, making part use of canal towpath.

Turn left beyond **Priors Hardwick**, and after two miles, bear left on to wider road (this is the Welsh Road, used by Welsh cattle drovers, taking their cattle to the London markets). Over **Oxford Canal** at **Marston Doles**. Lock to left is the last one between here and **Claydon**, and the start of the **Oxford Canal's** long summit level. Now head north-westwards along the Welsh Road, to return to **Southam**, completing Tour 10.

Tour 11
The Leam Valley and Blue Lias Country.

32 miles. Reasonable for cyclists.

Our route heads east out of Leamington Spa, and then turns north-east up the valley of the River Leam, through villages surpisingly remote from the nearby spa town which we have just left. We turn again at Weston-under-Wetherley, making use, beyond Eath-orpe, of a short stretch of the Roman's mighty Foss Way, before following the Leam eastwards as far as delightful Leamington Hastings. We now head south-westwards through blue-lias country, with canal-side inns and a large cement works much in evidence, and on past woodlands, to the large and attractive village of Harbury. Now to Chesterton, a hamlet with memories, mills and wildfowl, and beyond, into bumpy, wooded country through pretty Lighthorne and Moreton Morrell, to return northwards to Leamington Spa.

Leave **Leamington Spa** on the A425, Southam road, and cross the **Grand Union Canal** by old brewery at the entry to Radford Semele. Church down to left, not of outstanding interest. Fork left, off A425 in village, and after half mile re-cross **Grand Union Canal**. Fork left by woods, and bear left at T-junction by **Offchurch** church ... Norman origins, interesting associations. Turn right at junction, hospitable Stag's Head Inn on right. Bear left at T-junction, at end of village, on to smaller road (sign —

Hunningham). Occasional glimpses of River Leam over to left.

Bear left at entry to minute village of Hunningham. Church and River Leam to left. Bear left, and bear left again on to wider road, and over stout medieval bridge crossing River Leam. Straight, not left, joining B4453, at entry to Weston-under-Wetherley. Turn right, keeping on B4453 (Sign — Rugby), and after half mile, fork right with care, off B4453 (Sign- Wappenbury). Through little village of **Wappenbury** ... interesting Iron Age and Roman associations ... over-restored church, and small R.C. chapel, possibly the work of Pugin, one of the architects of the House of Commons.

Beyond **Wappenbury**, over River Leam by weir, and bear left twice in Eathorpe, on to the **Foss Way**, Roman road which once ran from Lincoln to Exeter. After half mile, over River Leam, and then turn right with care, on to minor road. Now turn right with care on to the busy A423 (sign — Southam). Over River Leam yet again, and into **Marton**. Turn left off A423 in village (sign — Birdingbury). (But stop here if you wish to visit the Museum of Country Bygones in Louisa Ward Close.) Fine medieval bridge crosses River Itchen, just to west of village ... walk to visit this.

Over main X-rds in Birdingbury (but turn left if you wish to visit village). **(Link with Walk 2.)** Straight, not right at end of village, and on to **Leamington Hastings**, delightful village, with 17th century almshouses, and an interesting church **(link with Walk 2)**. Well beyond village, turn right with great care on to A426. Now keep on A426 for over three miles. Over **Grand Union Canal** by the lively Boat Inn **(link with Walk 2)**, and then turn

Wappenbury Church.

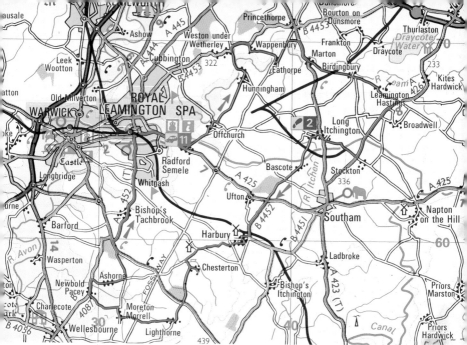

SCALE 1:190 080 or 3 MILES to 1 INCH

right at next X-rds, off A426. Re-cross **Grand Union Canal** by the ever popular Blue Lias Inn, an outstanding canal-side pub at the eastern end of a long flight of locks (**link with Walk 2**). Stop here to look at locks, and perhaps even lend a hand with some lock-work ... its all good for the thirst.

Into **Long Itchington**, bear right with care on to A423, and almost immediately bear left, leaving A423, close to attractive pond (**link with Walk 2**). Fork left near the Buck and Bell Inn, church soon on left ... worth visiting. Bear left beyond church, and over Grand Union yet again. Through Bascote hamlet. Over X-rds, and pass Fox and Hen on left. This is **Bascote Heath**, site of the first skirmish in the Civil War, 23rd August 1642. Through attractive woodlands, and over A425, with great care, joining B4452 (sign — Harbury).

Turn right, off B4452, at entry to **Harbury** ... a large village with a real country flavour and a bewildering pattern of streets (we hope you find your way out eventually). Bear left by church and immediately turn right at T-junction. Bear left by windmill, and then bear right soon after (yes, it is rather complex). Now go straight, not left, at T-junction, and leave village south-westwards. After one mile, bear right at Y-junction, and then turn left at T-junction. Small parking space here. to allow walk across field to the unique and beautiful **Chesterton** windmill.

Drop down small hill, with glimpse to left of **Chesterton** watermill, with its elegantly pedimented doorway, and its reed- bordered

mill pool. Turn left, and then bear left at Chesterton Green hamlet. Arrive at **Chesterton** church, and pool with wildfowl. Visit interesting church and possibly walk beyond. Then **turnabout** and bear left in Chesterton Green. Pleasantly open road beyond may unfortunately be affected by the M40 motor-way extension. Over X-rds with very great care, crossing A41. Into charming village of **Lighthorne** in a small hollow. Bear right by green in centre (Antelope Inn up to left). Church up to right at end of village is largely Victorian.

Over X-rds with great care, crossing the unclassified, but over-busy **Foss Way**, and turn right in **Moreton Morrell** (but turn left if you wish to visit the unspoilt church and/or the Sea Horse Inn). Royal tennis played in this village. At bottom of village, turn left at T-junction, and then bear right in hamlet of **Newbold Pacey**, on to B4087. Victorian church with interesting interior, pond by road junction. Over Woozeley Bridge, and turn right at T-junction off B4087 (sign — Ashorne). Through unspoilt hamlet of Ashorne, and turn left at X-rds.

Through wooded area, past gates to Ashorne Hill College, and bear left with care on to A41. Woods on left. Turn right with care on to A452 (sign — Leamington). Through **Bishop's Tachbrook**. Church up road to left contains interesting memorials, including one to author and poet, Walter Savage Landor, whose family home was here. Now move to **Leamington Spa** on A452, completing Tour 11.

Walks

Walk 1
The Hatton Flight . . . a Canalside Exploration.

Allow two hours.

This walk takes us beside the attractive Grand Union Canal, as it drops down into the Avon valley towards Warwick, through a long series of locks, known as the 'Hatton Flight'. Leaving the canal the walk loops round through largely unspoilt country, passing the pleasant, partly Norman church of Budbrooke. From here it passes over more open farming country before returning to the canal to complete its circle. This makes an ideal 'family walk'.

(A) Start from the vicinity of the British Waterways maintenance yard (24-66) which lies to the south of the A41, about two miles east of **Warwick**, in the parish of **Hatton**. (This can easily be reached from **Tour 2.**) Walk east, along the tow path on the north bank of the Grand Union Canal. Start to drop down into the Avon valley beside a long flight of locks (the Hatton Flight).

(B) After about a mile and a half, leave the canal at the third bridge (No. 53), which is on a sharp bend. Cross this road bridge and follow road for short distance. On sharp left hand bend, go through gateway on right (yellow FP arrow). After fifty yards, go over stile into field, and head for far left hand corner.

Go left through bridge under railway, and then head for top right hand corner in next field. Now over stile and head for Budbrooke church (this has Norman origins and handsome 18th century monument to Baron Dormer.) Through churchyard, and turn left on to road.

(C) After about fifteen yards turn right up track leading towards Church Farm. Now follow yellow FP arrows keeping to right-of-way.Turn right on to road, and eventually when road turns sharp right, **(D)**, go straight ahead up Budbrooke Farm track. Follow track right up to large yard close to farmhouse. Now turn right, over a gate, straight up beside hedge, and through gate into next field.

(E) Walk down field and cross bridge over stream. Follow right-of-way across next three fields, leading to pedestrian crossing of railway, and follow path leading back to the vicinity of the British Waterways maintenance yard **(A)**, thus completing the walk. The attractive Waterman Inn is situated on the A41 a short distance to the west of this point.

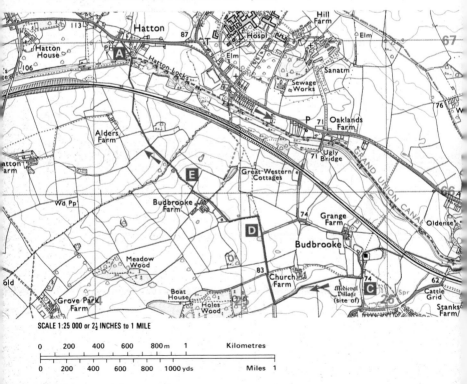

SCALE 1:25 000 or 2½ INCHES to 1 MILE

Locks on the Hatton Flight of the Grand Union Canal.

Walk 2
Blue Lias Country and the Stockton Flight.

Allow four hours. Wear stout boots or wellies.

This walk runs northwards across the fields from Long Itchington, to the village of Birdingbury, and then turns south-east, parallel with the River Leam, along a minor road to the charming village of Leamington Hastings. Southwards across country from here, to join the A426 for a short walk to the Grand Union Canal, where we follow the tow path beside the long Stockton flight of locks, before returning to Long Itchington. Several thirst quenching inns in the latter stages of the walk.

(A) Start from the village of **Long Itchington** (41-65), which is situated about six miles east of **Leamington Spa**, and which is on **Tour 11**. Walk north out of village, along A423. Turn right, off road, through gate opposite bus stop, along track. Turn right near Marton Road Farm, then turn left to walk across field. Now head N.N.E. across open country, keeping hedge and fence line on immediate left. Course of path not evident.

(B) When Debdale Woods are over to right, and ahead, bear left (north), across corner of field, and then bear right (N.N.E.), keeping Davenport Farm well over to left. Path not evident, but keep heading N.N.E. until reaching road. Now bear right, and go into Birdingbury.

(C) Over X-rds by war memorial in Birdingbury (sign — Frankton). Turn right, down road, just before bus stop. Leave road at corner by going straight, over stile and into farmyard, keeping to left of farm buildings. Through gate into field. Head S.W. across fields, to turn left on to road near stream on left. Now follow road into **Leamington Hastings**.

(D) Bear sharp right in village, and keep on road past church. Go straight, not left, leaving road at sharp bend. Now on track, past farm buildings. Head south across open

Village pond, Long Itchington.

country, keeping hedge and fence line on immediate right. Field House Farm well over to right. Join road at bend and then leave it at next bend, still heading south, on track. Walk through Malvern Hall farmyard, between house and barn. Over white fencing and through gate on opposite side of field.

(E) Turn right **with great care**, on to A426. Turn right at X-rds by canal bridge (but go just over bridge if you wish to visit the Boat Inn). Now turn left to follow **Grand Union Canal** tow path westwards. Pass long series of locks, the Stockton Flight, and beyond this, (F) the Blue Lias Inn. Now follow tow path to the Two Boats Inn, and turn right **with great care** on to A423, to return to centre of **Long Itchington (A)**, thus completing our walk.

SCALE 1:25 000 or 2½ INCHES to 1 MILE

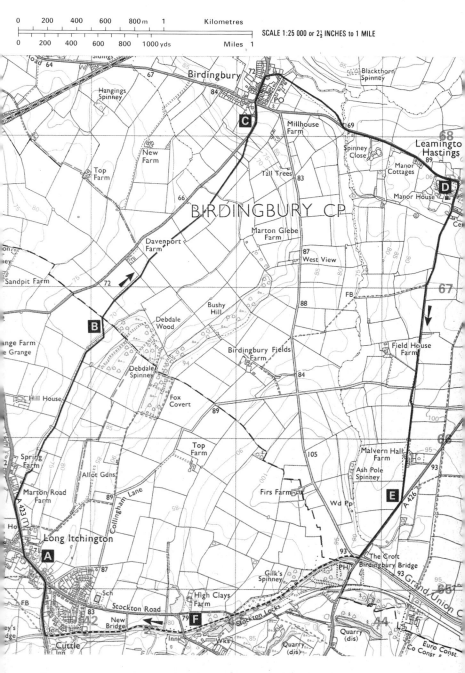

Walk 3
Cherwell Valley Country.

Allow two and a half hours.

This walk sets out eastwards from Cropredy, across the Oxford Canal and the River Cherwell, to the delightful village of Wardington, with its fine church and beautifully restored manor house, and with no fewer than three inns. From here it heads south across the fields, to Chacombe, and then north-west to Williamscot hamlet. More roads are used for this section of the walk than normally, due to paths being difficult to follow in places, but the roads will be found to be reasonably quiet, apart from the short length of the A361, where reasonable care should be exercised. Looping round to join the Oxford Canal near Bourton House, it then concludes by using the towpath, northwards to Cropredy, passing close to the bridge that gave its name to one of the Civil War's smaller, but most bitter encounters, the Battle of Cropredy Bridge (see page 33).

(A) Start from the charming canal-side village of **Cropredy** (46-46), which is situated some four miles north of Banbury, and which is on **Tour 8.** Leave the church and Red Lion Inn, and walk eastwards, crossing a small bridge over the attractive Oxford Canal, then turning left following sign to Prescote, on a small road northwards, parallel with the canal. Bend round to right, following road, until arriving near buildings, and now go straight ahead, leaving road which turns to left.

(B) Over cattle-grid, and after about 100 yards, over small footbridge crossing stream (the Cherwell). Now head for gateway ahead left. Through gate and head across fields following right-of-way, and aiming for a strip of woodland. Over 'cross-road' of tracks near corner of wood and head on towards road.

(C) Bear right with care, on to the busy A361. Bear right again, keeping on A361 by Hare and Hounds Inn at entry to **Wardington**. Take next turn left, following sign to Upper Wardington. Keep on road past church and school, and eventually turn left at T-junction, following sign to Upper Wardington. Keep on road past beautiful Wardington Manor, into Upper Wardington. Pass Plough Inn on left, Red Lion Inn on right.

(D) Near end of village, turn right off road, through small iron gate opposite gap between third and fourth houses in row on left. Now head S.S.W. across fields, eventually dropping down into valley. Go beneath old railway embankment, and cross over

Cropredy ... 'a canal-side village of great character'.

104

small stream. Up out of valley and arrive at northern edge of **Chacombe**. Keep to immediate left of fence-line in field adjoining church, and...

(E) Arrive at gate which has FP sign pointing north-west. Go south on road if you wish to visit George and Dragon Inn, but otherwise follow sign and head north-west across field. Note mounds of possible moated site in field. 14th century church is worth visiting. Over stream and turn right on to road by modern farmhouse (Glen Meadows Farm). Up road out of valley and then bear left at Y-junction, keeping on road.

(F) Turn right on to the busy A361, and walk with great care. After about 200 yards, turn left, and follow minor road into pretty Williamscot hamlet. Turn left at T-junction, and through the rest of Williamscot, noting minute early 19th century lodge to Williamscot House, and many pleasant, creeper-covered old houses.

(G) About half a mile beyond Williamscot, turn left off road where small power line crosses it, and head south-west down across field. Over river Cherwell, and then turn right on to canal tow-path, near Bourton House. Now follow tow-path northwards to complete walk at the bridge close to the Red Lion, **Cropredy (A)**.

Walk 4

Oxfordshire Cotswolds and a Roman Road.

Allow two and a half hours.

This walk runs south from Swalcliffe, along a very minor road, and then heads over open upland country. It runs westwards, briefly beside the infant River Stour, before going north up a side valley, and up over high ground to Sibford Ferris, and neighbouring Burdrop. From here it goes east and north, and then runs eastwards along the course of a Roman road. Finally, beneath the shadow of an Iron Age hill fort, it drops down into a valley to return to Swalcliffe.

(A) Start from the small stone village of **Swalcliffe** (37-30), which lies on the B4035 between **Banbury** and **Shipston-on-Stour**, and which is on **Tour 7**. Walk west on B 4035, keeping church on right. Turn down

High summer near Sibford Ferris ... 'the Oxfordshire Cotswolds at their best'.

small road to left just beyond petrol station on left and tithe barn on right. Turn left at T-junction by Swalcliffe Grange Farm, and follow FP sign to right immediately beyond, on to track.

(B) Follow track over open fields, then drop into valley and into wooded area. On reaching stream (the infant Stour), turn right and walk along north (right) side of it. After about half a mile, take left hand fork by gap and jump tributary stream. Turn right and follow edge of field. Through wooden gate, and follow undergrowth path through wood. Through gate into field, and keep hedge on left, heading for gate at top right-hand corner.

(C) Through gate and follow track towards Sibford Grounds farm. Just before reaching farm buildings, follow track to right, keeping to right-of-way marked on map, skirting to right of buildings. Now head directly towards school. Half way along fence at top of field,

go through gate, and over to a path up to right by greenhouses. Follow right-of-way carefully through school grounds and arrive at cross roads in **Sibford Ferris** village.

(D) Go over cross roads, following road signed 'Burdrop'. Drop into valley, take first right, and pass the Bishop's Blaize Inn. Turn right at T-junction, and follow road out of Burdrop. (But turn left if you wish to visit **Sibford Gower** and the Wykeham Arms). Now turn right with care on to B4035, and after about fifty yards turn left off it, following sign marked 'Shutford'.

(E) After about 1.5 miles, through small valley, and after climbing beyond, take well defined track to right. This follows course of Roman road (see **Epwell**, page 35). Follow track with view up to left of **Madmarston Hill** (Iron Age hill fort). Turn sharp right near Swalcliffe Mill, and follow small road back into **Swalcliffe**, completing Walk 4 **(A)**. The Stag's Head Inn not far away.

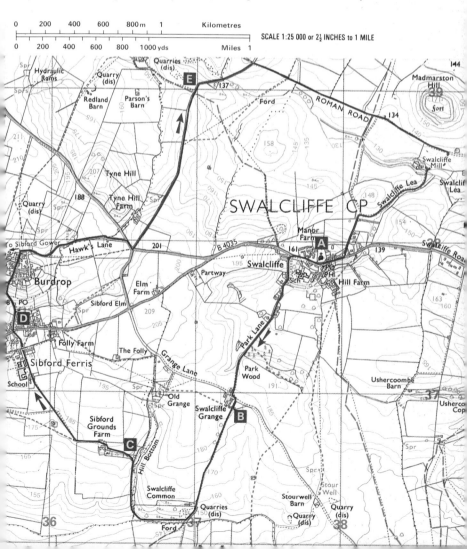

SCALE 1:25 000 or 2½ INCHES to 1 MILE

Walk 5

Dovedale and the High Wolds

Allow three hours

This walk takes us from Blockley, up a long wooded track, and emerges on to the busy A44 and A424, which we unfortunately have to use for a short while. We then drop down into a valley, and climb up again beside woodlands on to typical high Cotswold country. Turning north, we cross a minor road in a deep, wooded valley, and then up on to the wolds again, crossing the A44, before returning down a long track to Blockley.

(A) Start from the delightful village of **Blockley** (16-34), which lies to the south of

Chipping Campden, and which is on **Tour 5**, and **Tour 6.** Walk south-west along main street, past Crown Inn and 'No Through Road' sign. Russell Spring on right, inscription reads *'Water from the living rock, God's precious gift to Man'*. At FP sign straight ahead.

Follow track into wooded area, pass pumping station and through gate (**please fasten**). Now in thick deciduous woods. Stream on left. Up track, passing warning signs, and around corner. Coniferous plantation on left. Follow track up hill, beech trees now on both sides.

(B) Emerge on A44 and cross with great care near Trooper's Lodge Service Station, at same time, turning left to face oncoming traffic. Bear right beyond Service Station, on to A424, signed Stow. Take care of oncoming traffic. Over first (diagonal) X-rds, and then turn right at next X-rds. Fine views ahead.

Climbing roses and mellow stone, at Blockley.

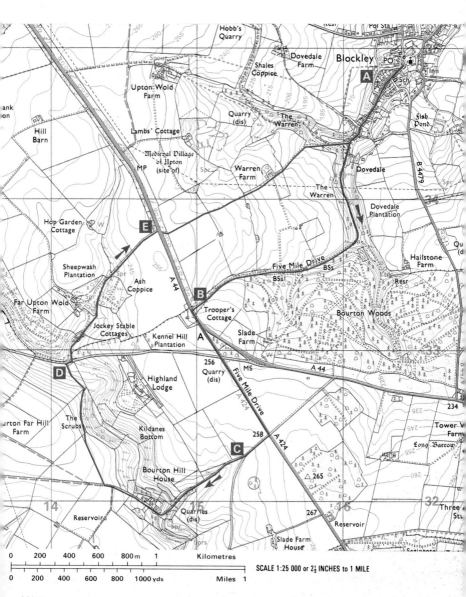

(C) Turn right, down drive marked 'Bourton Hill Farm'. Pass farmhouse, and then outbuildings, on up hill to top. Through gate and follow track ahead, not left. Go 100 yds then turn right, through small gate, and along upper edge of field. 'Highland Lodge' now visible to right. Through gate into next field, head towards bottom right-hand corner, through small coppice and along track to gate. Through gate and turn left , then head towards road, which is now visible.

(D) Through gate, and cross road by pond. Follow driveway signed to Far Upton Wold. Past derelict cottages, over cattle-grid, and follow road for 100 yds. Then turn right into field, jump stream, and follow path around

fenced-off shrubbery until reaching wooden gate. Through gate and follow wall along edge of field, aiming for gate immediately ahead. Through this and next gate opposite. Now follow grassy track up hill keeping fence to left. Through gate at end of field and turn right **with very great care**, on to A44.

(E) Cross A44 and turn left off it after only 10 yds, following exact direction of FP sign, going over gate and through small spinney. Straight across field, join clearly marked track, and follow it down hill. **Blockley** now visible ahead. Pass Warren Farm, continue down track through wooded area. Turn left on to **Blockley** main street, and complete walk near the Crown Inn. **(A)**.

Walk 6
Edge Hill and the Sanderson-Miller Country.

Allow three hours for full version, one hour for short version.

This walk starts from Radway and heads south-eastwards, and then south-westwards, up through woods to the Castle Inn, in Edgehill village. From here it runs across country, joining the Oxfordshire border near Uplands Farm. It then soon heads westwards, past Upton House, and partly uses the busy A422 road until reaching the top of Sunrising Hill. From this point it runs along the top of the thickly wooded scarp, and then, just below the Castle Inn, it turns north-westwards to drop back down through the fields into Radway, with fine views of Sanderson Miller's Grange in its well wooded park.

(A) Start from **Radway** (37-48), which is seven miles north-west of **Banbury**, and which is on **Tour 3**. Walk just to east of T-junction by bus stop and 'Village Stores', and then turn right up track to immediate right of Grafton Cottage. Through gate beyond allotments, and up long field towards woods. Fine views back over **Radway**. Through gate into woods, and turn right on to well defined path. Views of Radway Grange soon down to right. After about 50 yards, bear left and climb up rough path.

(B) Straight not right, just before Castle Inn (Edgehill Tower), but turn right if you wish to take 'short walk', by going down steep path to link with point **F** (see below). If you are taking the 'long walk', pass Castle Inn and turn left, and left again, up on to road in **Edgehill** village. Then cross road and turn right ,off it, at far end of small garage forecourt. (FP sign visible at back.)

Follow narrow path, first between stone walls, and then along spit of land between two depressions caused by past quarrying. Turn right on to road, quarry offices and yard

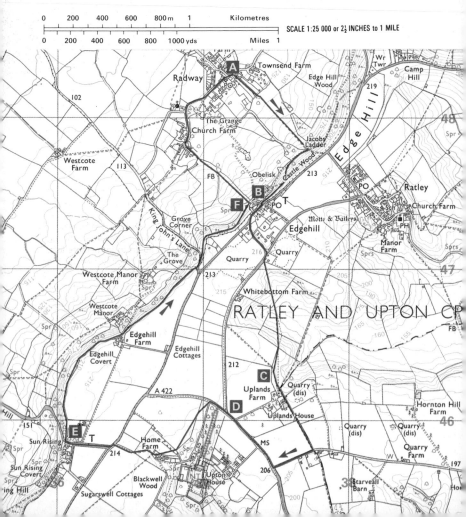

The church at Radway ... Sanderson Miller's village.

to right. Straight, not right, joining busier road, and almost immediately turn off left beyond stone bungalow (FP sign). Climb fence and head diagonally (south) across large field, into valley bottom. Up hill, on well defined track, and walk diagonally left at end of fence on left, heading for Uplands Farm.

(C) Arrive at Uplands Farm buildings, and keep to immediate left of them. Now following Warwickshire/Oxfordshire border. Walk parallel with power line as far as road, and then turn right, on to road by cottage. Turn right, with care, on to A422 (sign — Stratford).

(D) Straight, not right, keeping on A422. Entrance to **Upton House** (NT) on left. If clothes and footwear too rugged for house, why not visit garden? Immediately beyond Upton park wall turn left into driveway marked 'Home Farm', and immediately turn diagonally right, and head almost parallel with driveway to left.

Through two gates passing through end of long thin spinney, and head just to right of Home Farm farmhouse. Climb slight bank beyond farm, up track and turn right beyond gate. Keep to track on immediate left of wall, and turn left with care on to A422. Almost immediately bear right, keeping on A422. Layby and phone box on right.

(E) At top of Sun Rising Hill, turn right, off

road with great care (fast traffic coming up hill), into woods opposite house. Path may not be signed, and in summer it may be overgrown, but persevere, as it becomes clearer after short distance. Keep heading along path through woods, just above scarp face to left. Pass FP sign in woods. Over stile and then pass to left of Edgehill Farm. Bear left down driveway, between pillars marked Westcote Manor, and almost immediately fork right, up path by electricity pole with FP sign. Climb gradually upwards through woods, with scarp again to immediate left.

Bear left on to wider track known as King John's Lane, (could link to road by turning right), and then fork up right on to path with line of beech trees to right. Now follow path through woods, first along top of scarp, but later dropping down a little to turn left at bottom of path **(F)** leading down from Castle Inn, **Edgehill**, which the 'short walkers' will have reached from the Castle Inn at **(B)**.

Now through gate, and walk down fields, with views of Radway Grange and its park, to right. Through gate beyond fields, down track, and bear right by pond in **Radway** village green. Pass Radway Grange on right, with attractive pools, and bear right on to wider road, with church over to left. Now walk to T-junction by 'Village Stores', **Radway (A)**, completing Walk 6.

Walk 7

Combrook and some Capability Brown Country.

Allow two hours for full version, one hour for short version.

This walk starts from Combrook, heading northwards beside the shore of a well wooded lake, created by Capability Brown, as part of the Compton Verney parklands. After using a very short section of B4086, it again heads north, behind the mansion of Compton Verney, and eventually turns south, down the other side of the valley, cutting through woods on the edge of the Compton Verney estate, where there is another lake. Now over B4086, across a field and through further woods to return to Combrook.

Combrook ... 'a mellow village in a quiet valley'.

(A) Start from the attractive little tucked-away village of **Combrook**, which is seven miles east of **Stratford-upon- Avon**, and which is on **Tour 3**. From centre of village walk down little road keeping church on right. Beyond Victorian well-head on right, and just before Peregrine Cottage on left, turn down small path to left. Through small gate, over stream, and bear half right across field, with views of lake and dam over to right.

Through small gate marked 'Park Farm, Bridle Path', and on well-defined path through woodlands with glimpses of lake down to right. Through gate into field with trees, heading slightly left. Over small stile following bridleway sign, and keep to immediate left of fence-line. Through gate and bear right on to surfaced driveway by modern farm cottages. Now on Park Farm driveway.

(B) Turn left at end of Park Farm drive on to B4086, and walk beside road up hill. (But turn right on to B4086, follow between the

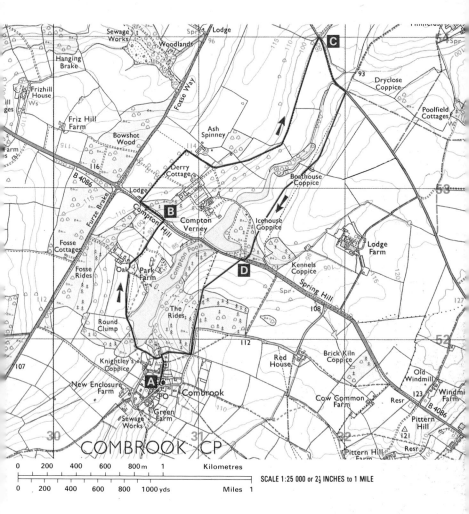

```
0    200   400   600   800m   1
                                        Kilometres
0    200   400   600   800   1000 yds          Miles   1

                              SCALE 1:25 000 or 2½ INCHES to 1 MILE
```

two lakes and turn right at point **(D)**, to cross field, if you wish to follow the 'short walk', see below.) Turn right at top of hill, through stone gate-posts beside old lodge, and on to farm track. Straight over 'cross roads' by small brick building to right, and then follow track as it bends to right, keeping modern farm building on left. Keep on track through small cast iron gate-posts, and then fork left, still on well defined track. Good views of lake, back down to right. Follow track for about a mile, and then ....

(C) Turn right on to road, by T-junction. Walk down road, and cross bridge over small stream (the one used by Capability Brown to feed his lakes). Turn right, off road, and walk parallel with, but well above stream. Through gap in hedge at end of long field, and then head across next field towards approximate centre of line of fir trees at far end. Views of **Compton Verney** (house) and bridge over to right. Over small stile and into rather dense wood known as Icehouse Coppice (no ice-house visible), and join B4086 road at point where driveway goes through fine wrought-iron gates.

(D) Over B4086 (this is where those taking the 'short walk', will join the route, having walked along the B4086 from the end of the Park Farm drive at Point **(B)**) and head diagonally across field, towards point just to left of where line of woods starts to curve inwards. Through gate at this point, and along well defined path through woods. At end of path bear left to join road, and turn right on to road. At end of wood on right, follow FP sign to right, and go through small gate into field. Keep to right hand side of field with good views of **Combrook** in valley, and at bottom over small stile on to path leading between two gardens **(garden on left has modern house with low pitched roof)**. Turn left on to road, pass Victorian well-head on left and complete Walk 7 by arriving at **Combrook** church, **(A)**.

Walk 8

Two Glorious Gardens, and the Cotswold Edge.

Allow two hours.

This walk starts from the village of Mickleton, and climbs the wooded slopes of the Cotswolds, beneath the lovely gardens of Kiftsgate Court. It then passes the even better known Hidcote Garden, and heads on upwards to the high country still known as Ilmington Downs. Now drop down across country, to the flower-filled hamlet of Hidcote Boyce, and then beside an orchard before crossing a stream which runs south, eventually to join larger tributaries of the distant Thames. Heading north through attractive woodlands, the walk then descends into the valley to return to Mickleton, the spire of its church acting as a fine landmark.

(A) Start from the village of **Mickleton** (16-43) which lies on the A46, seven miles south-south-west of **Stratford-upon-Avon**, and which is on **Tour 5**. Start from the vicinity of Mickleton church, which is situated on a side road to the south-west of the A46. Go through gate to left of entrance to 'new' cemetery, and walk around its wall. Then go through left hand of two gates, and walk straight up next field. **Kiftsgate Court** now visible up to left. Follow path up valley to reach road at top of hill by **Kiftsgate**

Court lodge. Do not miss a visit to gardens, if open.

(B) Go straight over road, and up wooded road towards **Hidcote Manor Garden**. Walk straight through car park (but walk to right if you wish to visit gardens, which should not be missed). Follow track straight up hill, pausing more than once, if not to catch one's breath, to take in the magnificent sweeping views. Take a turn to right and left, before reaching small road junction by TV transmitter. The hardest part of the walk is now completed!

(C) Turn right on to small road by TV transmitter, and after about 500 yards bear right again, on to wider road, but immediately turn right through gateway, and walk down to immediate left of wall. Into next field and walk just to right of small barn. Now walk down to join track leading to pretty hamlet of **Hidcote Boyce**. Walk down through hamlet, and at T-junction cross road and go straight through gate.

(D) At end of orchard and vegetable garden, turn right, and then turn left, following down field towards FP sign at far side. By FP sign, over bridge crossing small stream. Now up next field on left side of hedge, and then walk down track by right hand side of dutch barn, and...

(E) Turn right following FP signed 'Mickleton'. Follow path through woods for some distance, and then bear left into field, and head for gate over to left. Go through gate and down, over road, and into field opposite. Now follow path down to **Mickleton** church **(A)**, completing walk. Two inns and an hotel all within easy reach of here.

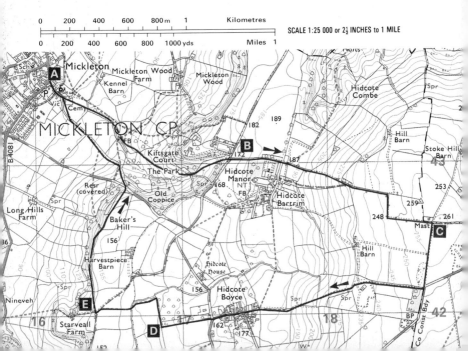

SCALE 1:25 000 or 2½ INCHES to 1 MILE

Hidcote Manor Garden.

CONVENTIONAL SIGNS

1:190 080 or 1 INCH to 3 MILES

ROADS

Not necessarily rights of way

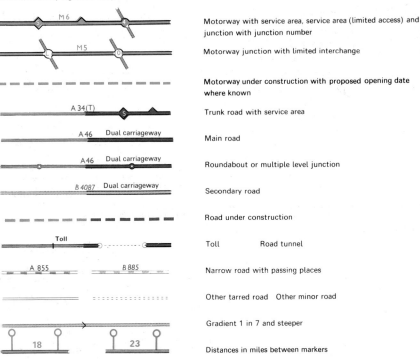

Motorway with service area, service area (limited access) and junction with junction number

Motorway junction with limited interchange

Motorway under construction with proposed opening date where known

Trunk road with service area

Main road

Roundabout or multiple level junction

Secondary road

Road under construction

Toll   Road tunnel

Narrow road with passing places

Other tarred road   Other minor road

Gradient 1 in 7 and steeper

Distances in miles between markers

The representation of a road is no evidence of the existence of a right of way

PRIMARY ROUTES

These form a national network of recommended through routes which complement the motorway system.
Selected places of major traffic importance are known as Primary Route Destinations and are shown thus **BANBURY**
Distances and directions to such destinations are repeated on traffic signs which, on primary routes, have a green background or, on motorways, have a blue background.
To continue on a primary route through or past a place which has appeared as a destination on previous signs, follow the directions to the next primary destination shown on the green-backed signs.

RAILWAYS

Standard gauge track

Narrow gauge track

Tunnel

Road crossing under or over

Level crossing

Station

WATER FEATURES

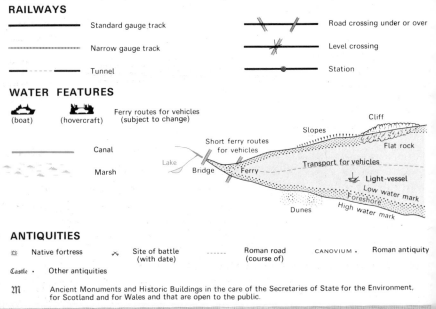

(boat)   (hovercraft)   Ferry routes for vehicles (subject to change)

Canal

Marsh

Lake   Bridge   Ferry   Short ferry routes for vehicles

Cliff

Slopes

Flat rock

Transport for vehicles

Light-vessel

Low water mark

Foreshore

High water mark

Dunes

ANTIQUITIES

☼ Native fortress   ✕ Site of battle (with date)   ------ Roman road (course of)   CANOVIUM · Roman antiquity

Castle ·   Other antiquities

ⅿ   Ancient Monuments and Historic Buildings in the care of the Secretaries of State for the Environment, for Scotland and for Wales and that are open to the public.

CONVENTIONAL SIGNS
1:25 000 or 2½ INCHES to 1 MILE

ROADS AND PATHS

Not necessarily rights of way

M I or A 6 (M)	Motorway
A 31 (T)	Trunk road
A 35	Main road
B 3074	Secondary road
A 35	Dual carriageway
	Road generally more than 4m wide
	Road generally less than 4m wide
	Other road, drive or track

Narrow roads with passing places are annotated

Unfenced roads and tracks are shown by pecked lines

.... Path

RAILWAYS

	Multiple track } Standard gauge
	Single track
	Narrow gauge
	Siding
	Cutting
	Embankment
	Tunnel
	Road over & under
	Level crossing; station

PUBLIC RIGHTS OF WAY

Public rights of way may not be evident on the ground

} Public paths { Footpath / Bridleway

+ + + + + Byway open to all traffic

Road used as a public path

The indication of a towpath in this book does not necessarily imply a public right of way
The representation of any other road, track or path is no evidence of the existence of a right of way

DANGER AREA
MOD ranges in the area
Danger!
Observe warning notices

BOUNDARIES

— · — · — · —	County (England and Wales)
— — — — —	District
⚬—⚬—⚬—⚬	London Borough
....	Civil Parish (England)* Community (Wales)
— — — — — —	Constituency (County, Borough, Burgh or European Assembly)

Coincident boundaries are shown by the first appropriate symbol

*For Ordnance Survey purposes County Boundary is deemed to be the limit of the parish structure whether or not a parish area adjoins

SYMBOLS

♦ Church	with tower
♦ or	with spire
+ chapel	without tower or spire
▨ ▲	Glasshouse; youth hostel
⬡	Bus or coach station
⚡ ⚓ ⚐	Lighthouse; lightship; beacon
△	Triangulation station
Triangulation point on	church or chapel / lighthouse, beacon / building; chimney
pylon pole	Electricity transmission line

VILLA	Roman antiquity (AD 43 to AD 420)
Castle	Other antiquities
⌖	Site of antiquity
⚔ 1066	Site of battle (with date)
	Gravel pit
	Sand pit
	Chalk pit, clay pit or quarry
	Refuse or slag heap
	Sloping wall

☐ Water	☐ Mud
	Sand; sand & shingle
	National Park or Forest Park Boundary
NT	National Trust always open
NT	National Trust opening restricted
FC	Forestry Commission

VEGETATION

Limits of vegetation are defined by positioning of the symbols but may be delineated also by pecks or dots

Coniferous trees	Scrub
Non-coniferous trees	Bracken, rough grassland
Coppice	In some areas bracken (σ) and rough grassland (⋯⋯) are shown separately
Orchard	Heath

Shown collectively as rough grassland on some sheets

Reeds
Marsh
Saltings

HEIGHTS AND ROCK FEATURES

50 ·	Determined by { ground survey
285	air survey

Surface heights are to the nearest metre above mean sea level. Heights shown close to a triangulation pillar refer to the station height at ground level and not necessarily to the summit

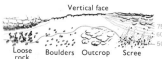

Vertical face

Loose rock   Boulders   Outcrop   Scree

75
60
50

Contours are at 5 metres vertical interval

ABBREVIATIONS

1:25 000 or 2½ INCHES to 1 MILE also 1:10 000 or 6 INCHES to 1 MILE

BP,BS	Boundary Post or Stone	P	Post Office		A,R	Telephone, AA or RAC
CH	Club House	Pol Sta	Police Station		TH	Town Hall
F V	Ferry Foot or Vehicle	PC	Public Convenience		Twr	Tower
FB	Foot Bridge	PH	Public House		W	Well
HO	House	Sch	School		Wd Pp	Wind Pump
MP,MS	Mile Post or Stone	Spr	Spring			
Mon	Monument	T	Telephone, public			

Abbreviations applicable only to 1:10 000 or 6 INCHES to 1 MILE

Ch	Church	GP	Guide Post		TCB	Telephone Call Box
F Sta	Fire Station	P	Pole or Post		TCP	Telephone Call Post
Fn	Fountain	S	Stone		Y	Youth Hostel

BOUNDARIES

+ — + — + — + — National

— — — — — — — — {County, Region or Islands Area

GENERAL FEATURES

Buildings

Wood

Lighthouse (in use)

Lighthouse (disused)

Windmill

Radio or TV mast

▲ Youth hostel

⊕ / ✦ Civil aerodrome { with Customs facilities / without Customs facilities

Ⓗ Heliport

☏ Public telephone

☏ Motoring organisation telephone

+ Intersection, latitude & longitude at 30' intervals (not shown where it confuses important detail)

TOURIST INFORMATION

✛ Abbey, Cathedral, Priory

🐟 Aquarium

⚑ Camp site

🚐 Caravan site

🏰 Castle

Cave

Country park

Craft centre

❀ Garden

⚑ Golf course or links

🏛 Historic house

ℹ Information centre

Motor racing

🖼 Museum

❗ Nature or forest trail

🦆 Nature reserve

☆ Other tourist feature

✗ Picnic site

Preserved railway

Racecourse

Skiing

Viewpoint

Wildlife park

🐘 Zoo

AREA COVERED BY SHEET 151

Henley in-Arden SP 06/16	Royal Leamington Spa SP 26/36 Warwick	Willoughby SP 46/56 Southam
SP 05/15	STRATFORD-UPON-AVON SP 25/35 Kineton	SP 45/55 Byfield
SP 04/14 Mickleton	Halford SP 24/34 Shipston on Stour	Cropredy SP 44/54 Banbury
Chipping Campden SP 03/13 Moreton-in-Marsh	SP 23/33	Bloxham SP 43/53 Deddington

The red grid and figures give the sheet lines and sheet numbers of the component 1:25 000 Pathfinder maps

The maps in this publication are reproduced from Ordnance Survey maps with the permission of the Controller of HMSO

© Crown Copyright Reserved

WALKS AND DRIVES
Applicable to all scales

🖊1 Start point of walk

→ Route of walk

——— Featured walk

- - - - Featured walk (not right of way)

🚗1 Start point of drive

→ Route of drive

——— Featured drive

1:50 000 ADJOINING SHEETS
The red figures give the grid values of the adjoining sheet edges

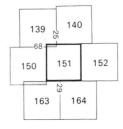

139	140
68— 25	
150	151	152
29	
163	164

Maps and Mapping

Most early maps of the area covered by this guide were published on a county basis, and to follow their development in at least one county, it is suggested that P.D.A. Harvey and Harry Thorpe's *The Printed Maps of Warwickshire 1576-1900* be studied in detail. The first significant county maps were produced by Christopher Saxton in the 1570's, the whole of England and Wales being covered in only six years. Although he did not cover the whole country John Norden, work-ing at the end of the 16th century, was the first map-maker to show roads. In 1611-12, John Speed, making use of Saxton and Norden's pioneer work, produced his *Theatre of the Empire of Great Britaine*, adding excellent town plans, battle scenes, and magnificent coats of arms. The next great English map-maker was John Ogilby, and in 1675 he published *Britannia, Volume I*, in which all the roads of England and Wales were engraved on a scale of one inch to the mile, in a massive series of strip maps. From this time onwards, no map was published without roads, and throughout the 18th century, steady progress was made in accur-

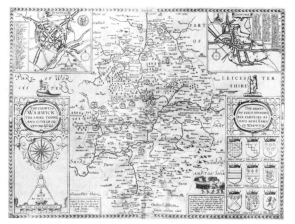

Allegorical map of Warwickshire which appeared in Michael Drayton's Poly-Olbion, *published in 1612.*

Map of Warwickshire, 1611, by John Speed.

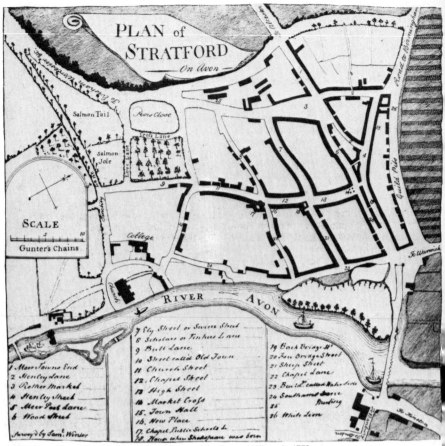

The first plan of Stratford-upon-Avon surveyed by Samuel Winter in 1759.

acy, if not always in the beauty of presentation.

The first Ordnance Survey maps came about as a result of Bonnie Prince Charlie's Jacobite rebellion of 1745. It was however in 1791, following the successful completion of the military survey of Scotland by General Roy that the Ordnance Survey was formally established. The threat of invasion by Napoleon in the early 19th century spurred on the demand for accurate and detailed mapping for military purposes, and to meet this need the first Ordnance Survey one-inch map, covering part of Essex, was published in 1805 in a single colour. This was the first numbered sheet in the First Series of one-inch maps.

Over the next 70 years the one-inch map was extended to cover the whole of Great Britain. Reprints of some of these First Series maps incorporating various later 19th century amendments, have been published by David & Charles. The reprinted sheets covering our area are Numbers 51, 52, 60 and 61.

The Ordnance Survey's First Series one-inch evolved through a number of 'Series' and editions, to the Seventh Series which was replaced in 1972 by the metric 1:50 000 scale Landranger Series. Between the First Series one-inch and the current Landranger maps many changes in style, format, content and purpose have taken place. Colour for example first appeared with the timid use of light brown for hill shading on the 1889 one-inch sheets. By 1892 as many as 5 colours were being used for this scale and at one stage the Seventh Series was being printed in no less than ten colours. Recent developments in "process printing" — a technique in which four basic colours produce almost any required tint — are now used to produce Ordnance Survey Landranger and other map series. Through the years the one-inch Series has gradually turned away from its military origins and has developed to meet a wider user demand. The modern detailed full colour Landranger maps at 1:50 000 scale incorporate Rights of Way and tourist information and are much used for both leisure and business purposes. To compare the old and new approach to changing demand, see the two map extracts of Stratford-upon-Avon on pages 122 and 123.

Modern Ordnance Survey maps of the area.

To look at the area surrounding our Landranger Sheet 151, the OS One-Inch to 4 miles, **Routemaster** Sheet 7 (Wales and the West Midlands), and Sheet 9 (South-East England) will prove most useful. An alternative will be found in the form of the OS Motoring Atlas, at the larger scale of One inch to 3 miles.

To examine our area in greater detail, and especially if you are planning walks, the Ordnance Survey publishes a modern Pathfinder map at 1:25 000 scale (2½ inches to 1 mile) which carries public rights of way information. The Pathfinder series is gra-

dually replacing the old 1:25 000 First Series (which does not show rights of way). Most of our area is covered by Pathfinder series maps. For even greater detail the OS 1:10 000, or 6 inches to 1 mile maps are most useful. They are available from OS Agents (Local Agent is shown on page 17, under 'Useful Addresses'), or direct from the Ordnance Survey, at Romsey Road, Maybush, Southampton, SO9 4DH. Each sheet covers a quarter of the area covered by the relevant First Series 1:25 000 sheet, and are coded NW,NE,SW,SE accordingly. In practice this relates to five-by-five grid squares on the Landranger map, with the two figure reference numbers ending in a zero or a five.

To place the area in an historical context the following OS **Archaeological and Historical maps** will also be found useful: **Roman Britain, Britain in the Dark Ages, Britain before the Norman Conquest, and Monastic Britain.**

Plan of Stratford-upon-Avon, drawn by Captain James Saunders in 1802.

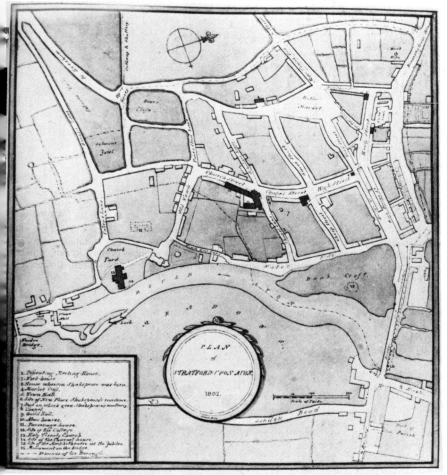

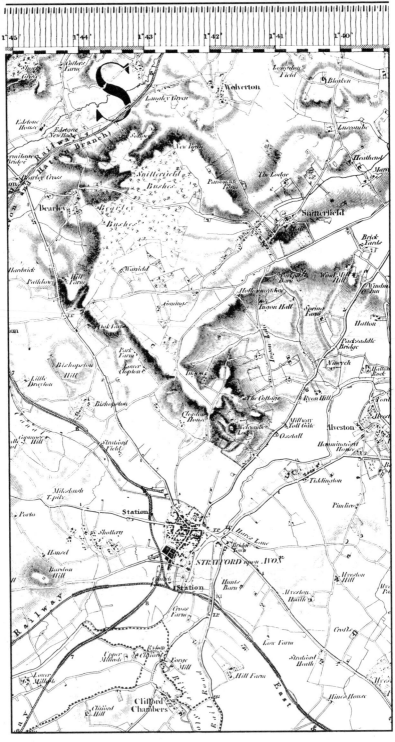

Published at the Tower of London 7th May 1831 by Lieut.! Colonel Colby of the Royal Engineers.

Engraved at the Ordnance Map Office in the Tower under the direction of Lieut.! Colonel Colby
by Benj.! Baker & Assistants.   The Writing by Ebenr. Bourne.

Printed from an Electrotype taken in 1885
Railways inserted to August 1884.

Scale of one Inch to a Statute Mile

0   1   2   Miles 3

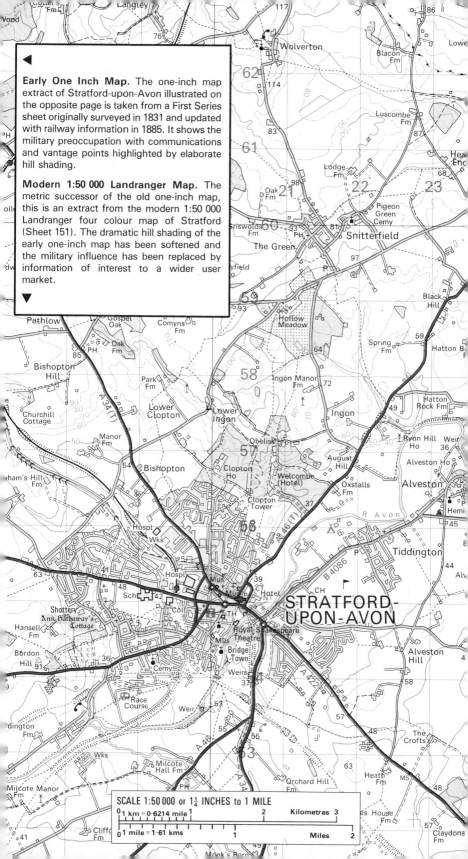

Early One Inch Map. The one-inch map extract of Stratford-upon-Avon illustrated on the opposite page is taken from a First Series sheet originally surveyed in 1831 and updated with railway information in 1885. It shows the military preoccupation with communications and vantage points highlighted by elaborate hill shading.

Modern 1:50 000 Landranger Map. The metric successor of the old one-inch map, this is an extract from the modern 1:50 000 Landranger four colour map of Stratford (Sheet 151). The dramatic hill shading of the early one-inch map has been softened and the military influence has been replaced by information of interest to a wider user market.

Index

Further Reading.... A List of Books.

General:

County Series ... Covering Gloucestershire, Northamptonshire, Oxfordshire and Warwickshire ... The Shell Guides. The Penguin 'Buildings of England' Series. 'The Queen's England' Series.

Beckinsale, R.& M. *The English Heartland.* Duckworth

Cave, L.F. *Warwickshire Villages.* Hall

Emery, F. *The Oxfordshire Landscape.* Hodder

Hoskins, W.G. *The Making of the English Landscape.* Pelican

Smith, B. *The Cotswolds.* Batsford

Stean, J. *The Northamptonshire Landscape.* Hodder

Sale, R. *A Guide to the Cotswold Way.* Constable

Art, Architecture & History

Ashby, M.K. *Joseph Ashby of Tysoe, 1859-1919.* Merlin

Beresford, M.W. *The Lost Villages of England.* Alan Sutton

Bird, V. *A Short History of Warwickshire.* Batsford

Clifton-Taylor, A. *English Parish Churches as works of Art.* Batsford

Dyer, J. *Prehistoric England & Wales.* Penguin

Fairfax-Lucy, A. *Mistress of Charlecote.* Gollancz

Hamilton, E. *The Mordaunts.* Heinemann

Harvey & Thorpe *Printed Maps of Warwickshire, 1576-1900.* Warks C.C.

Hawkes, J. *Guide to Prehistoric & Roman Monuments in England and Wales.* Cardinal

Horne, P. *Joseph Arch.* Roundwood

Kidson, P. *A History of English Architecture.* Pelican

Margary, I.D. *Roman Roads in Britain.* Phoenix House

Matthews, W. *Charles II's Escape from Worcester.* G.Bell & Sons

Miller, G. *Rambles round Edge Hill.* Roundwood

Payne, A. *Portrait of a Parish (Long Itchington).* Roundwood

Rainsberry, E. *Through the Lych Gate (Long Compton).* Roundwood

Seymour, A. *The Land where I Belong.* Roundwood

Seymour, A. *Fragrant the Fertile Earth.* Roundwood

Seymour, A. *A Square Mile of Old England.* Roundwood

Slater, T. *History of Warwickshire.* Phillimore

Smurthwaite, D. *Battlefields of Britain.* Ordnance Survey & Webb & Bower

Toynbee & Young *Cropredy Bridge, Battle of.* Roundwood

Wilson, R.J.A. *A Guide to Roman Remains in Britain.* Constable

Wood, E.S. *Field Guide to Archaeology in Britain.* Collins

Young, P. *Edge Hill, Battle of.* Roundwood

Stratford-upon-Avon and Shakespeare

Fox, L. *Stratford-upon-Avon: An appreciation.* Jarrold

Fox, L. *The Borough Town of Stratford-upon-Avon.* S-on-A Corporation

Fox, L. *Stratford, Past and Present.* Oxford Illustrated Press

Fox, L. *Shakespeare's Town and Country.* Jarrold

Jones, E.L. *The Origins of Shakespeare.* Clarendon Press

Wilson, J.D. *Life in Shakespeare's England.* Penguin

Railways

Christiansen, R. *The West Midland volume of the Regional History of British Railways.* David & Charles

Davies, H. *A Walk along the Tracks.* Hamlyn

MacDermot, E.T. *History of the Great Western Railway.* Ian Allan

Maggs, C. *Railways of the Cotswolds.* Peter Nicholson

Rolt, L.T.C. *Isambard Kingdom Brunel.* Penguin

Canals

Compton, B.J. *The Oxford Canal.* David & Charles

Hadfield, C. *The Canals of the East Midlands.* David & Charles

Hadfield & Morris *Waterways to Stratford.* David & Charles

Russell, R. *Lost Canals & Waterways of Britain.* Sphere

Rolt, L.T.C. *Inland Waterways of England.* Batsford

Nicholson/O.S. *Ordnance Survey Guide to the Waterways, Vol 2.*